Richard Neutra
and Brazil

Fernanda Critelli

Latin America: Thoughts

Romano Guerra Editora
Nhamerica Platform

Management Coordination
Abilio Guerra
Fernando Luiz Lara
Silvana Romano Santos

Translation
Odorico Leal

Translation Review
Noemi Zein Telles
Fernanda Critelli

Richard Neutra and Brazil
Fernanda Critelli
Brasil 7

Editor
Abilio Guerra
Fernando Luiz Lara
Silvana Romano Santos

Graphic Design and Formatting
Dárkon V Roque

Pre-press
Nelson Kon

To
Lilian, José Fernando and André

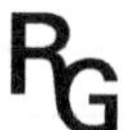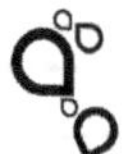

Richard Neutra and Brazil

Fernanda Critelli

Romano Guerra Editora
Nhamerica Platform

São Paulo, Austin, 2023
1st edition

Summary

Foreword
The "Uncanny" at South of Rio Grande
Abilio Guerra

Life and Work Intertwined

During my association with the graduate program of the
Faculty of Architecture and Urban Planning at Mackenzie
Presbyterian University, which dates back to 2005, I have
advised many students in monograph projects dedicated
to architects. Here I limit the notion of monographs to the
study of specific subjects – in this case, the feats of particular
figures –, usually an encompassing set of works developed
throughout their careers or a particular set related to a
period in time or a geographical region. And, even though
our focus has been on works developed within our national
territory, citizenship is not indispensable, for among these
figures we count many foreigners who have lived or worked
in Brazil, even if this connection only amounted to episodes
of cultural exchange. This does not imply a lack of interest in
the architecture developed abroad; it has to do with priori-
tizing deeper knowledge of the subject and easier access to
primary sources.

In 2007, a Master's thesis by Liana Paula Perez de
Oliveira, my second advisee, covered a very specific theme:
the transformation of an old drum factory into the Cultural and Sports Center SESC Pompeia by architect Lina Bo
Bardi.[1] Lina is also present in Patricia Nahas's 2009 dissertation on Brasil Arquitetura, playing the role of mentor to
architects Marcelo Ferraz and Marcelo Suzuki, founding
members – along with Francisco Fanucci – of the firm. Nahas
investigates their interventions in pre-existing structures,
from SESC Pompeia, a project on which Ferraz worked as
an intern, to the maturity achieved at the Museu do Pão,
formerly an old mill in the Rio Grande do Sul city of Ilópolis.[2]
Both researches start from a culturalist approach, where life
experiences and particular worldviews inform the choices of
the architects.

The trajectory and work of Rodolpho Ortenblad Filho,
who graduated from Mackenzie Architecture School in 1950,

is the subject of Sabrina Bom's 2010 Master's degree.[3] Ortenblad, active from the 1950s to the 1980s, worked as director of the magazine *Acropolis* from 1953 to 1955, achieving some notoriety in professional and academic circles; his house figures in Marlene Acayaba's 1957 book about residences.[4] Rescuing and rehabilitating important figures and works of our architecture is one of the most relevant roles of academic research. In this case, the formative period and the first years of Ortenblad's career as detailed by the author shed light on essential issues of the period, such as the modern North American single-family house – in particular, the Californian model disseminated by John Entenza in his *Arts & Architecture* magazine –, which influenced architects from São Paulo trained in the 1950s.

Contrasting with Ortenblad due to his international fame, Roberto Burle Marx was the subject in the dissertations of Marília Dorador Guimarães and Fernanda Rocha, both with a regional approach. The first one, defended in 2011, deals with the contributions of Burle Marx in works of Rino Levi, Marcello Fragelli, Miguel Juliano, Hans Broos e Ruy Ohtake in São Paulo.[5] The second, defended in 2015, is a product of Capes' Minter program, encompassing Mackenzie University and the University of Fortaleza – UNIFOR; it deals with the gardens designed by Burle Marx in the capital of Ceará state in partnership with architects Acácio Gil Borsoi, Luiz Fiuza, Delberg Ponce de Leon, Fausto Nilo and brothers Francisco and José Nasser Hissa.[6] Both works point out that there's still plenty to be discovered regarding the practice of our greatest landscaper, particularly his work dispersed throughout Brazil and foreign countries.

For his 2008 PHD in the Technical University of Catalonia – UPC, Marcio Cotrim tackled the residential works designed by Vilanova Artigas during the last two decades of his career.[7] The research prioritizes theoretical discussions based on original documents and the works themselves, followed by a careful typological analysis of each one of the selected residences. According to his advisors, Fernando Alvarez Prozorovich e Abilio Guerra, Cotrim "visited and experienced these houses, talked to owners and gathered valuable testimonies. Moreover, he carried out an impeccable analysis, highlighting the interest for these works and the need to reveal the *modus operandi* of the author."[8] Marcio Cotrim was my first advisee in the graduate program and his was the second academic work under my guidance to be published as a book.

Fausto Sombra's Master's thesis and PhD dissertation are also monographical works. The first one – from 2015, dealing with the restoration of Sítio Santo Antônio by Luís Saia[9] – sets up its presentation in two parts: a professional profile of the paulista architect, particularly his practical and intellectual production dealing with interventions in important historical buildings, marked by his relationship with Dina Lévi-Strauss, Mário de Andrade, Rodrigo Mello Franco de Andrade e Lúcio Costa, leading characters in the study and defense of our national historical heritage; the second part goes on to explore the restoration of the ranch, a estate which Mário de Andrade left to Iphan in his will. Sombra's dissertation, defended in 2020, surveys three pavilions designed and built by Sergio Bernades: the Volta Redonda Pavilion, in Ibirapuera Park, from 1955; the Brazil Pavilion in the Universal and International Exhibition of Bruxelas (1957-1958) and the Pavilion for the Exhibition of Industry and Commerce, built in São Cristóvão, Rio de Janeiro, between 1957 and 1960.[10] Both works prioritize primary documentation, research being carried out largely in the archives of Iphan (São Paulo and Rio de Janeiro) and the NPD of the Faculty of Architecture and Urban Planning of the Federal University of Rio de Janeiro – FAU UFRJ.

I have also advised four monographs which dealt with foreign architects who settled in Brazil, developing their work or a substantial part of it here. Tiago Franco's Master's degree, from 2009, reconstructs the path of Frenchman

Jacques Pilon in São Paulo, presenting an overview of his work, as well as a more detailed analysis of thirteen projects carried out between 1940 and 1947.[11] In turn, Marcelo Barbosa's dissertation[12] – from 2012, the first research under my guidance to be published as a book[13] – explores the architectural production of German Franz Heep. After starting his career in Paris in the 1930s as an employee of Le Corbusier and establishing a partnership with Jean Ginsberg, Heep migrated to Brazil, where he effectively contributed to the process of verticalization in São Paulo, both as an employee of Jacques Pilon, from 1948 to 1952, and through his own office, from 1952 to 1960. The third research is Mariana Puglisi's Master's thesis, defended in 2017, on three social housing projects – Conjunto Habitacional Rincão, 1989-1992; Rio das Pedras, Vila Mara, 1989-1998; and Parque Novo Santo Amaro V, 2009-2012 –, conceived or developed by Uruguayan architect Hector Vigliecca in the city of São Paulo between 1989 and 2016.[14] Finally, Felipe Rodrigues' master's degree, from 2018, explores Aurelio Martinez Flores, Mexican architect who took part in the project for the interior design of the palaces of Brasília in the 1960s. He settled in São Paulo, where he developed a successful career as an architect, designer and interior designer.[15] These four works deal with the question of how adapting to the Brazilian cultural environment shaped the careers of these architects.

Displaced with regard to theme among the studies I have supervised, Gustavo Lassala surveys with a biographical bent the life story and graffiti practice of Djan Ivson Silva.[16] Like the overwhelming majority of *"pichadores"*, "Cripta Djan" – a nickname that accompanied him to stardom – seeks notoriety by climbing tall buildings at great risk.[17] Lassala's text, based on concepts developed by Pierre Bourdieu for the study of social groups, reconstitutes the character's story, revealing the communicating vessels that unite the individual and collective spheres, the transformations regarding the social phenomenon of graffiti, how news coverage related to "pixo" migrated from crime reports to cultural events pages, and the growing interaction of this urban practice with the artistic environment. In this plot, we find a character with unusual predicates: a leader among "pichadores", an archivist with a significant collection of documents and great knowledge about the history of "pixação", qualities that lead to the invitation made by curators Agnaldo Farias and Moacir dos Anjos for him to take part in the 29th edition of the Art Biennial of São Paulo.[18]

The Master's thesis on João Filgueiras Lima – Lelé –[19] and the PhD dissertation on Aldary Henriques Toledo,[20] both by André Marques, are also monographic works. The latter, defended in 2012, became a book in 2020 – the third book to come out of academic work developed under my guidance.[21] In the introduction I survey Marques' considerations from two points of view: the intertextual dialogue with secondary sources that precedes and follows his text; and the great contact with primary sources regarding the works studied, all of them visited by the researcher.[22] The "dialogue" here with Richard Neutra and Jean Prouvé are metaphors expressing Lelé's bioclimatic and technical-constructive strategies, in complete harmony with two fundamental strands of Western architecture in the 20th and 21st centuries. The thesis is from 2018 and we will comment on it later.

The Flexible Cage

Among the professionals of the so-called "human sciences", the historian is the one who most engages with the episodic. For him, the precious stone to be discovered is the *fact*, which will later be polished in the form of an explanation. It's not an easy alchemy. An architectural object, for example, owes a lot to external and internal constraints; the historical circumstances that made it possible for it to materialize is as important as the dialogue with similar objects, when precepts, procedures and values are constituted and transmitted.

To reconstruct his character's path, the historian outlines the field of possibilities through which he moves. According to historian Carlo Ginzburg, a historical singularity has "very precise limits: there is no escaping the culture of one's class and of the times one lives in, except by entering into a state of delirium and lack of communication. Like language, culture offers the individual a horizon of latent possibilities – a flexible and invisible cage within which one's conditioned freedom is exercised.[23] In addition to the external ones, the internal constraints – or intermediaries, where the social and disciplinary spheres are intertwined[24] – are equally decisive for the qualities of a particular work. This, as I understand it, is the result of perpetually polishing formal principles and aesthetic values over time. Thus, the artistic process that takes place in the field continually interacts with society, incorporating its themes, tensions, doubts or anxieties, which are returned to it in a coded and sublimated way.

From a practical point of view, the historian of art and architecture has to carry out research that combines the internal and external phenomena of the discipline hoping to answer the basic questions that afflict him: what happened and how it happened. "What happened" puts us before the ontological fact, which took place in a specific space and time.[25] "How it happened" calls for an interpretation, which implies the ability to perceive and articulate the individual and collective forces that generate the ontological fact. Understanding these realms – which are defined by a specific area of philosophy, that is, epistemology – is essential for the historian.

The premises of any argument are – as they must be – verifiable; a fact can and must be proved; there can be no doubt about its existence – even if it is imaginary –, be it in regard to where it took place, or when it took place. Well-done research on primary sources ensures that the argument doesn't fall apart through negligence concerning dates or more mundane information. On the other hand, there is no way to categorically state that an argument, which concatenates its premises with the goal of explaining "how something happened", is indeed true, after all there are many forces at work, both at the individual level and in the social structure. An argument purports to be accepted by an interlocutor or by the social collective because it is credible; and yet it will always be subject to contradiction, doubt and distrust. Just as veracity is the domain of premises, verisimilitude is the ultimate end that any argument can aim for. This is one of the reasons for the distance between history and science; in the words of Carlo Ginzburg, history, as part of a "group of disciplines that we call evidential (which includes medicine), does not fall within the criteria of scientificity deducible from the Galilean paradigm. These are, in fact, eminently qualitative disciplines, which have as their object particular cases, situations and documents *seen as singularities*, and precisely because of this they have achieved results that imply an inescapable margin of chance."[26]

Primary sources must function as a secure foundation on which to build the edifice of argumentation. This, in turn, must be based on compatible theories that account for the understanding of the complex forces influencing society. But there is a hitch that takes us away from a reductive positivist view. If the historical fact itself has indeed a particular objectivity, the same cannot be said of the primary document where we glimpse its existence. The document is always marked by the "motivations" of those who produced it, whose freedom is conditioned by the "flexible and invisible cage" in which they inhabit. The historian's work at this point demands great patience to unravel the reasons for a particular event, which are not immediately visible, as individual and collective impulses and the interests of social groups, categories or classes get entangled in the various discourses that echo over time, and that were only partially registered in the available languages. The prudent historian, who moves away from overly abstract categories and maintains his constant interest in the episodic, finds his favorite building material in the concreteness of languages. The document – whether text or image – suffers from this ambiguity: just as much as it attests to the existence of the historical fact, it also embodies the tensions and contradictions of an era.

One more aspect of the document should also be mentioned, albeit an obvious one. The material heritage of the past expresses the social, cultural and economic complex that gave it form and content. The relationships between classes, the dynamics of production and appropriation of goods, technological development, the system for transmitting knowledge, the set of values, beliefs and customs that reinforce the ideological apparatus – in short, the set of phenomena that start from the materiality of life and that push forward the historical dialectic – must be available to the historian for his reconstructions. But the historian is much more interested in the capacity of dialectical materialism to make visible how these forces act upon the episodic, and less in its teleological and schematic narratives.

In order to delve into the individual and collective impulses that permeate an aesthetic appreciation, a formal decision or any other manifestation of the spirit, we must assume that those "all too human" factors are also at play, when actions and ideas are "responses to internal pressures, being, at least in part, translations of instinctual needs, defensive maneuvers and anxious anticipations."[27] A broad view of Freudian psychoanalysis, particularly the most historical, cultural and anthropological texts, is a very useful tool to understand how irrationality and thoughtlessness can inform decisions seemingly based on irreproachable logic. As Peter Gay points out, "the aesthetic documents accessible in a society – its novels, poems, or paintings – reveal, under the psychoanalytic lens, the way in which that society seeks to resolve, or refuses to recognize, issues that it finds too delicate to discuss frankly."[28] This is a perfect statement, even more so if we add "architecture" to the list.

When it comes to monographic texts dedicated to particular characters in the field of architecture, their life stories intertwine with the development of their work, just as the consolidation of their worldview is mirrored in the maturation (or improvement) of their designs and built works. But here, too, we observe a contamination of the history of an individual or discipline by external pressures. Here I'll use examples from the work of my advisees. In the development of his doctorate on Aldary Toledo, André Marques draws from concepts and analytical methods developed by or derive from Pierre Bourdieu, following in the footsteps of Gustavo Lassala in the study of the figure of the "pichador". In a situation similar to the trajectory of Rodolpho Ortenblad Filho, the considerable ostracism of the Rio de Janeiro-born architect ends a previous period of professional and academic recognition, even greater recognition in the case of Toledo, as he was part of the group of modern architects selected for the mythological 1943 exhibition at MoMA, New York, *Brazil Builds*, also being featured in the catalog that followed.[29]

According to Marques, following "the anthropological concepts found in Pierre Bourdieu's book *The Favored Circle*", historian Garry Stevens "explains the cultural construction of architecture as a profession. He deconstructs the idea of the creative genius by showing that, behind outstanding individuals, there is a social network that sustains them and in which they themselves take part."[30] If the recognition initially obtained by Aldary Toledo – his "symbolic capital", in Bourdieu's terms – reflects his inclusion in the group of first-generation Rio de Janeiro architects led by Lúcio Costa – his "social capital" –, these "capitals", however, are not enough to perpetuate the architect's recognition over time.[31] This is a theme that transcends any specific figure. Long-term recognition of an architect usually relates to the academic realm and class entities, but it is necessary that it be periodically renewed ithrough congresses, seminars, articles and occasional new books.

Richard Neutra According to Fernanda Critelli

My first interest in post-war North American architecture emerged while reading Hugo Segawa's 1997 text connecting the work of Oswaldo Bratke to Californian architecture.[32] After making the mistake of ignoring the book published in 2001 by Mônica Junqueira regarding Miguel Forte's trip to the United States,[33] which I read much later, I published in 2002 an interesting article by Claudia Loureiro and Luiz Amorim discussing Richard Neutra's influence in Brazilian architecture.[34] During this period, I expanded my limited knowledge of the subject with two important works by researcher Adriana Irigoyen: her 2002 Master's thesis,[35] which explores the relationship between Frank Lloyd Wright's thought and work and our country; and her excellent 2005 PHD dissertation, which showed how a whole generation of architects who graduated from the architecture faculties of Mackenzie University and the University of São Paulo, had been educated with their eyes set on America.[36] In the meantime, I took part of the thesis defense committee for Paulo Fujioka's 2003 PHD, which reiterated the interest of São Paulo architects in the North American masters.[37]

Half a decade later, when participating in three examining committees, I found that works with a similar perspective were on the rise. In 2008, Master's theses by Eduardo Ferroni[38] and Débora Foresti[39] established connections between the architecture of Salvador Candia and José Leite de Carvalho e Silva with US architects Mies van der Rohe and Frank Lloyd Wright, respectively. However, around 2007, while reading Patrícia Pimenta Azevedo Ribeiro's thesis on Richard Neutra's work, I realized how much still had to be done. In the introduction, the researcher outlined an association that seemed to me quite convincing between the Austrian

architect and Brazilian architecture, which she did not
develop in the following chapters.[40] However, it was indeed
in 2008, while participating in the examining committee for
Luz Marie Rodríguez López's PhD dissertation, which explores
Richard Neutra's presence in Puerto Rico,[41] that I felt the
need to better understand his presence in Brazil.

At the beginning of the new decade, I published Marcello Fragelli's book[42] and learned about the Master's theses
of Valeria Ruchti and Fernanda Ciampaglia; their focus was
on the works of their parents – Jacob Ruchti[43] and Galiano
Ciampaglia,[44] major Mackenzie architects. Even though this is
not the main concern of their texts, a point of convergence
was the relationship established between the works of Brazilian architects and North-American architecture. However, at
that moment, my first incursion on the subject was already
underway through my role as advisor for the aforementioned
Master's thesis by Sabrina Bom Pereira on Rodolpho Ortenblad Filho. Lacking the time and determination necessary to
undertake an in-depth research, I realized that I could follow
the expansion and deepening of the research on this topic as
an advisor.

It is during this period that luck came knocking. Fernanda Critelli, a young student at the Faculty of Architecture
and Urbanism of Mackenzie University, invited me to advise
her on her undergraduate research project. It was the year
2012, and we agreed to explore Richard Neutra's work.[45]
Thus, we started a partnership that has lasted a decade, sharing many interests and discoveries, such as reading historian
Antonio Pedro Tota's books, which, while not directly dealing
with architecture, outline the background surrounding
North American interests in Brazil,[46] or the first findings in
the collections of Museum of Art of São Paulo – Masp and
the families of Gregori Warchavchik and Henrique Mindlin.
The natural prominence of my role at the beginning dimin-
ished, as I secured the comfortable and privileged position of
being the first reader, marveling at these new and constant

discoveries that expanded even more during her Master's degree studies, especially when Fernanda was awarded a scholarship by The São Paulo Research Foundation – FAPESP to research Richard Neutra's life and work in North American libraries and collections.

The excellence of the finished work, defended in 2015,[47] motivated her to continue this inquiry during her PHD studies, now expanding the scope to Latin America and also elaborating on the presence of Brazilian architecture in the work of the Austrian architect.[48] The in-depth document research on the presence of Richard Neutra in Brazil – covering letters, messages, photographs, drawings, official documents, newspapers, magazines etc. – enjoyed at first the generous contribution of Adriana Irigoyen, who lent us her rich research findings, adding to Fernanda's lengthy inquiries in institutional and personal collections in Brazil and abroad. Many references to the presence of North American architecture in Brazil, as reported in articles, dissertations, theses and books, were compiled, ensuring a more accurate overview of the issue. The crossing of these data made it possible to describe Neutra's trips to Brazil and Latin America, pointing out the North American and Brazilian institutions involved, the main interlocutors, the repercussion of his presence in our territory and further developments in the United States. This rich material makes it possible to satisfactorily answer the question of "what happened"; it is not sufficient, however, to understand "how it happened". Thus, Fernanda Critelli's final interpretation encompasses several aspects that clarify the subject in question, especially in the following topics that I outline here.

The first one refers to Richard Neutra's many visits to Latin America. These visits are carried out in the interest of the US government, which, via the Department of State and the Office of the Coordinator of Inter-American Affairs, headed by Nelson Rockefeller, put into practice the Good Neighbor Policy, focusing on countries "below the Rio

Grande" and encompassing intellectuals and artists from both hemispheres. What Critelli's argument convincingly demonstrates is that the nature of Neutra's interest in establishing a dialogue with its Latino peers changed over time, to the point of transcending the diplomatic and strategic interests of the US government. In addition to the official nature of the visits, there is a genuine interest on the part of Neutra for the architecture of the region, especially the Brazilian one — an interest that is revealed in articles that highlight the many qualities of our architecture and also in his inviting Roberto Burle Marx to do some work together.

One of the most interesting aspects of this book, this ambiguity detected in Neutra's behavior translates into Neutra's willingness to let himself be influenced by Brazilian architecture. The presentation of this hypothesis – and its confirmation – is the next special moment of the argument. According to Critelli, because he is a major architect, when he incorporates architectural elements typical of modern Brazilian architecture, Neutra reinterprets them according to a particular way of looking at a problem. Thus, the incorporation of brises, vaults, artistic panels and landscaping moves away from certain Brazilian attributes; however, the bonds with their origin are never completely lost.

Finally, a third aspect to be highlighted is the clash with North American criticism and historiography, which see Neutra's late works as impoverished examples of his architecture. Starting from an interesting adaptation of the Freudian concept of the "unheimlich", or the "uncanny", Fernanda Critelli confronts Barbara Lamprecht and Thomas Hines – two major scholars of the Austrian architect – pointing out that what appears to them as unintelligible, or even strange, in the late work of Neutra, and which led them to underestimate it, actually reveals a kind of repression promoted by these intellectuals, so as to hide the undesirable influences of a lesser architecture. Critics who present themselves as impartial, as if concerned exclusively with the architectural object, hide the feeling of cultural aesthetic superiority, a process of concealment so effective that it is no longer visible to the authors themselves.

This preface is yet another expression on my part regarding the value of academic research, which is marked by a collective dimension and the intertextuality of the final accounts. Nevertheless, I also reiterate here that I feel very fortunate to have taken part in a work marked by extreme personal commitment and to be able to publicly express my enormous appreciation for the text that follows, the product of a decade of hard work.

Notes

1. Liana de Oliveira, "A capacidade de dizer não. Lina Bo Bardi e a Fábrica da Pompeia."
2. Patricia Nahas, "Brasil Arquitetura: memória e contemporaneidade. Um percurso do Sesc Pompeia ao Museu do Pão (1977-2008)."
3. Sabrina Souza Pereira, "Rodolpho Ortenblad Filho: estudo sobre as residências."
4. Marlene Milan Acayaba, *Residências em São Paulo 1947-1975*, 95-100.
5. Marília Guimarães, "Roberto Burle Marx: a contribuição do artista e paisagista no Estado de São Paulo."
6. Fernanda Cláudia Rocha, "Os jardins residenciais de Roberto Burle Marx em Fortaleza: entre descontinuidades e conexõe."
7. Marcio Cotrim, "Construir a casa paulista: o discurso e a obra de Vilanova Artigas entre 1967 e 1985."
8. Fernando Alvarez Prozorovich and Abilio Guerra, "Construindo a casa paulista. O rigor e a clareza de Marcio Cotrim na análise da obra de Vilanova Artigas."
9. Fausto Sombra, "Luís Saia e o restauro do Sítio Santo Antônio: diálogos modernos na conformação arquitetônica paulista."
10. Fausto Sombra, "Três pavilhões de Sérgio Bernardes: Volta Redonda, Bruxelas e São Cristóvão. Contribuição à vanguarda arquitetônica moderna brasileira em meados do século 20." The thesis was the basis for the exhibition "Three pavilions by Sérgio Bernardes", curated by Abilio Guerra and Fausto Sombra at Mackenzie Historic and Cultural Center, São Paulo, from September 18 to November 14, 2019.
11. Tiago Franco, "A trajetória de Jacques Pilon no Centro de São Paulo. Análise das obras de 1940 a 1947."
12. Marcelo Barbosa, "Franz Heep. Um arquiteto moderno."
13. Marcelo Barbosa, *Adolf Franz Heep. Um arquiteto moderno.*
14. Mariana de Carvalho Puglisi, "Habitação e cidade – espaços coletivos na habitação de interesse social. Análise das obras do arquiteto Hector Vigliecca em São Paulo – 1989 a 2016."
15. Rodrigues, Felipe Silva. "Aurelio Martinez Flores: a produção do arquiteto mexicano no Brasil (1960-2015)."
16. Gustavo Lassala, "Em nome do pixo. A experiência social e estética do pixador e artista Djan Ivson."
17. For more information about Djan Cripta, see the interview: Gustavo Lassala and Abilio Guerra, "Pixar é crime num país onde roubar é arte."
18. Guss De Lucca, "Those responsible for the attacks on the event in 2008 will take part in the next edition to debate the '*pixo*.'"

19. André Marques, "A obra de João Filgueiras Lima, Lelé: projeto, técnica e racionalização."

20. André Marques, "Aldary Toledo – entre arte e arquitetura."

21. André Marques, *Lelé*: diálogos com Neutra e Prouvé.

22. Abilio Guerra, "Como se escreve uma dissertação."

23. Carlo Ginzburg, *O queijo e os vermes: o cotidiano e as ideias de um moleiro perseguido pela Inquisição.*

24. We believe that it is impossible to circumscribe the autonomy of art, since its very status is socially defined, as can be seen from a precious and precise passage by Bourdieu: "The distinction between works of art and other elaborated objects and the definition (inseparable from it) in a properly aesthetic way of approaching objects socially designated as works of art, that is, objects that demand and deserve to be approached according to a proper aesthetic intention, capable of recognizing them and constituting them as works of art, imposes itself with the arbitrary necessity of normative facts whose contrary is not contradictory, but simply impossible or improbable". See: Pierre Bourdieu, "Os modos de produção e modos de percepção artísticos," 271.

25. A fact that is materially non-existent, yet consistent in the social imagination, can be as effective as any other. In this case, its existence takes place in the symbolic, ideological or psychological spheres, and it is from these circumstances that it must be studied. "The historical relevance of such events, which never happened, is based on their symbolic efficacy: that is, on the way in which they were perceived by an anonymous crowd". See: Carlo Ginzburg, "Controlando a evidência: o juiz e o historiador," 346.

26. Carlo Ginzburg, "Sinais: raízes de um paradigma indiciário," 156.

27. Peter Gay, *Freud para historiadores*, 16.

28. Ibid, 153.

29. "Hermenegildo Sotto Maior Residence, Fazenda São Luís, State of Rio de Janeiro, project by architect Aldary Henriques Toledo, 1942." In *Brazil Builds: Architecture New and Old 1652-1942*, edited by Philip L. Goodwin, 176.

30. Marques, "Aldary Toledo – entre arte e arquitetura," 26-27.

31. Pierre Bourdieu's concepts – symbolic goods, fields, social capital, habitus etc – are especially operative in the two aforementioned doctoral theses. See: Pierre Bourdieu, *A economia das trocas simbólicas.*

32. Hugo Segawa and Guilherme Mazza Dourado, *Oswaldo Arthur Bratke*, 1997.

33. Miguel Forte, *Diário de um jovem arquiteto: minha viagem aos Estados Unidos em 1947.*

34. Claudia Loureiro and Luiz Amorim, "Por uma arquitetura social: a influência de Richard Neutra em prédios escolares no Brasil."

35. Adriana Marta Irigoyen De Touceda, "Frank Lloyd Wright e o Brasil" (master thesis, EESC USP, 2000). Resulting book: Adriana Marta Irigoyen Touceda, *Wright e Artigas: duas viagens* (São Paulo: Ateliê Editorial, 2002).

36. Adriana Marta Irigoyen Touceda, "Da Califórnia a São Paulo."

37. Paulo Yassuhide Fujioka, "Princípios da arquitetura organicista de Frank Lloyd Wright e suas influências na arquitetura moderna paulistana."

38. Eduardo Ferroni, "Aproximações sobre a obra de Salvador Candia."

39. Débora Foresti, "Aspectos da arquitetura orgânica de Frank Lloyd Wright na arquitetura paulista: a obra de José Leite de Carvalho e Silva."

40. Patrícia Ribeiro, "Teoria e prática. A obra do arquiteto Richard Neutra."

41. Luz Marie Rodríguez López, "¡Vuelo al porvenir! Henry Klumb y Toro-Ferrer: proyecto moderno y arquitectura como vitrina de la democracia – Puerto Rico, 1944-1958" (PhD diss., Universitat Politècnica de Catalunya, 2008).

42. Marcelo Fragelli, *Quarenta anos de prancheta.*

43. Valeria Ruchti, "Jacob Ruchti: a modernidade e a arquitetura paulista (1940-1970)."

44. Fernanda Ciampaglia, "Galiano Ciampaglia. Razões de uma arquitetura."

45. Fernanda Critelli, "Richard Neutra no Brasil."

46. Antonio Pedro Tota, *O imperialismo sedutor: a americanização do Brasil na época da Segunda Guerra*; Antonio Pedro Tota, *O amigo americano: Nelson Rockefeller e o Brasil.*

47. Fernanda Critelli, "Richard Neutra e o Brasil." In 2014, Fernanda won a scholarship from Fapesp, spending three months at the University of Austin under the mentorship of Fernando Luiz Lara, and another three months conducting research in Los Angeles collections.

48. Fernanda Critelli, "Richard Neutra: conexões latino-americanas."

Travel Sketches

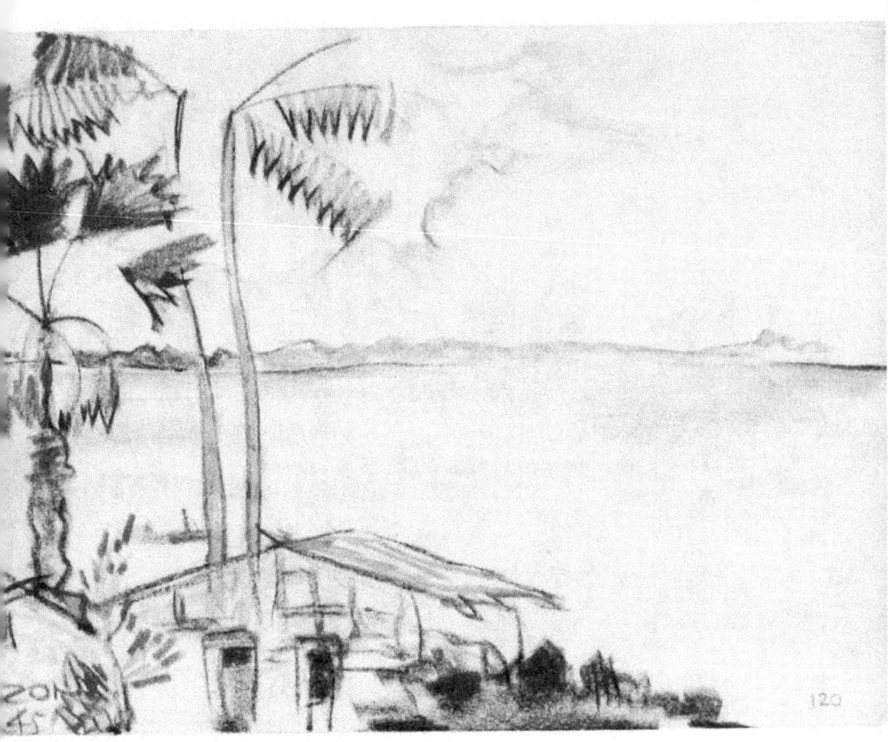

Travel sketch, view of single attached houses and palm trees on Amazon River's banks. Richard Neutra, 1945

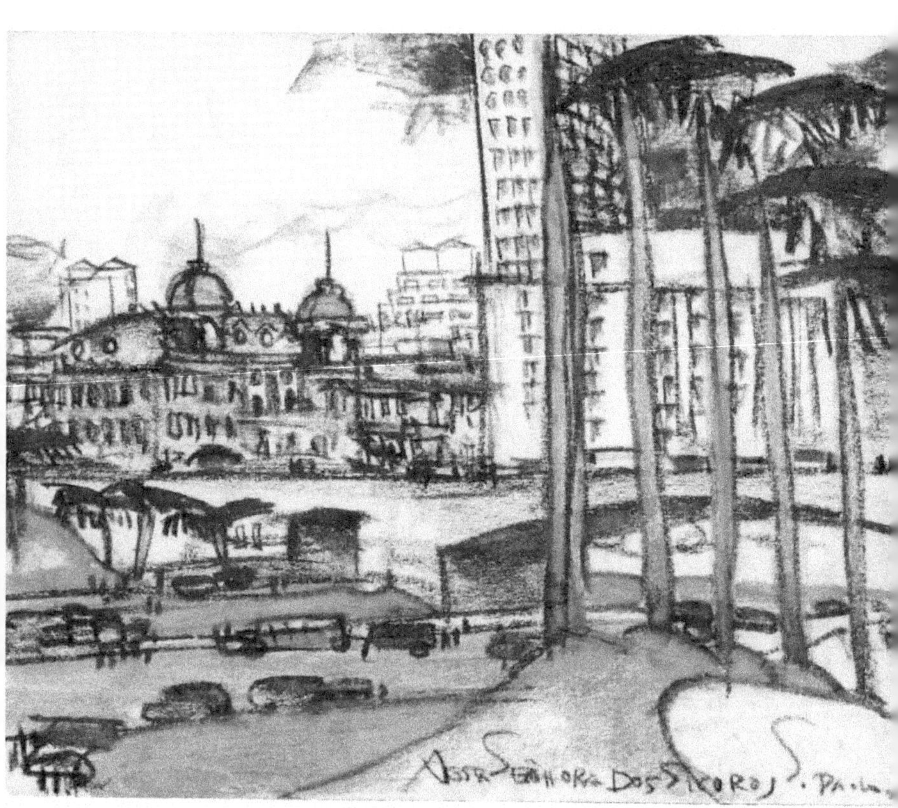

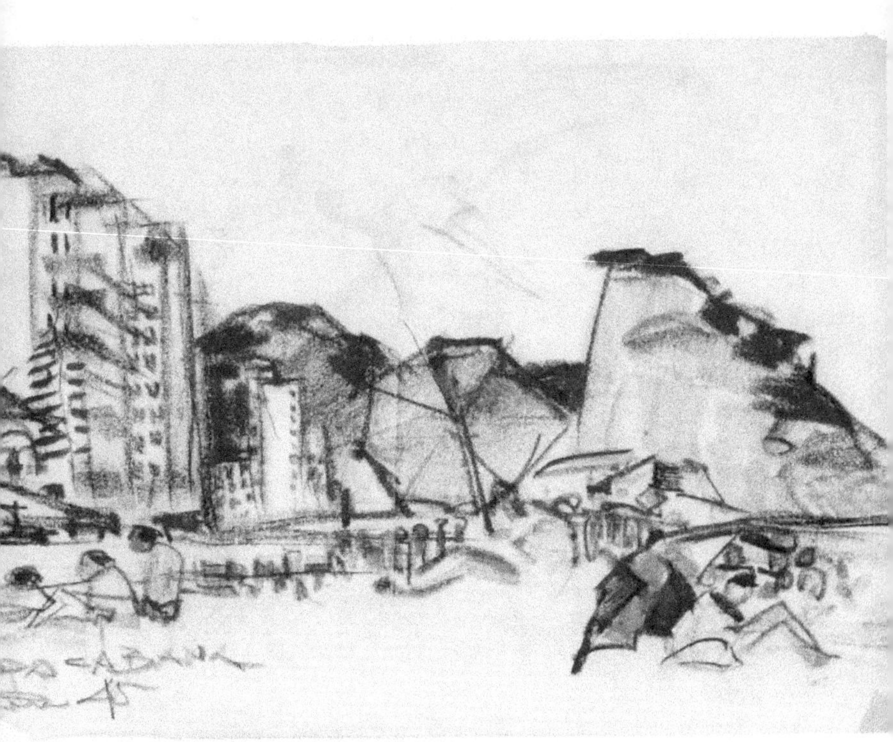

Travel sketch, Morro dos Dois Irmãos,
Leblon, Rio de Janeiro. Richard Neutra,
1945

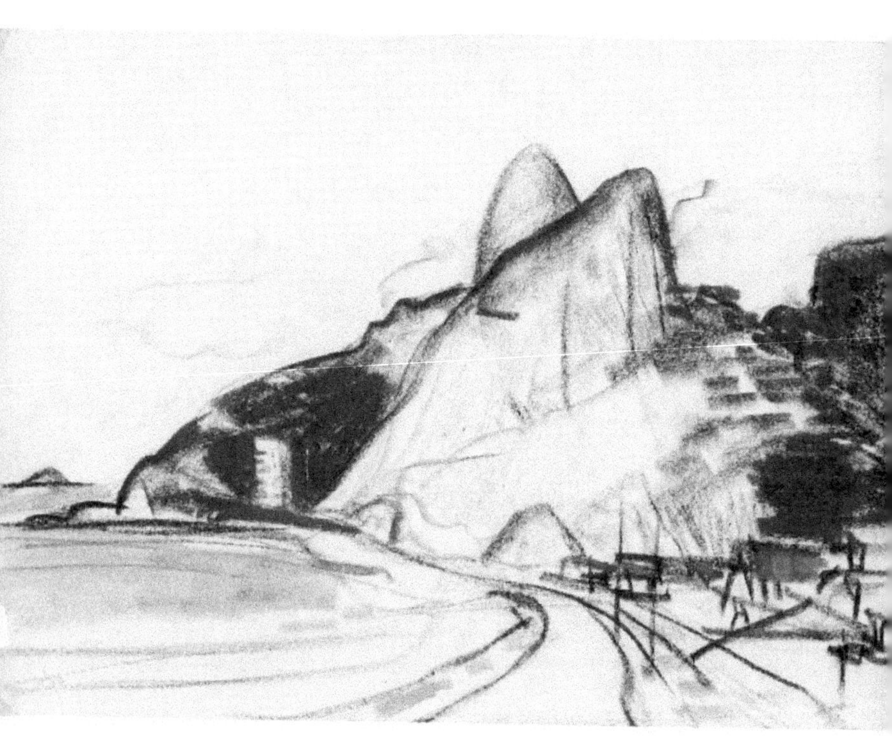

Trevel sketch, elevated view from Rio
de Janeiro. Richard Neutra, 1945

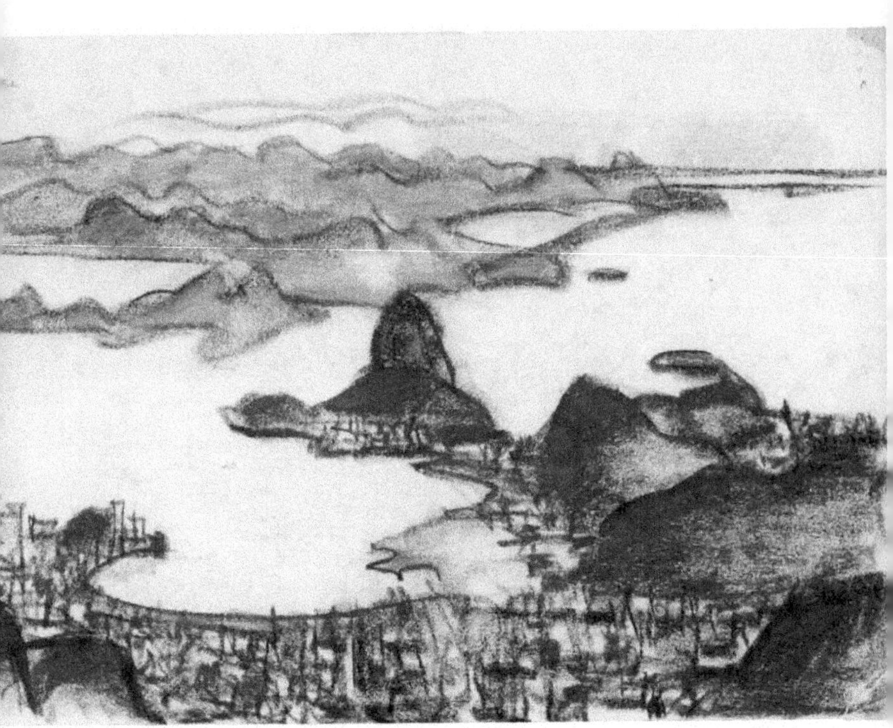

Travel sketch, Carioca Street, Rio de
Janeiro. Richard Neutra, 1945

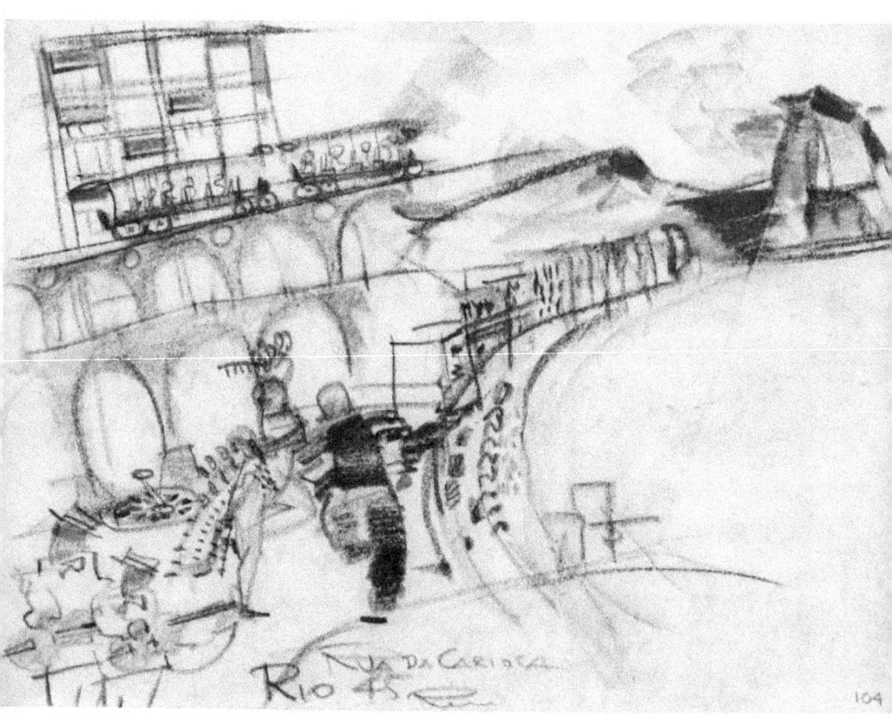

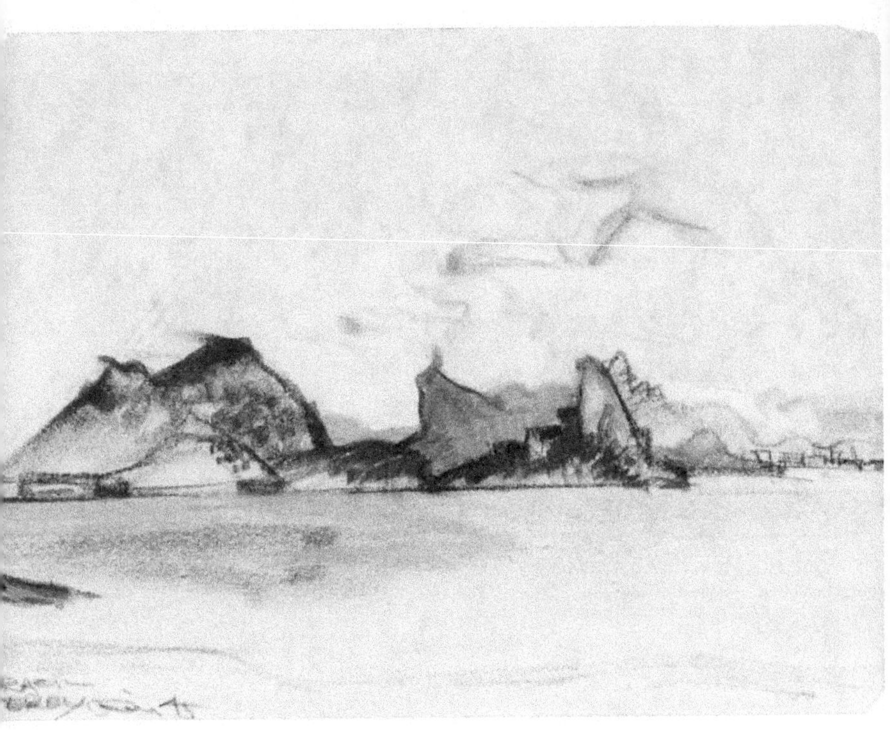

Travel sketch, Niterói. Richard Neutra, 1945

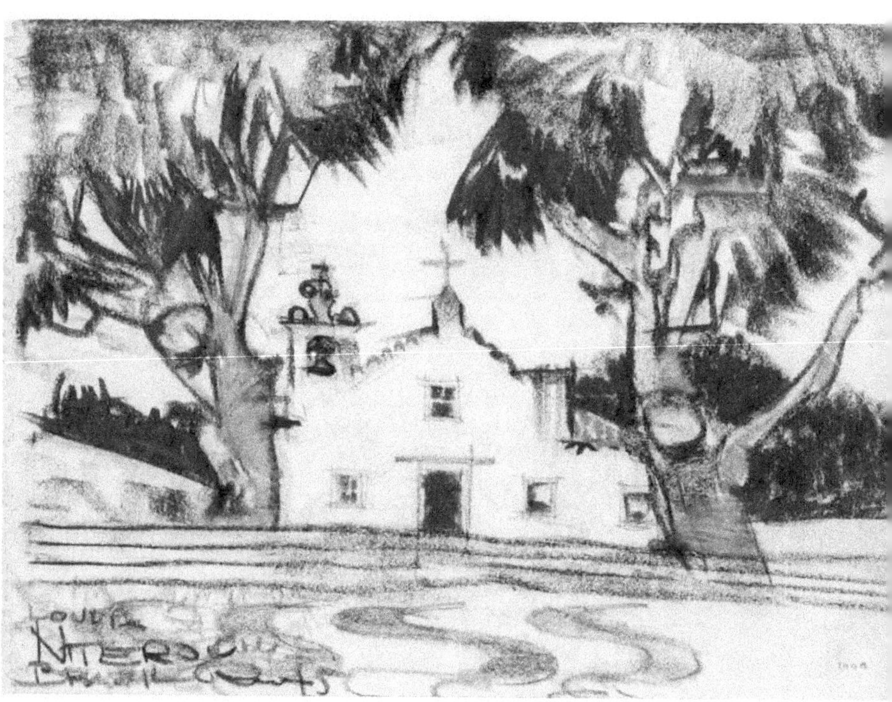

Travel sketch, litter. Richard Neutra,
1945

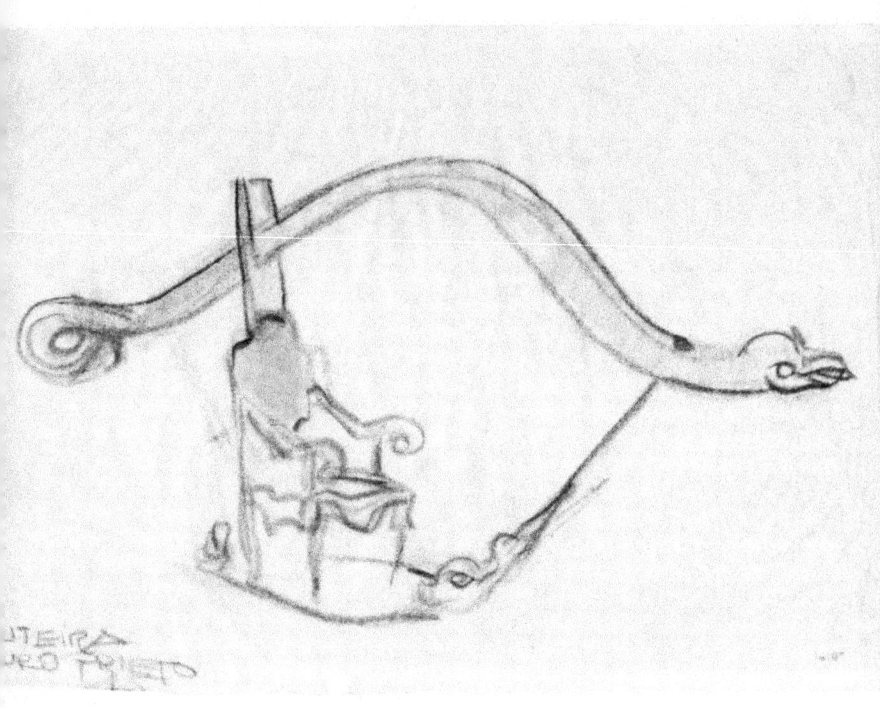

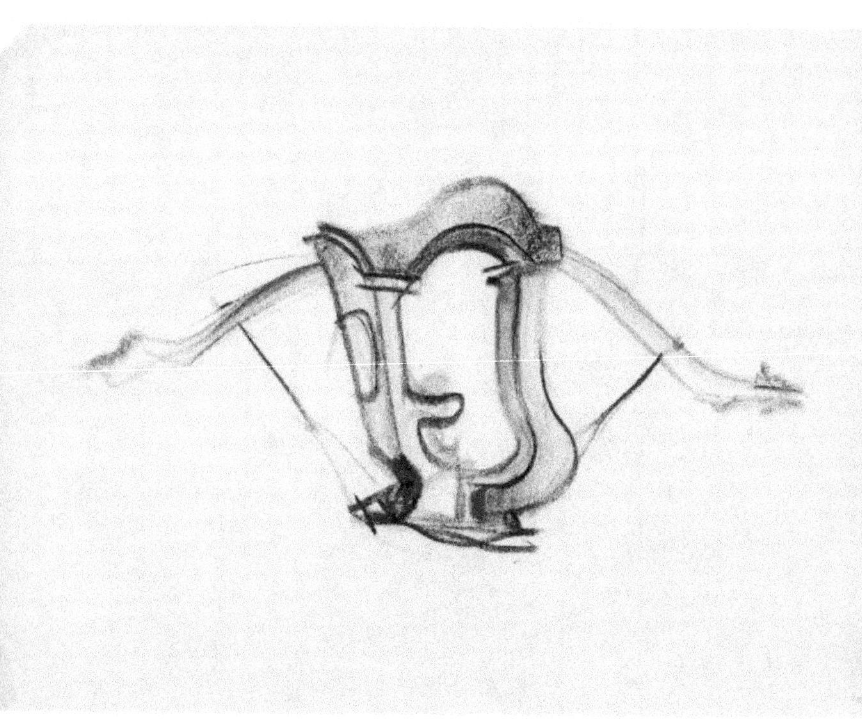

Travel sketch, litter. Richard Neutra, 1945

Travel sketch, Grande Hotel Ouro
Preto. Richard Neutra, 1945

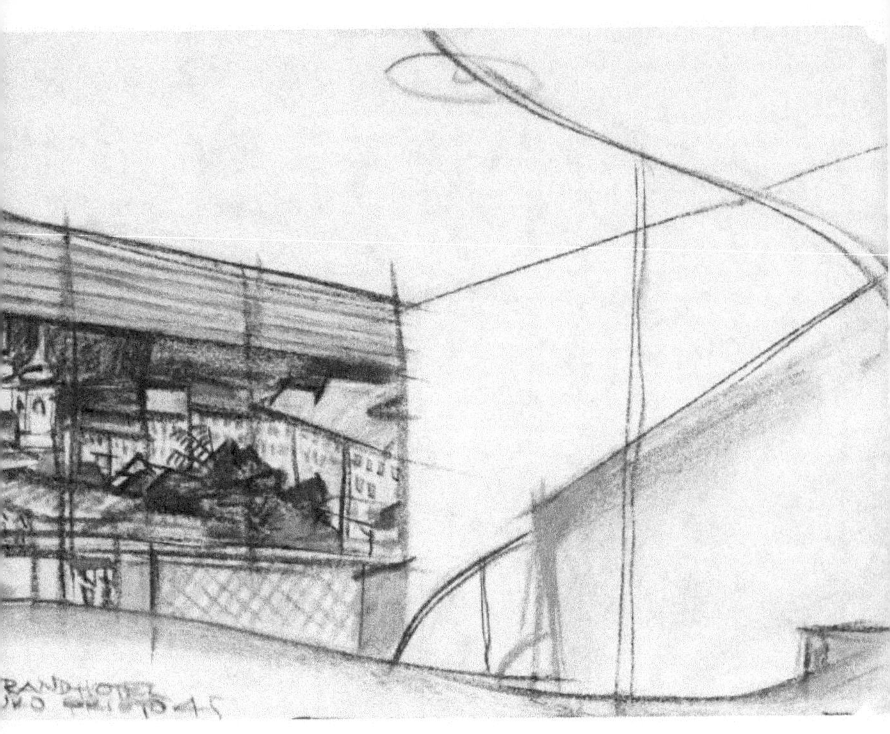

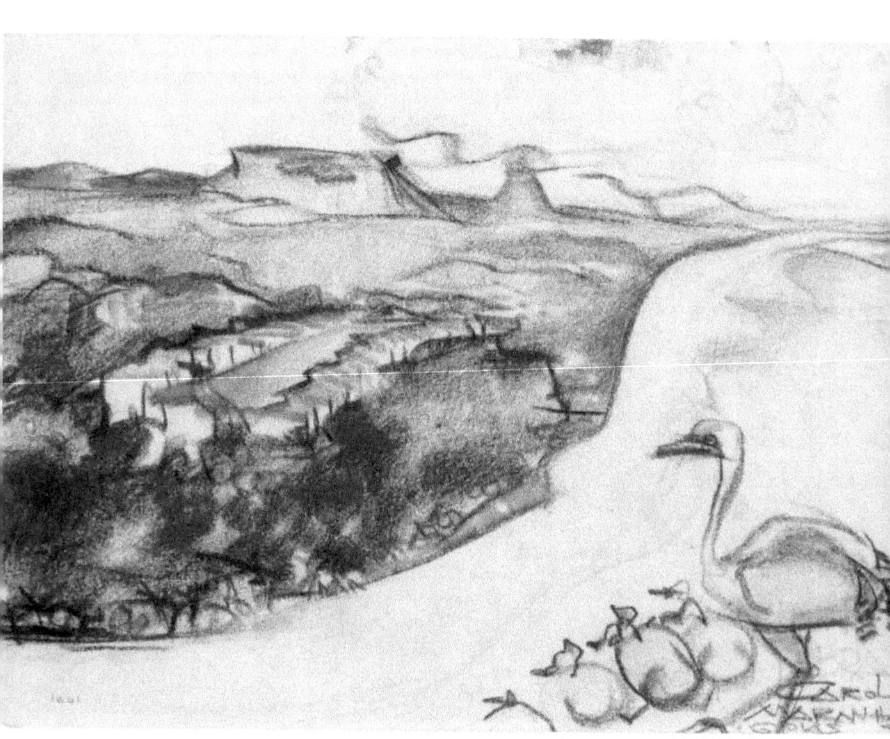

Travel sketch, view of the city of
Carolina MA surrounded by the forest
and the Morro do Chapéu. Richard
Neutra, 1945

Travel sketch, Aspen. Richard Neutra,
1952

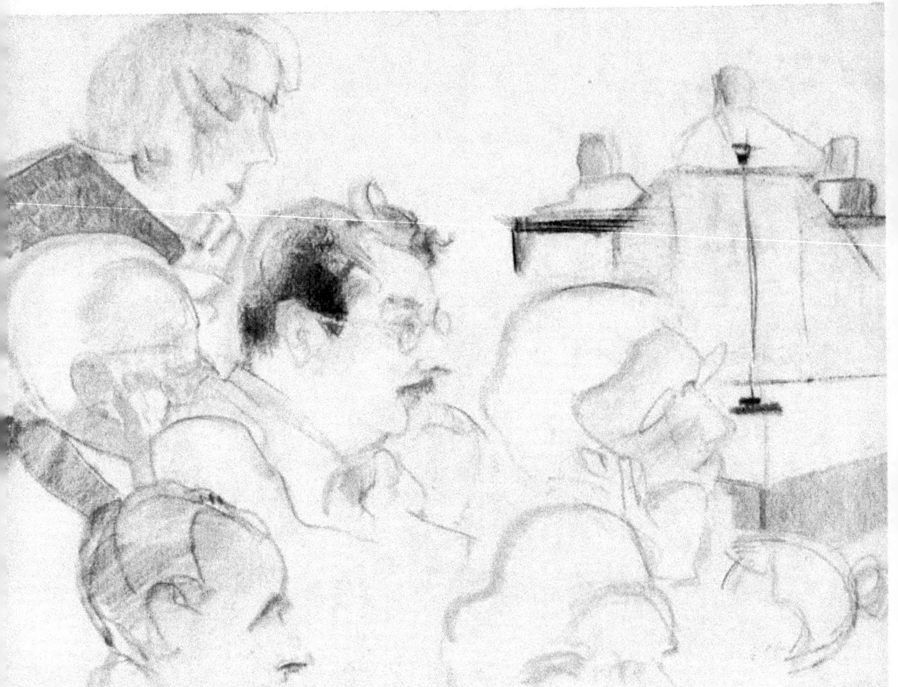

Travel sketch, Diego Rivera and Frida
Kahlo. Richard Neutra, 1937

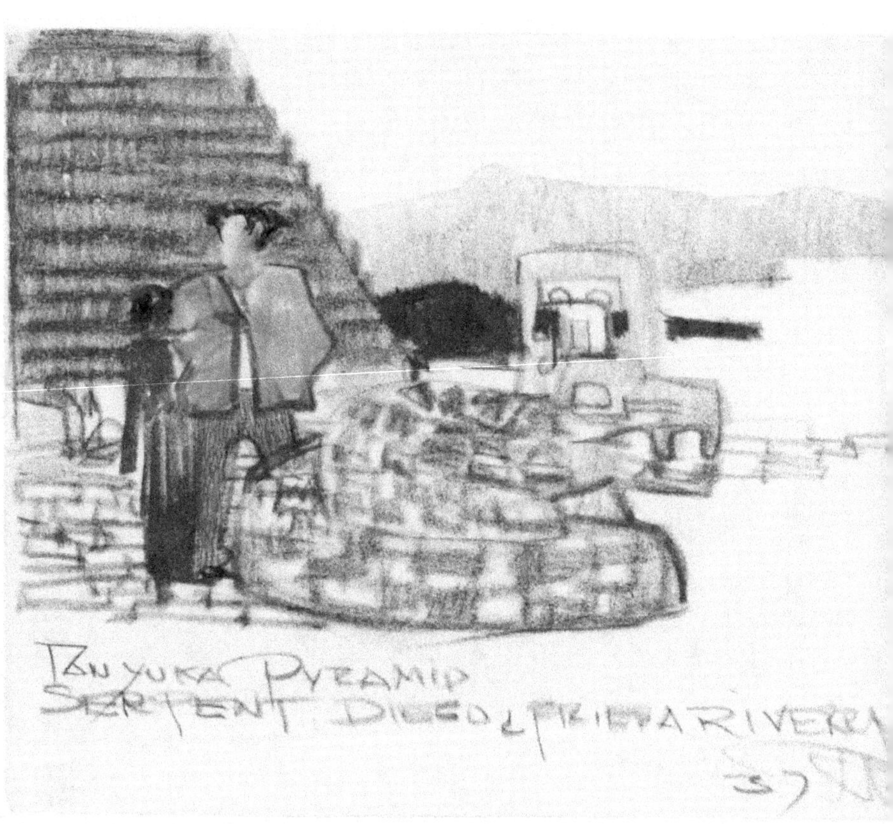

38

Travel sketch, Machu Pichu. Richard
Neutra, 1945

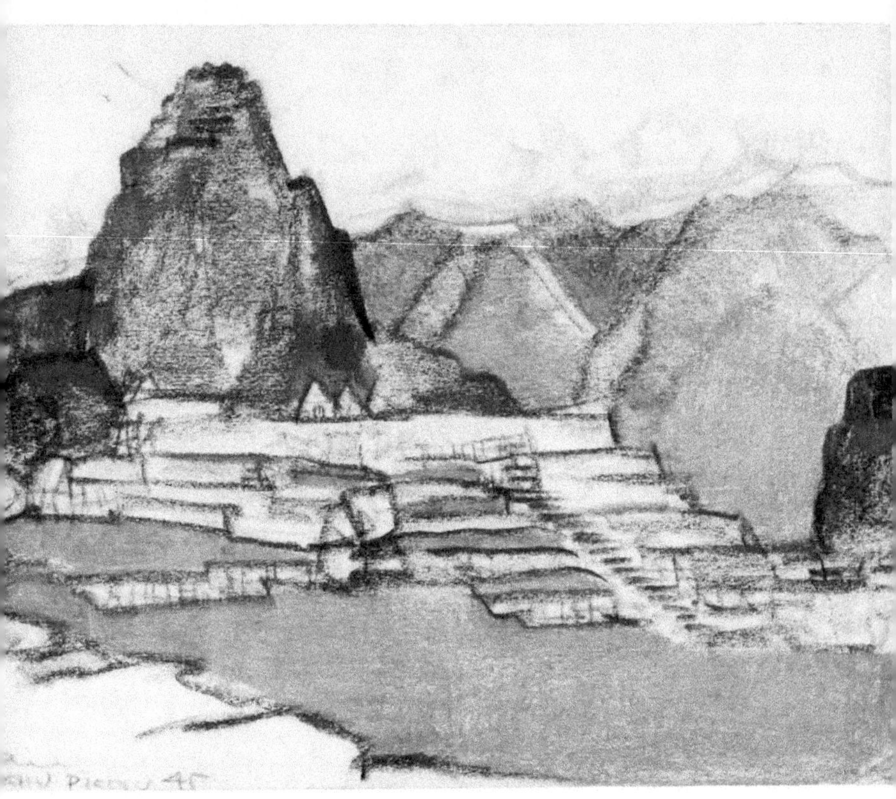

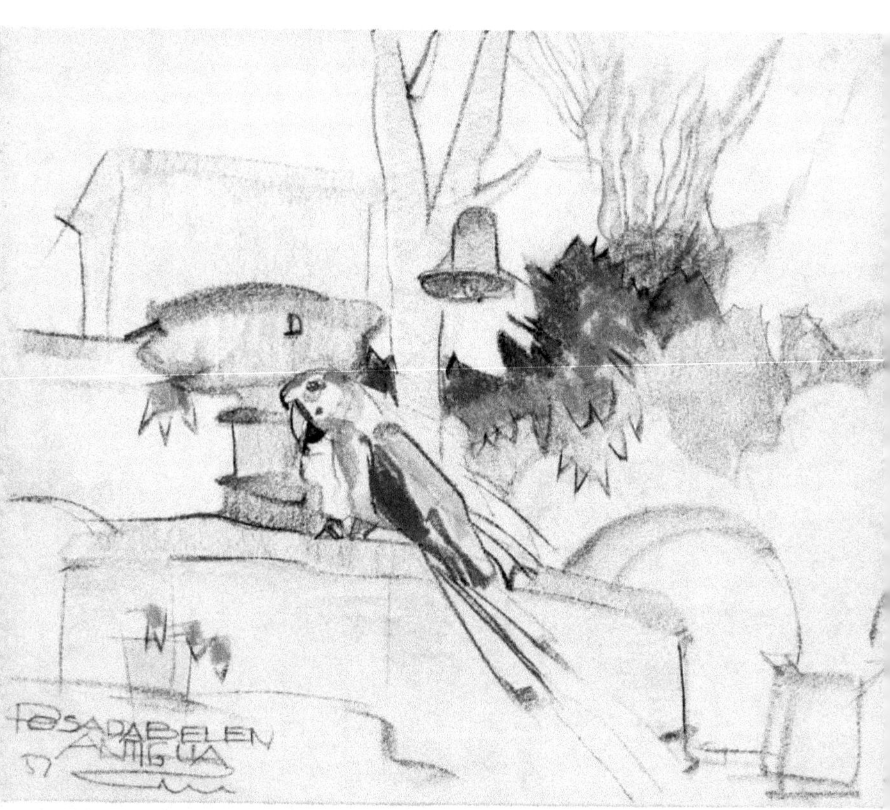

Travel sketch, Posada Belén, Antigua
Guatemala. Richard Neutra, 1957

Richard Neutra's drawings here presented are part of a
bigger amount of, approximately, 240 travel sketches done
throughout his life. This material, along with greater part of
the architect's archive (correspondences, articles, newspapers
and magazines clippings, designs and photographs), is held
by UCLA Charles E. Young Research Library, Department of
Special Collections, at the "Richard and Dion Neutra Papers"
Collection.

Introduction

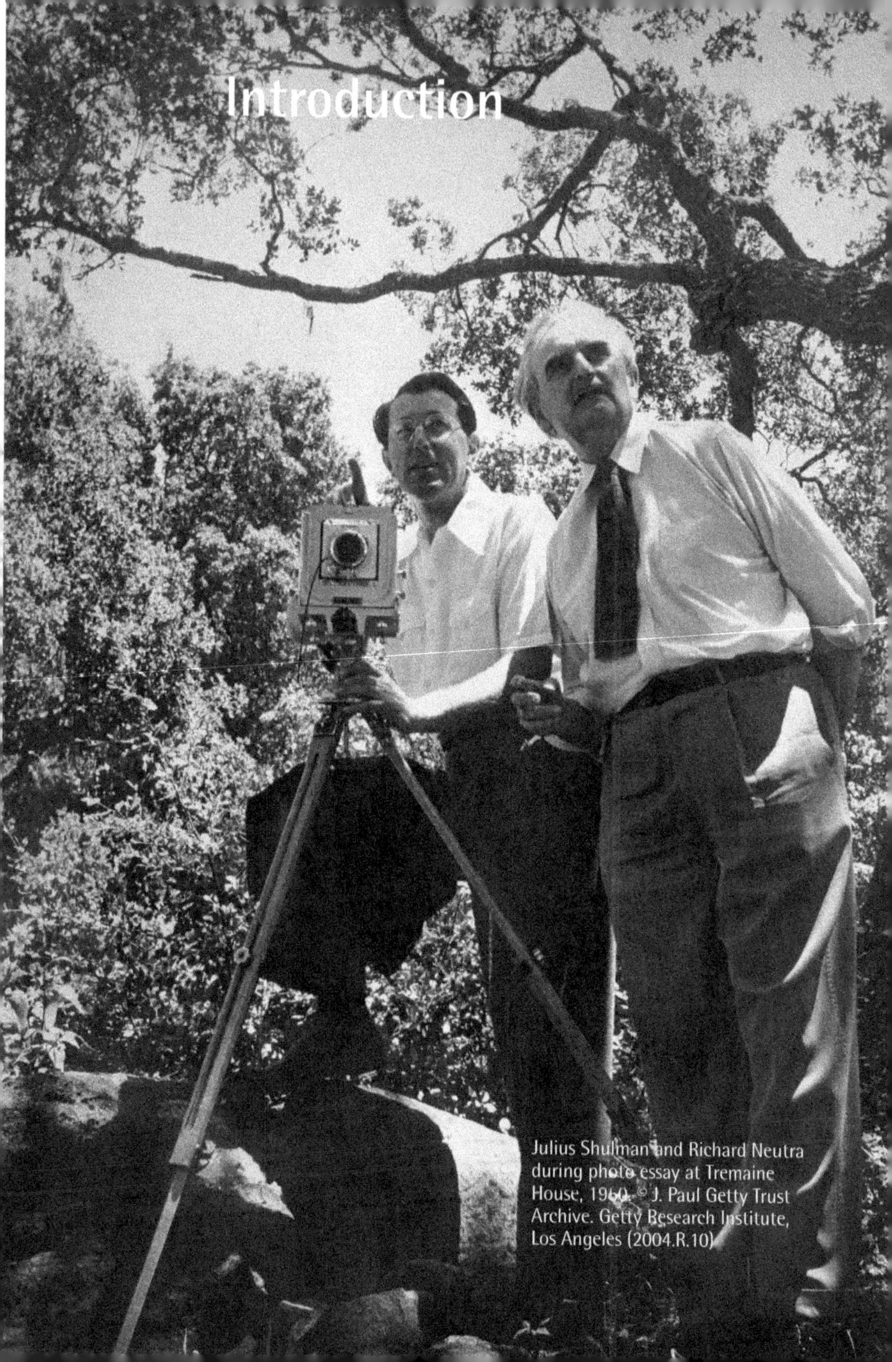

Julius Shulman and Richard Neutra
during photo essay at Tremaine
House, 1960. © J. Paul Getty Trust
Archive. Getty Research Institute,
Los Angeles (2004.R.10)

Neutra empirically observed all his life. Just as his client interrogations allowed him to inspect the individual, his never-ending international trips, commissions, lectures and appointments ensured that Neutra did not patronize local cultures but attempted to work with them.
Barbara Mac Lamprecht, "The Obsolescence of Optimism?"[1]

Richard Joseph Neutra (1892-1970), Austrian architect based in the United States, sought throughout his works to correlate modern, rationalist and industrialized architecture to particular conditions of culture, climate, landscape and technology, as well as to local resources. Ever since settling in Los Angeles, on the US West Coast, he explored ways to integrate architecture with its surroundings, bringing the natural landscape into the built environment while at the same time extending the interior to the exterior. In parallel, he pursued his interests in new construction technologies, enhancing efficiency and rationalization in his project at lower costs.

The wanderer architect – as Adriana Irigoyen[2] has put it, borrowing the term from Hugo Segawa[3] – saw each trip not only as a way to advertise his work, but much rather as an opportunity to observe local cultures and architecture and extract the best from them. He did this in every drawing, every photograph taken, and every text he wrote about the works and/or architects that caught his attention. His attentive eye did not even miss the work of young architects such as Jacob Ruchti, much less the major contributions of Oscar Niemeyer and Roberto Burle Marx.

Richard Neutra's first contact with South America took place between October and November 1945, through a diplomatic mission entrusted to him by the US Department of State. The relationships that were established there ranged from the personal to the professional and lasted until the mid-1960s. Either because of the political transformations that most Latin American countries underwent at that period of time, or because of Neutra's health condition and his long stays in Germany during the last few years of his life, the fact is that these relationships emerged, flourished, and eventually withered over a period of approximately twenty years. It is safe to say, however, that they went beyond what was stipulated – and even expected – by the US government.

In order to grasp the circumstances that led Richard Neutra to Latin America, we will delve into the historical plot of the period, with special attention to North American foreign policy and its efforts to build closer relations with its sister republics. The Good Neighbor Policy, established in 1933 by the newly elected President Franklin Roosevelt, brought about a period of cultural and intellectual exchange in the Americas: The exhibitions and accompanying catalogs *Brazil Builds* (1943) and *Latin American Architecture Since 1945* (1955), organized by the Museum of Modern Art of New York – MoMA; the exhibit, also at MoMA, of the works of Cândido Portinari, in 1940; the travels of Walt Disney and Orson Welles that resulted in the creation of characters and films about Latin America; the multiple trips and extended stays of Erico Verissimo (1905-1975) in the United States;[4] as well as Richard Neutra's multiple visits to South American countries, starting with his recognition trip in 1945, under the auspices of the Department of State.

In the specific case of Brazil, Neutra landed there for the first time in November 1945 and visited iconic projects of modern architecture, such as the headquarters of the Brazilian Reinsurance Institute and the building of the Brazilian Press Association, designed by the Roberto brothers, and the Seaplane Station, by Atílio Correa Lima, in Rio de Janeiro; the Esther and Leonidas Moreira buildings, respectively by Álvaro Vital Brazil and Eduardo Kneese de Mello, in São Paulo; the Grande Hotel in Ouro Preto and Oscar Niemeyer's Pampulha works, in Minas Gerais. He took pictures and made several drawings – not only of Brazilian landscapes, but of all the countries he visited – which served as illustrations for two articles published in 1946 by *Progressive Architecture* magazine: "Observations on Latin America," where he wrote about landscapes and customs of the Latin American people; and "Sun Control Devices", in which he discussed architectural solutions developed by Latin American architects to control solar incidence and ventilation in buildings. But these were not the only articles that Neutra wrote. A few months after his return to the United States, he delivered a full report on his trip to the Division of Cultural Cooperation of the US Department of State, describing the places he visited and the people he met, as well as lectures given at universities and institutes of architects.

As properly verified in the *Neutra Collection* of the University of California, Los Angeles – UCLA Library Special Collections, during this recognition trip, several personal contacts were established between Richard Neutra and Brazilian architects and intellectuals: Henrique Mindlin, Eduardo Kneese de Mello, Marcello Fragelli, Vilanova Artigas, Gregori Warchavchik, Miguel Forte, Pietro Maria Bardi, Roberto Burle Marx, Lucjan Korngold, Sérgio Bernardes, among others. In addition, some important events followed this first visit, such as: The publication of the book *Architecture of Social Concern in Regions of Mild Climate*, in São Paulo, in 1948, where he dwells on his experiences in projects for hospitals, health centers and schools as a consultant on the Committee on Design of Public Works in Puerto Rico; the exhibition *Neutra: Residências/Residences* at the São Paulo Museum of Art – Masp, in 1951; his participation in the II Bienal of the Museum of Modern Art of São Paulo, in 1953; the works in partnership with Roberto Burle Marx – the Schulthess House in Havana and the panel for the Amalgamated Clothing Workers of America building in Los Angeles, both in 1956. In addition, there were also his consecutive trips back to Brazil, in 1957, 1958 and 1959, when Neutra visited São Paulo, Rio de Janeiro and Brasília – still under construction –, as a participant in the Extraordinary International Congress of Art

Critics; finally, the design and construction, between 1958 and 1965, of the González-Gorrondona House, in Caracas, Venezuela.

Barbara Lamprecht, author of a series of books about Richard Neutra published mostly by Taschen, pointed out the relevance of the travels and works developed by the architect abroad and how this experience formed his way of taking advantage of the local culture in his projects – as noted in the epigraph at the beginning of this introduction. This statement corroborates the hypothesis presented here and is the starting point for our investigation. The fact that Neutra "empirically observed" each place he visited throughout his life – the practice of making drawings and taking photographs is already an indication, perhaps even proof of this – shows that he was in a continuous search for transformation. And, although the hegemonic discourse refuses to address, in its analysis, Neutra's relationship with Latin America (his travels, his personal and professional contacts, his studies carried out here), this experience nevertheless transformed his later work.

Even more important is the fact that Richard Neutra identified with the Latin American people he met. In the preface to the Spanish edition of *Survival Through Design*, published in Mexico in 1957, Neutra states that he felt culturally "familiar with these people who thought in Castilian" comparing the history of Argentina and Peru with that of Vienna in the post-Renaissance period. In addition to pointing out this similarity around his motherland, the architect also recalled the Spanish origins of the city that had welcomed him in 1925.[5] This was not condescending talk from an European, based in the United States, pandering to Latin American readers; rather, this was a genuine statement from someone who understood the meaning of being *the other* and who identified with it. Perhaps because of his Jewish origins and the historical persecution they suffered in Europe, or perhaps because of his status as a German-speaking immigrant in the US. In any case, Neutra's attitude makes it even clearer that his interest in Latin American architects and architecture was genuine and that his presence here went far beyond a mere diplomatic mission.

Nevertheless, a careful reading of the main historiography about the Austrian architect and his work reveals that the relationship between Neutra and Latin America has been largely overlooked in the main discourse, at the very least insofar as it is not seen as a two-way street. Besides dismissing some of the transformations that the architect underwent throughout his trajectory, historians commonly impose on Latin American countries a unidirectional view which insists that modern architecture emerged and consolidated in Europe and the United States, only later being transplanted to Latin America and adapted to our regionalist condition. Such ideological interpretation of historical facts is the "historiographic problem" that Marina Waisman refers to and that this book seeks to challenge:

> Historical problems are resolved through research. Critical operations are performed to ensure data accuracy and relevance. These are technical problems. Historiographic problems, on the other hand, are directly linked to the historian's ideology, since, in order to define the structure of the historiographical text, they favour a particular aspect of their subject matter and make use of particular critical instruments – that is, all that will lead them to their interpretation of the facts and meanings and, eventually, to the formulation of their own version of the chosen theme.[6]

In our analysis of hegemonic historiography, the first *loose end* is found in the compilation of the architect's works by Barbara Lamprecht. In the book *Richard Neutra: Complete Works*, González-Gorrondona House, which in the first edition is reduced to an image of the façade, was mistakenly swapped with Alfred De Schulthess House. That is, instead of a photograph of the Venezuelan house, we would find a photo of the Cuban house. Naturally, the problem was fixed for the second edition; however, the absence of any technical drawings or more precise analysis of the work has not been corrected, despite the project being extensively featured in the third volume of the collection edited by Willy Boesiger.[7]

In Thomas Hines' narrative, *Richard Neutra and the Search for Modern Architecture*, both Latin American projects are mentioned only as an excuse for the historian to point out what he considers to be a bad example of large-scale residential projects (Schulthess House) and a good example (González-Gorrondona House).[8] Further reading of Hines' text provides even more evidence that a new look at Richard Neutra's work is indeed necessary and might as well suggest revisions and new reflections.[9] Important projects that somehow bear the mark of his relationship with Latin America are described by Hines as merely the consequence of Neutra's conflicts with partners. It's almost as if the evolution of an architect in a continuous search for modern architecture – the very title of Hines' biography points this out – could hurt the image of the architect who pioneered the International Style.

In addition to treating Neutra's relationship with Latin American architects and architecture as secondary, historians also seem to overlook the evolution of his work. In an essay on the society and culture of the 19th and 20th centuries, Marshall Berman notes that to be modern is to be in constant search for growth, self-transformation and transformation of the world around us.[10] Richard Neutra was no different: His constant travels, his efforts to understand the styles of architecture he saw and to stay connected with colleagues around the world, pay tribute to his constant quest for transformation.

From his formative period and his first works on the American continent, the architect has sought to incorporate to his projects technological innovations, as well as his fascination with landscape, his appreciation for the arts and even his restlessness in the face of the challenge posed by the climate and the social conditions of the places where he worked. On numerous occasions (articles, correspondence and unpublished texts), he freely expressed his belief in the importance of transforming others and himself. He also did not hide his admiration for the work of his colleagues – whatever their origins – or even his desire to keep in constant contact with them. The immense collection of correspondence stored in the UCLA Library Special Collections and the numerous books and articles he has written are ample proof of this.

Even so, the existing historiography on Richard Neutra's trajectory and his works insists on denying the transformation process throughout his whole career, at least with regard to what he took from Latin America. The recognition trip through South American countries is neither seen nor described by historians with as much enthusiasm and importance as, for example, his tour through Asia and Europe in 1930. Perhaps because the trip was financed by the United States government; or perhaps because, for such historians, the Bauhaus means much more than Latin America. It is worth noting that the role of the US Department of State as the promoter of the 1945 trip is treated with contempt by both foreign and national historians.

The discourse on the architect's work and trajectory has been based on the premises laid by Thomas Hines in the book, and also in subsequent debates which did not advance any critical review – even those by historians from Latin America. With regard to Latin American architecture in general, our position is currently being duly reevaluated by important researchers who dare to discuss history tackling new points of view. However, in the specific case of Richard Neutra, this effort is still incipient. Even researches developed by Latin Americans that deal with the relationship between

the architect and their own countries have the dominant
view that this influence was a one-way process instilled in
their discourse.

This book intends to carry out an analysis that takes
into account the existing historiography on the architect,
going beyond a simple – although it is never really simple –
design analysis. The projects, in fact, provide the basis for our
investigation of the impact that Latin American architecture
had on Neutra's work. The opposite is much easier to see:
Just take a look at the several publications of the architect's
projects in Latin American magazines; his books published
in Portuguese and Spanish; and even the testimony of those
who, at the time of his visits, were still young architects and
students. But, how to understand the opposite point of view,
if the existing discourse, whenever possible, ignores it or even
denies it?

Starting from apparently insignificant and overly specific
identifications, it was possible to bring to light a new aspect
of Richard Neutra: His intense contact with Latin American
architects, landscapers and intellectuals was in fact reflected
in his work after 1945, and not only thanks to the period in
which he developed designs for hospitals, schools and health
centers in Puerto Rico – as the hegemonic historiography
tends to insist –, but also because he found interlocutors in
Latin America who shared his concerns, as well as, and this is
even more important, architectural answers for the questions
he was battling with.

Although his first contact with the "other American
republics" – as the official documents of the US government
used to refer to the countries South of Rio Grande – was
to carry out a diplomatic mission in the post-World War II
period, the contacts he established there and the references
he took – in the form of drawings, photographs and studies – had nothing to do with the political situation or The
Good Neighbour Policy of the time. In fact, these elements
represent his genuine interest in Latin American architecture.

More than that, they demonstrate how influence unravels through a complex network, being the opposite of the fateful process of contamination that the academy usually conceives.

In the excerpt of the January 11, 1962 issue of the *Los Angeles Times*, which accompanies the publication regarding the Los Angeles Hall of Records building – in the third volume of Boesiger's collection –, one reads: "One of the most striking features of the well-articulated building mass are the 125-foot-high movable aluminum louvers which Neutra has used for a quarter of century to shield glass fronts that are exposed to the direct rays of the sun."[11]

A quick calculation leads us to the first project in which movable louvers were applied – Kaufmann House (1946-1947) – and the basis for its use: The article "Sun Control Devices." Under the title on page 88 of the October 1946 issue of *Progressive Architecture* magazine is the following sentence: "A presentation based primarily on examples collected in South America by Richard Neutra."[12] At the top, crowning the page, is a generous photo, taken by Neutra, of the North façade (the sunnier one) of the model for the Maternity Hospital of University of São Paulo, by Rino Levi. In the photo, the vertical louvers, as shown both in the taller and in the lower volume, are the protagonists.

Thus, from the reading of the two main researchers – Barbara Lamprecht and Thomas Hines – and the detection of their resistance regarding Neutra's work in relation to Latin America, it was observed that the same patterns of thought and interpretation were repeated in subsequent research. Having identified the issue, a subversion of the hegemonic discourse on Richard Neutra is proposed, inverting the point of view of traditional historiography and opening up the possibility for new analyzes that highlight the influence of Latin America. In the words of Marina Waisman:

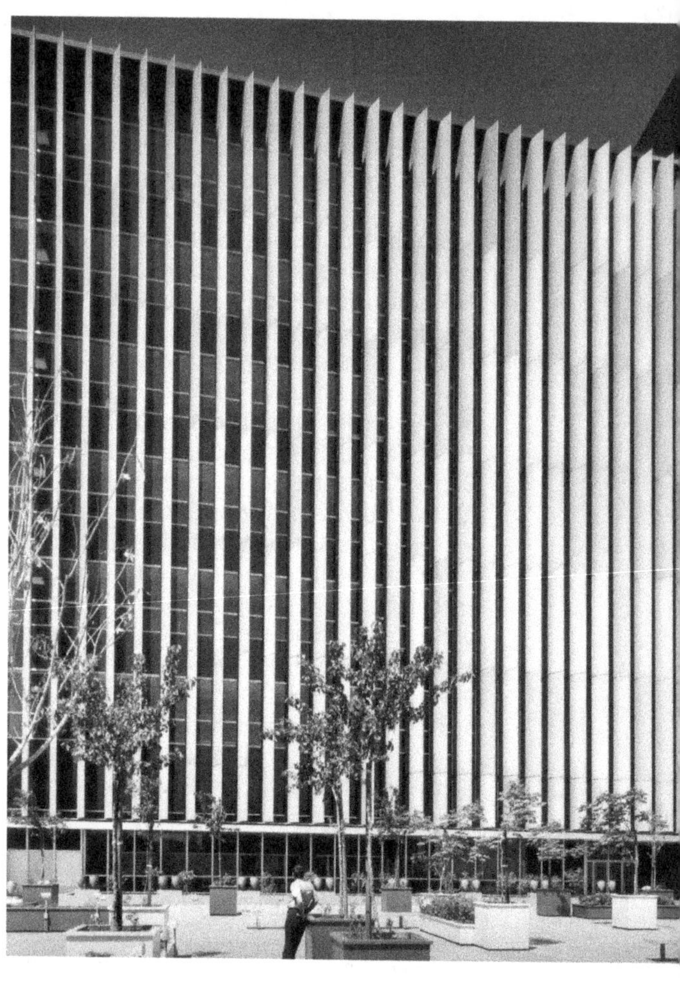

Los Angeles Hall of Records, Los
Angeles EUA. Richard Neutra, 1962.
Photo Julius Shulman. © J. Paul Getty
Trust Archive. Getty Research Institute,
Los Angeles (2004.R.10)

The dismantling of the mechanisms of historiography
is a fundamental operation for a critical reading that
makes it possible to become aware of one's own position
in relation to architecture. History is never a definitive
thing, it keeps rewriting itself through each present,
each cultural circumstance and also through the convictions of each historian. Learning how to unravel the
motivations, intentions, ideologies that, in each case,
preside over a historiographic work, is the essential first
step towards knowledge.[13]

If history is a succession of judgments[14] and historiography is the study of the development of history over time,
never immune to the historian's ideological preconceptions,[15]
this research aimed to deconstruct the historiographical
discourse, presenting a new reading and a new interpretation of the data. Our hypothesis is that Latin American
architecture had as much or even more impact on Richard
Neutra's production than Richard Neutra had on Latin
American architects. Thus, our aim is to question the existing
historiographical discourse, as well as any repetition devoid
of critical revision, while repositioning Latin America in
order to bring it to a well-deserved prominence – no longer
as the site of regionalist and marginal interpretations of a
supposedly central modern architecture, but as the place
where particular responses to modernity were produced and
that would greatly influence the modern architecture of the
Northern hemisphere.

Taking on the role of the unwary and nosy researcher
– a character created by Ruth Verde Zein in her short-story
about the historiographical documentation of architecture[16]
–, this book sets itself the difficult task of presenting a new
reading, from a Latin American point of view, in the debate
regarding Richard Neutra. It started off as an undergraduate
research – *Richard Neutra no Brasil*, developed between
August 2011 and July 2012 with the aid of a Pibic-CNPq

scholarship –, later being developed during my master's degree – *Richard Neutra e o Brasil*, presented in August de 2015 and which had two FAPESP scholarships – and also my PhD – *Richard Neutra: conexões latino-americanas*, presented in February 2020 – with the aid of a scholarship from the Mackpesquisa Fund. These three stages were developed at the School of Architecture and Urbanism of Universidade Presbiteriana Mackenzie, under the supervision of Professor Abilio Guerra.

Notes

1. Barbara Mac Lamprecht, "The Obsolescence of Optimism? Neutra and Alexander's U.S. Embassy, Karachi, Pakistan."

2. Adriana Marta Irigoyen Touceda, "Da Califórnia a São Paulo."

3. Hugo Segawa, "Arquitetos peregrinos, nômades e migrantes," 9-13.

4. Carlos Cortez Minchillo, *Erico Verissimo, escritor do mundo: circulação literária, cosmopolitismo e relações interamericanas.*

5. Richard Joseph Neutra, *Planificar para sobrevivir,* 9-10.

6. Marina Waisman, *O interior da história: historiografia arquitetônica para uso de latino-americanos,* 5. Free translation.

7. Willy Boesiger, *Buildings and Projects: Richard Neutra, 1961-1966.*

8. Thomas S. Hines, *Richard Neutra and the Search for Modern Architecture,* 303.

9. Cf. Ruth Verde Zein, "When Documenting is not Enough. Buildings, Dates, Reflections, and Theoretical Constructions."

10. Marshall Berman, *Tudo que é sólido desmancha no ar. A aventura da modernidade,* 15.

11. Boesiger, *Buildings and projects: Richard Neutra, 1961-1966,* 200.

12. Richard Joseph Neutra, "Sun Control Devices," 88.

13. Waisman, *O interior da história,* xv. Free translation.

14. Cf. Renato de Fusco, *História y arquitectura,* 77, quoted in Waisman, *O interior da história,* 3.

15. Waisman, *O interior da história,* 4-5.

16. Zein, "When Documenting is not Enough," 102-125.

Richard Neutra and Brazil

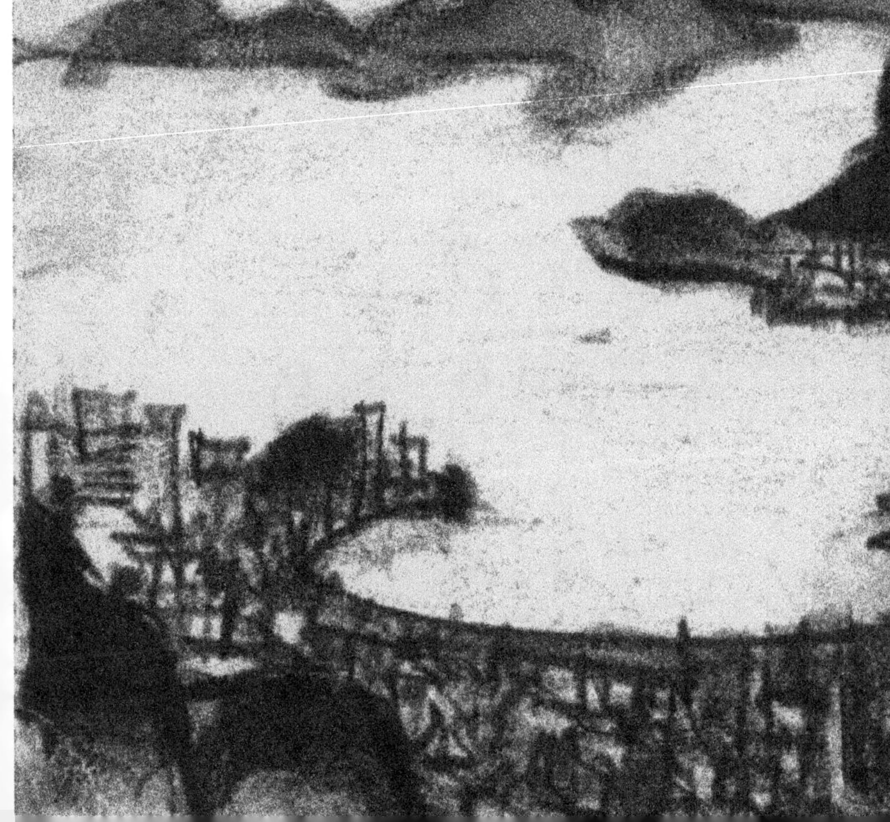

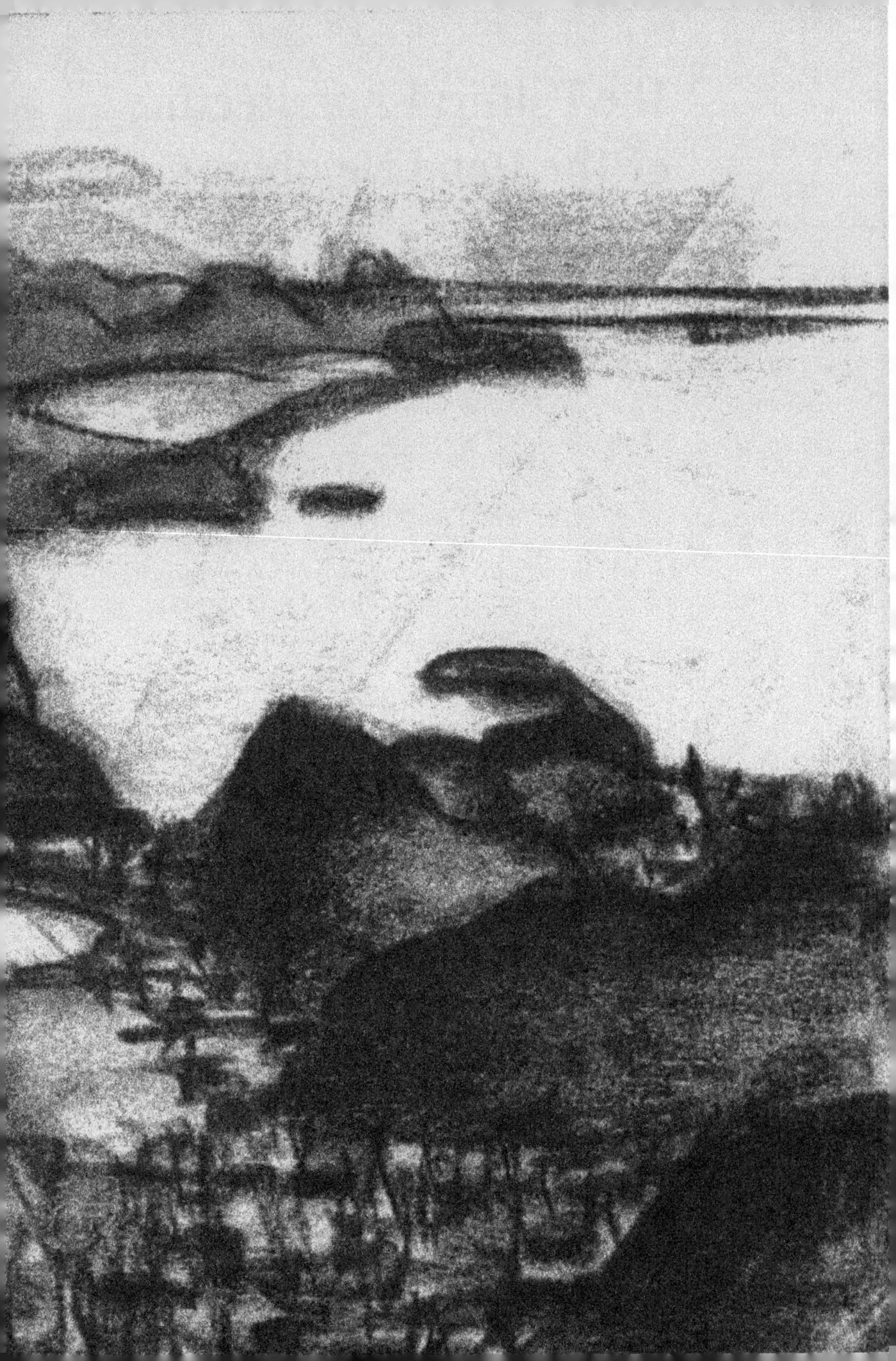

The Political Architecture of the Good Neighbors

America began as an empire during the nineteenth century, but it was in the second half of the twentieth, after the decolonization of the British and French empires, that it directly followed its two great predecessors.
Edward W. Said, *Cultura e imperialismo*[1]

Topics regarding US diplomatic policies and efforts for cultural convergence between the United States and Latin America have been debated by several authors, many of them either of direct or indirect interest to this research: Gerson Moura,[2] Antonio Pedro Tota,[3] Luis Alberto Bandeira,[4] Fernando Atique,[5] Lauro Cavalcanti[6] and Carlos Minchillo,[7] in Brazil; Jorge Francisco Liernur,[8] in Argentina; Anaioly Glinkin,[9] in Russia; Michael Blumenthal,[10] Patrício Del Real,[11] Thomas Leonard,[12] Justin Hart,[13] Jenifer Van Vleck,[14] Gisela Cramer and Ursula Prutsch,[15] in the United States – to name just a few. From this range of researchers dealing with a variety of strategies for approximation – from convergence through the arts (such as cinema and literature) to efforts at economic cooperation –, Fernando Atique, Jorge Liernur and Lauro Cavalcanti are the authors who best engage with architecture. However, it is Patrício Del Real who deals in greater depth with the impact of North American foreign policy on the architecture of Latin America.

Following the efforts for post-war reconstruction and consolidation of the United States hegemony, American architecture started to receive strong governmental stimulus and sponsorship,[16] a process that entailed the participation of groups such as Congrès Internationaux d'Architecture Moderne – CIAM and American Institute of Architects – AIA, as well as internationally recognized architects, such as, for example, José Luis Sert, Paul Lester Wiener and Richard Neutra. These three architects were particularly involved with projects from the US Department of State aiming to solve economic and social issues on the American continent – issues that were seen as possible gateways for communism in the Western Hemisphere. After the defeat of Nazism, US policy turned to fight the expansion of the influence of its former Soviet allies.

José Luis Sert and Paul Lester Wiener, partners at Town Planning Associates from 1942 to 1959,[17] had great roles as consultants in the planning of cities in Latin America, as is the case of Cidade dos Motores (City of Engines) in Brazil.[18] This 1942 project for National Engine Factory – which would be implemented in the lowlands of the Rio de Janeiro state (*Baixada Fluminense*), between the capital and Petrópolis[19] – was the result of an American political operation set to establish a closer relationship with South America countries as a response to recent Nazi victories and fear of German expansion in America. Appointed by his father-in-law and Treasury Secretary in the Roosevelt administration, Henry Morgenthau, Wiener would be named adviser of the US Department of State in the cultural field for architectural planning in Latin America.[20] Thus, he traveled along with Sert through the countries south of Rio Grande,[21] establishing contacts and working on urban planning projects.

Brazil was to be the first country of destination in South America, and Sert and Lester were to be its visitors, charged with spreading the "good news". [...] The trip must have made quite an impression in certain Brazilian university circles, as can be deduced from the letters that Lester regularly received from that country. The practice continued to be encouraged by the North American Department of State throughout 1943, the year in which Lester wrote an opuscule with the unequivocal title: *Uma nova era cultural para as Américas* [A new cultural era for the Americas].[22]

Richard Neutra's relationship with the US government, which dates back to the early 1930s when the architect worked on projects for public schools and social housing, consolidated with his hiring as a consultant to the Committee on Design of Public Works in Puerto Rico, followed by his trip through South America. Hence, in order to better explore Neutra's relationship with Latin America – and, in particular, with Brazil –, we should start our discussion by clarifying the foreign policy adopted by Franklin Roosevelt towards the sister republics on the American continent, as well as the origins of this policy.

As pointed out by Edward Said in our epigraph, the project of the United States of America to establish itself as an empire began in the 19th century with the Monroe Doctrine, following the protectionist policies adopted by then-president James Monroe, who sought to isolate America from the influence of European politics. The project went much further after the Second World War, which had devastated Europe.[23] While seeking dominance, the United States suffered an economic setback with the stock market crash in 1929. In 1933, as a response to the serious crisis that swept the country, the newly elected President Franklin Delano Roosevelt (1881-1945) adopted a strategy of intense state intervention in the economy: "With the New Deal, the construction of the welfare state began, entailing a strong presence of the State in society; the goal was to plan and regulate the American capitalist system in the general interest of the nation, as never before in American history."[24]

Contrary to how it is depicted in history books, the New Deal was not as successful or assertive as we imagine it. It consisted, in fact, of a series of attempts, with varying degrees of success, at State interventionist measures in the economy, ranging from the creation of numerous state agencies that sought to regulate prices and working hours in large industries to emergency injections of financial stimulus.[25]

> [The New Deal] did not end the Depression and the massive unemployment that accompanied it. It did not – the complaints of conservative critics notwithstanding – transform American capitalism in any genuinely radical way. Except in the field of labor relations and a few other areas, corporate power remained nearly as free from government regulation or control in 1945 as it had been in 1933. The New Deal did not end poverty or effect any significant redistribution of wealth. Nor did it do much to address what became some of the principal domestic problems of the postwar era, among them the problems of racial and gender inequality.[26]

Through this new economic policy, Roosevelt sought to expand foreign markets for manufactured goods and secure the supply of raw materials, as well as new investment possibilities. To that end, he turned to Latin America as a logical response in order to make up for his losses in Europe.[27] However, maintaining the Latin American economic market was not his ultimate goal. This strategy sprang from a greater concern: to ensure the maximum collaboration and alignment of the sister republics under US leadership.[28] As the United States struggled to win over the economic crisis, in

Germany, the Nazi Party took power, appointing Adolf Hitler as Prime Minister. The growth of the Nazi threat brought a new challenge to the maintenance of US hegemony in the Western Hemisphere, especially in Brazil, where three of the largest contingents of immigrants – Italians, Germans and Japanese – came from countries that would constitute the enemy bloc in the Second War.

Therefore, the concern with the global image of the United States increased; consequently, the need to adopt diplomatic policies, either through dissemination or exchange, also intensified.[29] Thus, Roosevelt chose to set aside direct intervention policies (such as the *Big Stick* and *Dollar Diplomacy*), favoring more subtle forms of domination and ideological influence over Latin-Americans.[30] At this point, it is important to insist upon the notion that the ideal of "projecting America" as a world power pre-dates the war and the Nazi or the socialist threat, but it was the eminent expansion of these threats that shaped US foreign policy and made Latin America its laboratory for broader actions. In other words, consolidating a united America from North to South under a Yankee leadership, during the period of the Nazi rise in Europe, served as an opportunity for trying out modes of action that would later be extended to the European continent.

> As much as the Soviet threat amplified and modified these initiatives after the war, the desire to 'project America' throughout the world would have existed irrespective of the Soviet Union's emergence as a geopolitical rival. Of course, the fact that the Soviet Union posed both a geopolitical and an ideological threat made that rivalry all the more intense and, perhaps, all the more likely.[31]

In order to guarantee its hegemony in the Western Hemisphere, the United States sought to encourage mutual collaboration between countries on the American continent, a solidarity that required some initiative on the part of the North Americans in order to get "other American republics" back on their feet in economic terms. Here, it's well worth explaining two expressions referencing countries on the American continent that speak Latin languages. The term Latin America – the more commonly used – arose from a French attempt to exert influence among peoples of Latin origin – that is, of French, Italian, Spanish and Portuguese descent – in America, as a way of opposing the Anglo-Saxon advance.[32] Both Simon Bolivar and José Marti defended a union of the former Iberian colonies in the 19th century, but it was the French intellectuals who gave life to the term. The expression "other American republics", on the other hand, was how the United States government officially referred to the countries south of Rio Grande, as evidenced in the reading of a report produced as part of a government program to collect information on administrative experiences during World War II.[33] The use of both expressions, as well as the consolidation of the term "Americans" to designate the people of the United States, marks a greater distance between this country and the others, also pointing out to a common identity among Latin-speaking countries.[34]

This estrangement, added to the economic depression caused by the stock market crash, and also the advance of the Nazi threat, demanded from the United States a greater effort to secure the continent. For this, aiming to reverse its "bad neighbor" image, Franklin Roosevelt sought to implement a foreign policy of cultural approximation and economic solidarity – the Good Neighbor Policy. In this context, in December 1938 – during the 8th Inter-American Conference in Lima –, the Inter-American Financial and Economic Committee was created, with the goal of solving economic and financial issues imposed by the war, guaranteeing inter-American trade agreements and promoting economic growth in Latin America.

In June 1940, under the auspices of this Committee, the Inter-American Development Commission was created, set to promote – again, as stated in the official guidelines – the broad organization of the economic potentialities of the American republics. This commission, under the chairmanship of Nelson Aldrich Rockefeller (1908-1979), sought to foster a number of studies, gather information and establish the necessary relations for the development of the Latin-American republics. In addition to economic issues as delineated in the Good Neighbor Policy, military resources were made available to guarantee the defense of the Western Hemisphere. This strategy did not anticipate a joint participation of the North and Latin-American armed forces: the security of the continent fell on the United States, the remaining republics contributing in accordance to its resources. The concession of air and naval bases from Latin-American countries to the United States relates this agreement.[35]

It is important to emphasize that two countries deserved special attention from the US government: Mexico and Brazil. In the first case, besides the obvious question of the borders, there was an interest in the extraction of oil and rubber – key products for the war effort – and in the availability of cheap labor.[36] As for Brazil, the country played a major political role in South America, and this alliance could guarantee a North-American hegemony in the region.[37] Furthermore, the Brazilian coast – due to its dimension and position in the Atlantic Ocean – represented a strategic point for defending the continent against a possible Nazi attack from Africa.[38] Hence, the North American air base Parnamirim Field was built in Natal RN, in 1942.

In economic terms, the measures adopted at the Lima Conference were not enough, given the success and advancement of Germany. Emergency measures were necessary in order to absorb surpluses from Latin-American agricultural and mineral production. A report written in 1947 by the historical official Donald Rowland makes it clear the position adopted by the United States government of investing in Latin-American economies to preserve their trade balance, thus avoiding weak spots that could represent a gateway for the advance of Nazism in America.

> Increased investment in the other American republics should be undertaken by the United States, both to secure raw materials and to aid in maintaining a balance of trade. The problem of external debts should be faced realistically and should not stand in the way of a constructive financial and trade program.[39]

But it was not just German territorial expansion that the United States was concerned about. A great number of Latin-American republics were ruled by leaders with authoritarian proclivities, and this fact was also seen as a vantage point for Nazism in America: "Democracy had not taken root in most of the countries South Rio Grande, and while knowledgeable analysts distinguished between Latin-style authoritarianism and the newer brands of European totalitarianism, they still viewed them as being rather compatible in practical policy terms."[40]

That was the case with Brazil. The government of Getúlio Vargas (1930-1945) was characterized by a duality in its relation to the two powerhouses:[41] while it did sign the Treaty of Reciprocal Assistance with the United States (1935), it also negotiated the Compensation Agreement with Germany (1934 and 1936).[42] And even though this agreement represented everything that Roosevelt was trying to combat, the growing threat of a world conflict inspired the US government to avoid retaliation, according to historian Antonio Pedro Tota.[43] Even after the 1937 coup, when Vargas established a dictatorship, Roosevelt maintained his support for the government, considering that "Brazilian stability was essential to the hemispheric defense plans of the United States and to American trade."[44]

In mid 1940, the advance of the German forces in Western Europe – which resulted in the capture of the Netherlands and Belgium, the victory over the British army on the continent and the fall of France and the following establishment of the Vichy regime – posed a threat even more acute for US hegemony in the Western Hemisphere and, consequently, demanded more incisive actions from the Roosevelt administration in Latin America. Up to that point, the various government departments and agencies (Department of State, Treasury, Commerce, Agriculture and Export-Import Bank Eximbank) had developed distinct and often conflicting programs to help the sister republics.[45] Thus, on August 16 of that year, a new emergency government agency was created, aiming to produce anti-Nazi and pro-American propaganda, secure trade agreements between the American republics, and also to promote a Pan-American identity, that is: the idea that the American republics should work together, under the *benevolent* American leadership, given their sharing of the same history and geography.[46]

This new agency – the Office for Coordination of Commercial and Cultural Relations between the American Republics, which was known for almost all of its existence as the Office of the Coordinator of Inter-American Affairs[47] – had the expressed purpose of "formulate and execute a programme to increase hemispheric solidarity and farther the spirit of inter-American co-operation."[48] The same order of Democratic President Franklin Delano Roosevelt, which established the creation of the Office, named Nelson Rockefeller as its coordinator. Son of tycoon John D. Rockefeller and heir of Standard Oil – an oil company that monopolized the sale of kerosene, lubricants and gasoline in the United States and in several other countries for many years[49] –, Nelson Rockefeller, a member of the Republican Party, was also President of the Museum of Modern Art of New York – MoMA, as well as advisor to the Metropolitan Museum of Art. His involvement with Latin America first took place in 1935, when he traveled to Venezuela to visit the local Museum of Modern Art, where a group of artists who received financial support from MoMA exhibited their works. This trip brought him closer to the International Division of the Rockefeller Foundation, responsible for developing a health program for Latin American countries.[50]

In 1937, now with some knowledge of the Spanish language, he made a second trip to Latin America to solve problems related to Standard Oil. On board the Sikorsky S42B seaplane, Nelson Rockefeller and his entourage left Miami in the morning of March 30, arriving in Barranquilla, Colombia, in the late afternoon of that same day. The next morning, they traveled to Maracaibo, Venezuela, to inspect their newest investment: the oil fields of Creole Petroleum Corporation, a subsidiary of Standard Oil. There he felt concerned about the quality of life and working conditions of Latin Americans, which led Nelson Rockefeller to take part in the creation of a development company, whose objective was to promote the agricultural and the industrial sectors in the country.[51] Then the group traveled to Port of Spain, capital of Trinidad and Tobago, where they stayed until April 13, flying that morning to Belém, in Pará. The next day, they went to Recife and, from there, to Rio de Janeiro. Between April 15 and 23, they visited São Paulo and several other cities in the interior of the state. Finally, on April 23, 1937, they boarded a seaplane in Santos bound for Buenos Aires and, from there, the group flew back to the United States.[52]

On this trip, Rockefeller realized the need to adopt a social welfare policy aimed at Latin America, to neutralize anti-American sentiments and promote the unification of the continent.[53] According to historian Antonio Pedro Tota, "young Nelson Rockefeller was clearly aware that there should be changes in the relationship between his own country and Latin America."[54] This background, in addition to his personal and professional relationships, made him the perfect man to assume the position of coordinator of the Office.

> His optimism, directness, and enthusiasm and interest in the Latin American field and the good neighbor idea had gained him the post despite the fact that he was a Republican, rather youthful, and lacking experience in governmental administrative practices. Particularly in the cultural field, the Rockefeller name was also considered an asset.[55]

At the Office of the Coordinator of Inter-American Affairs – OCIAA –, Nelson Rockefeller worked to put into practice the objectives of the program for solidarity and financial and economic aid. To that end, he re-examined existing laws, coordinated research from various federal agencies, and, when necessary, recommended new laws to the Interdepartmental Committee. In addition, for the "formulation and execution of this program which, *by effective use of Governmental and private facilities in such fields as arts and sciences, education and travel, the radio, press, and cinema, would further national defense and strengthen the bonds between the nations of the Western Hemisphere,* he was instructed to cooperate with the Department of State."[56] That is, despite being an independent agency that blended private and state interests and used them to carry out Franklin Roosevelt's good neighbor policy as part of the war effort, the Office was expected to work together with the Department of State. However, as an independent agency, Rockefeller reported directly to the president, submitting reports and recommendations to him.[57]

Despite the close relationship between agency and department, the creation of the Office was seen by Department of State officials as a suggestion that it was not capable to manage the emergency demands of war in Latin America on its own. Even though they would admit the lack

of physical space and trained personnel for such projects,
they felt that the appropriate solution was not to create
a new branch, but rather to invest in improvements in the
department itself. In a statement, Donald Rowland alleges
that there is no material available in the Office's collection
pointing out this particular stance; however, when inter-
viewing people who worked at the Department during that
period, it became clear that Department of State officials
linked to Latin American affairs saw the arrival of the Office
in that environment with a lot of apprehension and distrust.[58] The inevitable dispute for space between the agency
and the department only came to a halt when, in a letter to
Rockefeller from April 22, 1942, President Roosevelt established the limits of the Office:

> As you know, it was my thought in the establishment of
> an Office of the Coordinator of Commercial and Cultural
> Relations between American Republics that such an
> office was especially desirable as a coordinating organ
> for certain emergency measures rendered advisable by
> the course of events [illegible] the outbreak of war. But
> in order that our foreign relations may be conducted so
> as to advance the security and welfare of the country,
> it is now more than ever essential that the Secretary
> of State be apprised of all Governmental undertakings,
> whether carried on directly by Governmental agencies
> or indirectly through private agencies, relating to foreign
> countries. The Department of State is charged with
> responsibility under the President for the conduct of the
> foreign relations of the country. This centralization of
> responsibility is of the utmost urgency today. Without
> it, the maximum result of the combined efforts of the
> executive agencies cannot be attained.[59]

In the field of cultural relations, Roosevelt's letter
resulted in an agreement between the Office and the

Department of State: Rockefeller's agency would be responsible for emergency programs – which were always discussed by members of both teams and approved, or not, by the department –, such as activities in the fields of vocational and adult education; on the other hand, the department's Cultural Relations Division would focus on those programs considered to be long-term projects. After the attack on Pearl Harbor and with the de facto entry of the United States into World War II, the US government expressed the need to "double all cultural efforts and speed up their execution, but with new accent tuned to new developments."[60] According to the minutes of the Executive (or Policy) Committee meeting, a study was carried out to order these cultural projects into four categories: those with an immediate impact on national defense issues (class A); those of secondary impact on national defense, including direct propaganda efforts (class B); those that would exert an immediate influence on improving Latin American sympathy for the United States (class C); and those aiming at promoting solidarity on the continent in the long-term (class D).[61]

With this study by Donald Rowland, it became clear that only a few of the projects developed by the Cultural Relations Division of the Department of State belonged in class A; besides that, the ones that focused on advertising – that is, class B – had health and safety issues as their central concerns. As for those projects in category C, the Cultural Division had developed a series of programs for cultural exchange, enlisting influential people from Latin America and the United States working on different areas, in an attempt to instigate interest and enthusiasm for solidarity efforts on the continent. In the same proportion, the projects in category D – which should be kept in place – sought to demonstrate the sincere interest of the Americans in the hemisphere as a whole.[62]

During the first half of 1943, a new agreement on
the division of responsibility between the appropriate
divisions of the two agencies was carried out. In general,
the Division of Cultural Relations of the Department of
State was to assume full administrative responsibility
for that part of the program generally to be developed
on a long-range basis, such as projects concerning the
arts, music, student interchange, cultural institutions
and American libraries, and American-sponsored school
programs. The Division of Science and Education of the
Coordinator's Office was granted the right-of-way in
the areas of literacy and education at the elementary,
secondary and teacher and school administrator training
levels, including interchange of teachers and school
administrators, and development and distribution of
instructional materials. This field was interpreted to be
more nearly an emergency typo of activity.[63]

Still in the realm of cultural exchange, the outbreak of
the war in Europe and the Nazi and socialist threat to North
American hegemony brought new insights on the image
of the country nationally and internationally. A side note
on this subject: government propaganda acquired a new
dimension during World War I, when it was used by the most
eminent powers as a form of persuasion through mass communication inside and outside the country. Making use of
everything from print media to film, the aim was to promote
and disseminate a message of unity during the conflict. Nevertheless, such a strategy of pushing an *official history* of the
country was rejected by the American people, especially after
the end of the war, culminating, in 1919, in the extinction, by
then-President Woodrow Wilson, of the so-called Committee on Public Information – CPI. However, unlike the United
States, the other countries involved in the war – France,
England, Germany, Italy and, later, the Soviet Union – continued to spread their official histories in order to maintain their

influence on their colonies, expand their imperialistic reach and promote proletariat revolutions around the globe.[64]

Over the course of the 1930s, the US goal of projecting itself as a world power consolidated. Faced with an encroaching new war, the government resumed its advertising efforts to spread its own version of history to the rest of the world, starting with Latin America. Through mass media, it presented itself to its neighbors as a solidary country, one genuinely interested in the well-being of the continent as a whole. At the same time, these efforts introduced the American people to the curiosities, beauties and lifestyle of Latin American countries, in an attempt to unify efforts and prevent German penetration in America. It was this spirit that led Rockefeller's Office to finance the visit of Walt Disney and his team of designers to the countries of Latin America in 1942, which resulted in the creation of two new characters – the Brazilian Zé Carioca and the Mexican Panchito – and two new films: *Alô, amigos* (1942) and *Você já foi à Bahia?* (1943). The same spirit informed the cultural travels of artists – such as Cândido Portinari, Carmen Miranda, Frida Kahlo and Diego Rivera – and Latin American writers – such as Érico Veríssimo[65] – to the United States, as well as the Fulbright program of cultural exchange and sponsorship.

Even before the end of World War II, Nelson Rockefeller expressed – in a letter to Under Secretary Sumner Welles, dated back to May 17, 1943 – his concern with the continuity of the work carried out by the Office. According to him, it was necessary to consider the need for headquarters and organizational arrangements to handle the many activities developed by the Office as soon as possible, for he believed that the United States should not renounce the advances achieved, albeit through emergency measures, in the field of solidarity and mutual trust. According to Donald Rowland, a memo sent in August of that year by Office agents made clear the general feeling pervading both the agency and the Department of State that their projects would be discontinued once the war ended. Rockefeller also pointed out that Nazi propaganda was already attacking the Office's programs, pushing the idea that the much-professed goodwill would be readily abandoned by the United States once the war effort was over.[66]

Finally, on April 10, 1946, President Truman signed an order extinguishing the Office as an independent agency, put to effect on the 20th of that same month. In that ten-day period, all activities of the Office were either transferred to the Department of State or discontinued.

> On May 20, 1946, the agency established in August 1940 as the Office for the Coordination of Commercial and Cultural Relations between the American Republics, then renamed the Office of the Coordinator of Inter-American Affairs, and finally entitled the Office of Inter-American Affairs, ceased to exist as an entity. All operations, however, did not end.[67]

According to historian Justin Hart, changes in US diplomacy and foreign policy in order to soften them as to avoid resentment from other countries were meant to project the country as a powerful and dominant nation – a goal that became ever so strong with the Second World War and the Nazi and Socialist threats. "With these exchanges, the Department of State clearly intented to uso Latin America as the *laboratory* for honing an approach that it would eventually deploy worldwide."[68] In this context, the North American embassies started to play a major role in the efforts of solidarity and economic and financial aid, and even more so in the dissemination of the American Way of Life and in the attempt to bring foreign peoples closer to the US. Thus, with the input of architecture, the embassy construction program was part of the efforts of the US foreign policy to project America[69] – its dominance and ideals – to the world. And it

must be emphasized in this book for it highlights the impact
of American diplomacy on modern architecture.

During a period of international conflicts, modern architecture became a symbol for prosperity and the possibility of
a better future. By taking this ideal as a motto the US foreign
policy – more specifically, the US Department of State –
veered towards consolidation as a world power after the war
and during the Cold War period. Architecture, cinema and
cultural exchange were valuable weapons in the fight against
Nazism and, later on, communism, as well as tools in international cooperation and in building the country's image as
a successful and friendly leader.

According to Patrício del Real, it was necessary to cele-
brate Latin America as a culturally recognized region capable
of delivering a unique contribution to Western culture.[70] In
this context, Brazilian modern architecture was seen as a
possible representation of Latin American (regional) values
within the context of consolidation of Western (international) culture:

> The Second World War fueled the need in the United
> States to construct a regional category capable of nego-
> tiating cultural differences within a unified Pan Amer-
> ican geography. [...] This period manifested what I call
> a metonymic drive, a hermeneutical reading of images
> that facilitated dual and ambiguous interpretations and
> eventually allowed Brazil to represent Latin America in
> the 1940s and 1950s. This was possible because Brazilian
> modernism had the capacity to be ambiguous, to oper-
> ate both as a national and regional marker.[71]

In 1939, the Brazil Pavilion at the New York World's Fair
– a project by Lúcio Costa and Oscar Niemeyer in partnership
with the American architect Paul Lester Weiner – took the
best of Brazilian art, culture and architecture to the United
States: panels by Cândido Portinari were exhibited inside the

structure; in the garden, gigantic water lilies represented
the flora of the Amazon; in the restaurant, one could have
a taste of a brand of Brazilian coffee; the music was by
maestro Villa Lobos; and even Carmen Miranda – well-known
by the American public – showed up. A few years later, in
1943, MoMA set up the exhibition *Brazil Builds: Architecture
New and Old, 1652*-1942,[72] not only to represent the modern
Latin American style, but also to offer a possible model for
the post-war world.[73] This promise, which had already been
introduced during the war, was actualized when, in 1955, the
museum organized the exhibition *Latin American Architecture since 1945.*[74]

> With MoMA, modern architecture was first brought into
> the fold of cultural relations between Latin America and
> the United States. The notion of a Latin American mod-
> ernism is fundamental to understanding how modern
> architecture in the region appeared in the international
> stage. Between 1939 and 1955 architectural historians
> and critics outside the region noticed not only specific
> buildings but also the contours of a Latin American
> modern manner, not necessarily as homogeneous but
> certainly as an identifiable style.[75]

This appropriation of architecture as a political tool for
demonstrating the power and benevolence of the United
States in foreign territories was described by the American
historian Ron Robin as *political architecture.*

> Political architecture, a symbolic illustration of American
> power and willingness to intervene forcefully in the the-
> ater of international relations, played a significant role
> in the complex mission of orchestrating world affairs
> while refraining from an enduring and large physical
> presence abroad. Thus an analysis of the symbolism of
> American architecture abroad reveals the crystallization

of fundamental American goals in the international arena.[76]

The use of architecture as a political tool for domination is not an exclusive feature of the historical period studied in this book. Ever since the beginning of the 20th century, the United States had been systematically erecting monuments and consular buildings abroad. However, after the two great wars, and the country's emergence as a powerhouse in the New World Order, this policy gained much more traction.[77] In this sense, and on the verge of a new conflict, Franklin Roosevelt considered the embassy building program, coordinated by the Office of Foreign Buildings Operations – FBO, as essential for his government and for the foreign policy it envisioned, alongside programs for cultural exchange and economic aid.[78]

Like the Fullbright educational exchange program – designed to promote international understanding and widely praised as a goodwill gesture – new embassies have been hailed as evidence of American goodwill and commitment, and their modern architecture, introduced in the late 1940s, has come to symbolize the openness of public diplomacy.[79]

By expanding an American presence through the establishment of information libraries, the Voice of America, academic exchange programs, and cultural centers, the United States hoped to influence the elites of the postwar years. Elaborate legation buildings complemented this effort. They provided a condensed glimpse of American foreign policy objectives, particularly for the proverbial man in the street who had no access to the elite-oriented information programs of the Department of State, and who was liable to construct a pistol-packing, gangster-ridden, Hollywood-inspired version of life in the United States.[80]

Starting in 1926 through an act of Congress,[81] the embassy building program came to meet a demand for international representation for a country with increasing world power. Up until that moment, there were some embassies and consular buildings – functions that operated separately until 1924 –, but these were few and quite apart from each other; in any case, insufficient given the changing political landscape, especially after World War 2.

The ideological battle waged against the advance of communism required the US government to invest massively in foreign policy in order to expand and advertise the pro-American flag; hence, the necessity of building official headquarters for the diplomatic model that would be adopted by the United States at that time of conflict.

The United States also had to wrestle with its own perceived need to maintain and expand free market economies and the concomitant need to increase pro-American sentiment and build worldwide support for the democratic model. Military and diplomatic objectives included postwar plans for an array of military bases, strategic defense pacts, economic aid, and information dissemination. Each of these had direct or indirect impact on the foreign building program, which became part of a larger effort by the United States to strengthen its postwar position and the position of its allies.[82]

As Jane Loeffler says, this initiative brought a number of benefits to the embassy building program. With the end of World War II, the debt of foreign countries to the US Treasury amounted to millions. In 1946, Congress authorized the use of so-called "frozen funds" or "locked funds" for the purchase and construction of diplomatic buildings around the world.

Thus, the program would receive the necessary investment without, however, using dollars from taxes paid by the American people. "It would be fair to say that congressional interest in the bill (H. R. 6627) was less an endorsement of the foreign buildings program itself than it was approval of means of recouping American assets."[83]

Thus, the FBO headquarters, which was previously limited to a sole base in Washington, branched out, establishing offices in Paris, Hague, London, Bonn, Tokyo and Rio de Janeiro, in addition to planting supervisors in Eastern Europe, North Africa and the Middle East.[84] Thus, Leland W. King Jr., architect and project director at FBO, invited architects with private offices to develop the projects of these embassies and diplomatic buildings. By offering commissions to renowned modernist architects, King believed he was generating positive publicity for the program, which from 1948 to 1958 gained a reputation for being a showcase of modern architecture.[85]

> Between 1949 and 1953, the number of projects assigned to private architects grew from five to twenty-one, and with the completion of working drawings for seventeen additional projects, the total reached thirty-eight. Through these designs modern architecture became symbolically associated with the postwar effort to find new and better ways to represent American interests abroad.[86]

For the embassies in Rio de Janeiro (1948-1952) and Havana (1950-1952), King hired the New York office Harrison & Abramovitz, which at the time supervised the construction of the United Nations headquarters – a project developed in 1947 by a team of eleven architects, notably Oscar Niemeyer and Le Corbusier, led by the American. The choice of Wallace Kirkman Harrison (1895-1981) for these embassy projects was not random at all: renowned among his peers,

Harrison was deeply involved in the foreign policy of cultural convergence adopted by the United States. Besides having developed several projects in Latin America – such as the Hotel Avila in Caracas (1941) and the United States Air and Submarine Base in Panama (1942) –, in 1945 the architect was appointed head of the Division of Cultural Affairs of the OCIAA, the agency directed by Nelson Rockefeller.

The suspicion that the choice of Wallace Harrison was due to his personal relationship with the Rockefeller family – that is, his social capital – is not corroborated by Jane Loeffler. In her book *The Architecture of Diplomacy: Building America's Embassies*, the author stated that the commissioning of Harrison was not explained by some social advantage, rather by his skills as an architect; after all there was a consensus that his designs would draw attention to the building program of embassies. However, without questioning the merit of his architecture, it is conceivable – following the analysis of Garry Stevens, anchored in the concepts of Pierre Bourdieu – that his personal relationships were also quite important for his professional success in the architectural environment.

> Naturally, the more capital vested in the particular members of one's social network the higher the value of that network, and thus the privileged classes have an inherent advantage over the lower classes, simply because their social capital is so much higher. Moreover, upper-class individuals have more *weak ties* to others than do the less privileged. That is, they have bigger networks of acquaintances, people who they do not know very well, but who can be of invaluable assistance in business.[87]

In the excerpt above, Stevens applies Bourdieu's concept of social capital to analyze the social environment in which architectural activity takes place. The nature of the dispute for power between artists and the bourgeoisie in the 19th century, mentioned by Bourdieu – that is, "the power relations between social positions that guarantee their occupants a sufficient amount of social force – or capital – so that they have the possibility to engage in the struggles for the monopoly of power"[88] – translates here into disputes over project commissioning. Architects with greater social capital, with a larger network of influential acquaintances, are offered better and/or more important commissions.

To clarify the presence of Garry Stevens and Pierre Bourdieu in this argument, a side note is needed. In the early 1930s, New York architecture firm Corbett, Harrison & Mac-Murray was invited to join the team of architects responsible for developing the Rockefeller Center (1932-1939). Wallace Harrison's leading position on the team brought him closer to Nelson Rockefeller – who had been tasked with managing this particular venture by his father, John D. Rockefeller Jr. According to the *New York Times*, "it was the beginning of a long association that would bring Mr. Harrison commissions ranging from houses for the Rockefeller family to such huge projects as the Empire State Plaza, constructed during Nelson Rockefeller's tenure as Governor."[89]

In addition to the Rockefeller Center – the building in which he himself established an office in 1940, soon after his partnership with Max Abramovitz – and the aforementioned United Nations headquarters, Harrison was also part of the team that designed the 1939 New York World's Fair, whose theme was *Building the World of Tomorrow*. Working along J. André Fouilhoux, he designed the Trilon and the Perisphere, a monumental structure that became a symbol of the fair.[90] Now, it is clear that, apart from the merits of the architectural quality of his works, Wallace Harrison's relationship with Nelson Rockefeller was crucial for these large commissions, such as the projects for the embassies in Havana and Rio de Janeiro. It is also important to highlight that, despite being separate agencies, the Rockefeller Office and the

Department of State (responsible for the embassy building program) collaborated with each other.

Now to the issue of the embassies: for the United States, the years that followed the end of World War II – formalized with the official surrender of Japan in September 1945 – were a period dedicated to strengthen former alliances and also to build new ones, in an attempt to block the advance of communism to other nations. The program for the construction of embassies and consular buildings was directly impacted by the new scenario, which increased the presence of US citizens and investments abroad in quite an unusual measure:

> The State Department increased the number and size of its embassies and consulates in part to meet the needs of American military men and women and their families stationed abroad – with enlarged offices for passport, visa and immigration, and public health service operations, for example – and also in part to provide space for the administration of new programs, ranging from those that offered immediate hunger relief to those that supplied long-term economic assistance and training.[91]

In the aftermath of the conflict, Europe faced the need for massive reconstruction in its own territory, while a series of movements for independence emerged in its colonies. Over the next two decades, new nations were formed and the UN, founded in 1945 by 51 countries, added another 66 by 1965.[92] "The new nations, eager to attract financial and technical assistance for their development became fertile grounds for the ideological competition between the Cold War rivals."[93] US policy with regard to its embassies changed, and the rented buildings were replaced by new ones, built on land purchased by the country.[94] As an example, in 1954, Republican politician Prince H. Preston Jr. noted the unsatisfactory conditions of the Embassy in Karachi, Pakistan's capital at the time – which operated in a rented office on top of a mechanical garage – and pointed out the pressing need to build a brand new building on a piece of land that had already been purchased by the United States for this purpose.[95] Soon the new buildings would be designed – including security measures against theft and fire,[96] but none against terrorist attacks, which, until then, were unheard of.[97]

In 1955, when the US Congress approved a budget of $3 million to be spent on embassies that fiscal year, half of that amount went to the "construction of an impressive new chancery in Karachi."[98] To carry out such a task, FBO hired the Neutra & Alexander office. According to historian Thomas Hines, this project ranks among the three most important endeavours in the partnership between Richard Neutra and Robert Alexander, alongside the Cyclorama Center at the Lincoln Memorial Museum, in Gettysburg, and the Los Angeles County Hall of Records.[99] Completed in 1959, this project, unlike other US embassies, addressed from its very conception local particularities in terms of labor, available materials and, above all, climate.[100] This embassy stands out in our analysis not just because it was designed by Neutra, but for adding into its project a series of climate concerns that, to a certain extent, relate to Latin America, as will be explored below.

Given the analysis presented so far, it is important to realize that political interests and needs affect, to some extent, the fields of art, architecture, cinema, music and lit-erature. More specifically, it must be noted that US ambitions to become a world power turned modern architecture into an expression of prosperity, well-being and social advance-ment. In this process, modern Latin American architecture gained international visibility, as in the case of the Brazil Pavilion at the New York International Fair (1939), the par-ticipation of Oscar Niemeyer in the team responsible for the United Nations headquarters (1947) and the two exhibitions at MoMA: *Brazil Builds* (1943) and *Latin American Architecture Since 1945* (1955).

Now moving on to our subject: within the general scope of North American policy towards Latin America, it is possible to point out the role of Richard Neutra in the development of modern Latin American architecture. In Brazil, his teachings are quite significant for our constructive culture. However, it is a two-way relationship, as Neutra takes with him architectural solutions that he saw – and studied – on his visits to Latin American countries.

This exchange, made possible by the diplomatic mission under the auspices of the Department of State, did not amount to mere bureaucracy but ended up developing into a relationship of mutual interest. Once again, it is worth noting that Richard Neutra indeed brought architectural possibilities to Latin America; nevertheless, once he meets local peers interested in the same issues as him, he demonstrates a genuine curiosity and interest in their work. As already pointed out in my master's degree thesis,[101] each work visited yielded photos, drawings and detailed studies of solutions, and these were eventually absorbed in his own projects.

Character Construction

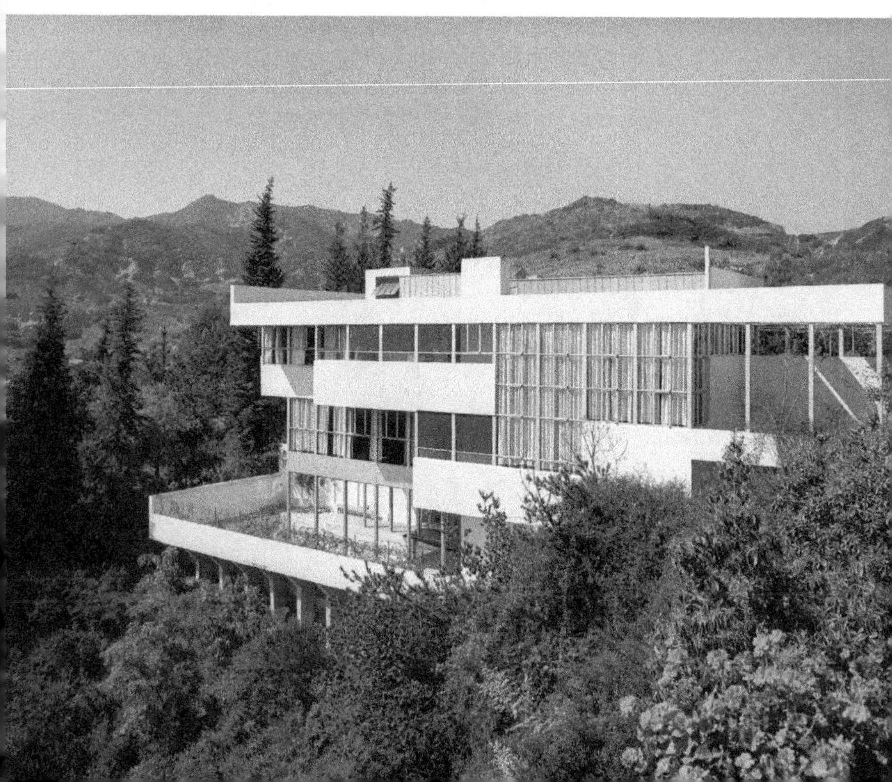

Lovell House, Los Angeles. Richard
Neutra, 1927. Photo Julius Shulman.
© J. Paul Getty Trust Archive. Getty
Research Institute, Los Angeles
(2004.R.10)

The many contacts with government, with public service, and business have seasoned Neutra's thinking, and together with his continuous concrete technical designing work and building creation, have helped him never to lose himself in isolated theory or to separate himself from real life. In the midst of all grand and theoretically posed problems, Neutra likes to keep his attention on even the smallest structure entrusted to his care, and none of them is without lively interest to him. He is not only a researcher who patiently and methodically tests the applicability of each newly-emerging building element; he is also a sociologist and psychologist who is profoundly attracted by the intrinsic and the essential requirements of the groups and individuals for whom he builds.
Gregori Warchavchik, "Introduction"[102]

To understand Richard Neutra's role in North American foreign policy, it is first necessary to understand the relevant facts in his trajectory that led him to be chosen by the State Department's Cultural Relations Division to head a diplomatic mission in Latin America.[103] Much influenced by Adolf Loos (1870-1933) and his colleague Rudolph Schindler (1887-1953), Neutra graduated from the Technische Hochschule in Vienna in 1918 after having served in the Austrian Imperial Army during World War I, when he was stricken with malaria during a mission in the Albanian border.[104] Professional hardships and Schindler's encouragement led him to consider emigration.

In October 1923, still a young man, Neutra immigrated to the United States aboard the S.S. Laconia.[105] After a brief stay in New York, he moved to Chicago, where he quickly began working at the prestigious Holabird and Roche. There, through editor Ralph Fletcher Seymor – a personal friend of Frank Lloyd Wright (1867-1959) and Schindler –, he met and became friends with Louis Sullivan (1856-1924), who, at that time, besides his old age and illnesses, was virtually broke and living in some random hotel room.[106] Later on, at Sullivan's funeral in April 1924, Richard Neutra had the opportunity to personally meet Wright, whom he had admired since the publication in Berlin of *Wasmuth Portfolio* (1910) – a collection of lithographs with perspectives and plans of houses and commercial buildings designed by Wright between 1893 and 1909.[107]

Neutra then received the long-awaited invitation to visit the master at Taliesin East, Wisconsin. In his autobiography, first published in 1962, Neutra rolls up in the same paragraph his appreciation for Wright's work and the desire to settle in California:

> Once when I was walking down the Bahnhofstrasse in Zurich, I saw in a travel-office window a folder with a palm tree printed on it, and the words, *California calls you.* I knew only a little English then, and I wasn't quite sure what this meant, but I put two and two together and concluded that I was supposed to come to California. After I had been in New York, Chicago, and Taliesin – more or less a guest of Mr. Wright's, as he had no work or projects – I began restlessly to think about California. I knew it was the only place where he had had anything under construction during my American sojourn.[108]

In June 1924, his wife Dione Neutra landed in New York; she had obtained a professional visa as a musician – she was a cello player. However, her newborn son, Frank Lucian Neutra[109] had not been allowed to travel with her, because he was born in Germany, forcing her to leave him under the care of her mother, Lilly Niedermann. Still, due to an immigration issue, she could not leave Elis Island until a hearing which Neutra attended, when he claimed to be able to support her young wife.[110] From there, the couple traveled to Spring Green, where they hoped Richard Neutra would be offered a job opportunity. Dione wrote about her impressions upon arriving at Taliesin in her book *Richard Neutra: Promise and Fulfillment, 1919-1932*:

> It is impossible to describe the first impression. Immense astonishment is paramount. Then one becomes somewhat anxious at the thought to be soon in the presence of a genius, to meet him at any moment...[111]

The offer indeed came, but only in September 1924: "My dear Richard Neutra, a hundred and sixty dollars per month and your board is what I had in mind. [...] Will try it for a while and if you like it and I like you and all goes well we will discuss a contract."[112] In addition to the job, Wright helped the young couple bring little Frank Neutra to the United States, through a senator in Wisconsin.[113] Neutra worked with Frank Lloyd Wright for only a short period of five months: the few projects and the dream of establishing himself as an architect in California led the couple to say goodbye to Taliesin and leave for Los Angeles in February 1925.[114]

There, Rudolph Schindler and his wife Pauline were of the utmost importance. The Neutra family rented the North apartment of the Kings Road house, designed by Schindler for himself in 1921. The place encompassed two independent apartments with a shared kitchen.[115] The professional partnership between Neutra and Schindler intensified in 1926, when they joined forces to establish a collaborative office for non-residential projects: the Architectural Group for Industry and Commerce – Agic. Until then, Neutra had developed only landscaping proposals, namely one for the project of the Schindle's How house (1925), in Los Angeles, and the Lovell house (1926), in Newport Beach.[116]

He found a quite propitious scenario in California, which had a great impact on his future trajectory. Within the Schindlers' close circle of personal and professional relationships

Lovell House, ground floor (acess), lower floor and pool floor plans, Los Angeles. Richard Neutra, 1927. Croquis Fernanda Critelli

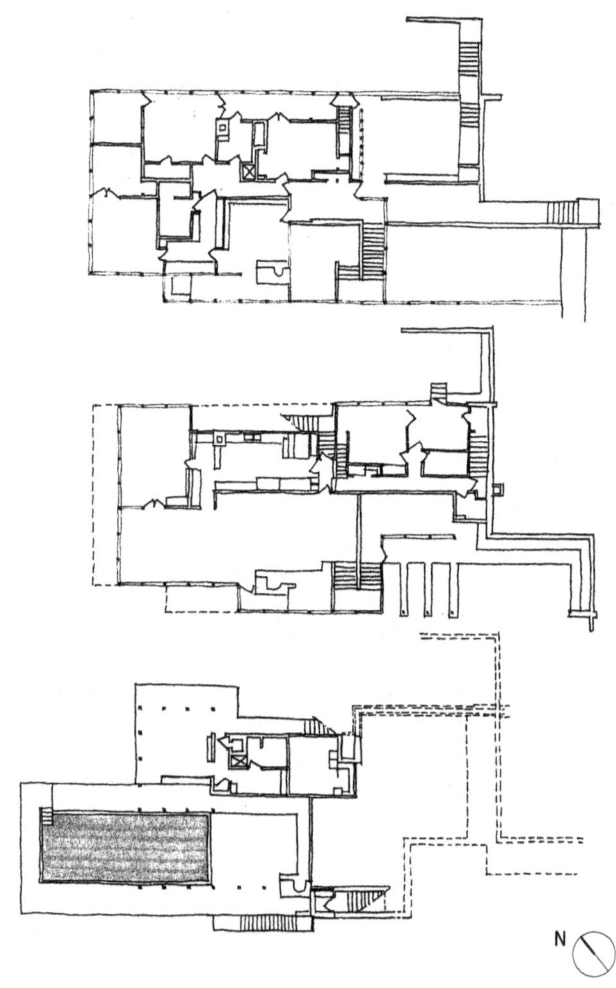

Lovell Beach House, Newport Beach.
Rudolph Schindler, 1922-1926. Photo
Julius Shulman. © J. Paul Getty Trust
Archive. Getty Research Institute, Los
Angeles (2004.R.10)

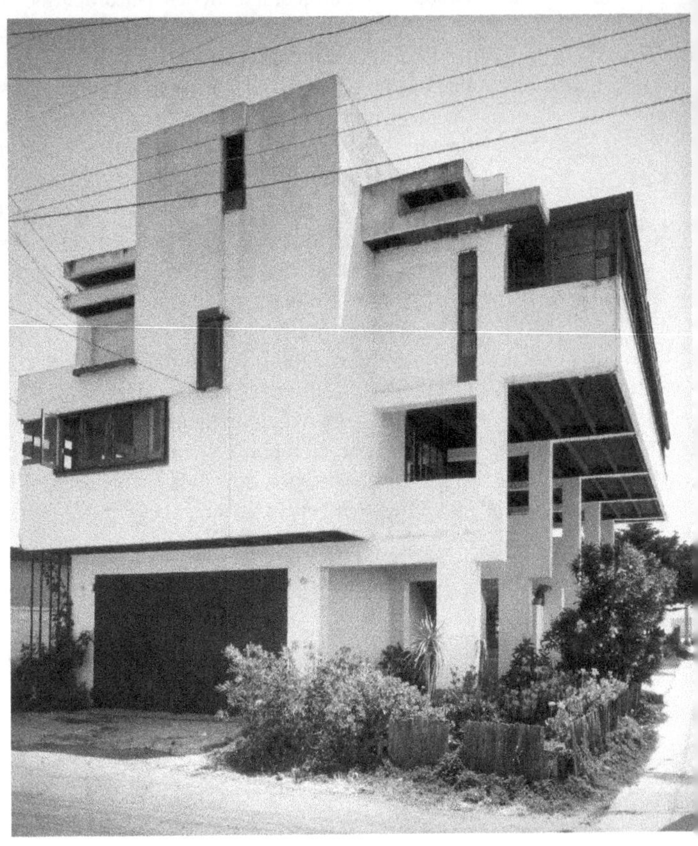

one could count Aline Barnsdall and Harriet Freeman – both of whom had homes designed by Frank Lloyd Wright – and the couple Philip and Leah Lovell, whose importance in Richard Neutra's career goes far beyond the opportunity to build his first project in America. Naturopathic physician, Philip Lovell advocated for the prevention of disease through healthy eating and daily sunbathing. According to writer Lyra Kilston, in addition to his office in downtown Los Angeles, Dr. Lovell had a column in the *Los Angeles Times*, where he wrote about food, health, and even architecture, with contributions from Rudolph Schindler.[117] Their client-architect relationship bore three fruits: a cabin in the Wrightwood Mountains the roof of which collapsed in the first blizzard; a house in the Fallbrook Desert, which would end up destroyed in a fire; and the landscaping project for the famous beach house in Newport.[118]

It is also worth noting that at that time both Leah Lovell and Pauline Schindler taught at an informal school run very progressively by Aline Barnsdall and designed by Frank Lloyd Wright, as part of a home, theater and school complex built in the East Hollywood area. It is not surprising that here, too, Philip Lovell's health ideals had been implemented as part of everyday school life:

> A photograph of Leah and Pauline shows an idyllic scene in a sundrenched garden where they are holding hands in a circle with their young students (including two sons of the photographer Edward Weston). Most of the children are barefoot and naked but for underwear. Not surprisingly for the wife of Dr, Lovell, it appears that sunbathing was part of the school's curriculum. *All classes outside*, she had told Wright.[119]

The impact that this naturalist trend in California had on Richard Neutra is not negligible. With training and professional background in countries whose intense cold called for more enclosed, isolating architectures, such a contrast of

climate and landscape was a formative discovery. His projects
now open generously to the sun, the breeze and the surrounding landscape, working with these elements to improve
the environmental quality and, as a result, the lives of the
inhabitants. This change of perspective can be observed in
the very first work built by Neutra in America: the Philip
and Leah Lovell house at Griffith Park. Besides an innovative
technological experiment – the steel skeleton of the structure, never before applied in residential works, was erected in
just forty hours[120] –, the house was also an opportunity for
Neutra to translate the naturopathic doctor's ideas of health
and well-being into architecture. At the inauguration, as
Lyra Kilston describes, Lovell used his newspaper column to
invite his readers to visit the house. The reception would be
crowned by daily tours guided by the architect himself.[121]

Ever since he moved to California, Richard Neutra had
been looking for projects and/or job opportunities that would
help him establish himself as an architect in the United
States, so he could support his family. Between jobs at major
Los Angeles architecture firms and projects in partnership
with Schindler, Neutra also aspired to teach classes. In order
to fulfill this dream, he founded the Academy of Modern Art
in 1925:

> When I first arrived Southwest and looked for a job, I
> also thought of teaching. I wanted to teach about my
> search and convictions, but no college would have me.
> Then in 1925 the tiny Academy of Modern Art was set
> up in an old Victorian residence, and I found four or five
> students. Harwell Hamilton Harris, then a very young
> sculptor, and Gregory Ain, who had dropped his regular
> studies in dismay, were among them, and they soon
> joined my diminutive office in loyal effort.
>
> Regular college students began to give me extra-
> curricular, unorthodox but cordial attention, like Raphael

Soriano from Rhodes, and as time went on, others from
many places and in ever-increasing numbers.[122]

As Frank Lloyd Wright in 1932, when he founded Taliesin
Fellowship[123] – it seems that Wright first envision this idea
in 1929[124] –, Richard Neutra set up his own school where he
could transmit his beliefs regarding architecture to young
students, many of whom were dissatisfied with what was
taught in regular courses.[125] Interestingly enough, the three
best historians to explore Neutra's life and work – Esther
McCoy, Thomas Hines and Barbara Lamprecht – treated
the creation of the Academy of Modern Art as a secondary
issue in their narratives.[126] However, despite this apparent
unimportance, the fact that he set up his own school, where
he could transmit his ideals, actually made it possible for
Neutra to establish a circle of disciples, thus influencing a
new generation of architects. Shortly after settling in a new
country, he sets up this school, soon becoming a *master* and
a reference in modern California architecture. If we consider
the words of Garry Stevens – "symbolic power, operating in
the field of culture, is used by the dominant classes in society
to maintain their dominance"[127] –, this search of the Austrian
architect for symbolic cultural capital might be understood
as a personal project – also a family one –, the goal of which
was to establish a place for himself in the highest spheres of
North American society.

Another interesting point in his trajectory is the project for a futuristic utopian city – Rush City Reformed –,
which he developed between the 1920s and 1930s, with the
occasional help from his young apprentices at the Academy
of Modern Art. According to Thomas Hines, the revolution-
ary ideas applied here were organized in a relatively unified
system,[128] putting Neutra side by side with Antonio Sant'Elia
and his *Città Nuova* (1914) and Le Corbusier with his *Plan
Voisin* (1925).

Rush City Reformed was a growing cluster of studies on urban affairs, on downtown and suburban communities, on housing and traffic, on recreation and education in the picture of a stimulating prognostics. It prophesied that comprehensive urban renewal would have to take place; and much later I should become member and even chairman of our State Planning Board [...]

They [the drawings and ideas] were ridiculed by those who saw them, as was the time I spent on their development. Some quarter of a century later Lewis Munford in *The New Yorker* graciously recommended these never-ending comprehensive studies of Rush City Reformed to young planners and architects as an early, almost forgotten prelude to urban renewal, and I felt gratefully vindicated. My friends Harris, Ain, Soriano, and more and more others [...] watched the then quite lonely lecturing effort of mine, listened with constructive minds, and further developed these fragments. Slowly thoughts were improved, jelled, and fused to a panorama of inescapable urban reform, but much still is left to the future.[129]

As one can gather from Richard Neutra's own words, the fact of having developed a project for a futuristic utopian city represents, once again, the acquiring of symbolic cultural capital. From the moment he became a reference for his students and, later on, for other students, Neutra became a dominant figure capable of influencing new generations of architects and urban planners. His convictions and ideas about what modern architecture and the city should look like were therefore widespread and would continue to be disseminated for many more years through lectures and books published around the world throughout its trajectory. With Harold Bloom's theory in mind, we might say that the influence here happens in an active way and should not be seen as a harmful contamination, but rather as a conscious act of "poetic misprision."[130]

After the publication of *Wie baut Amerika?*, in 1927, and the completion of the Lovell House, in 1930, Richard Neutra left for a journey through Asia and Europe. In Japan, he was received by fellow architects Kameki and Nobu Tsuchiura – colleagues who had stayed and worked in Taliesin in 1924 – and gave lectures in Tokyo and Osaka. He then traveled through Macau, Hong Kong and Singapore and from there to Switzerland, where he met Dione and her two children, Frank and Dion. He gave lectures in each city he visited: Vienna, Zurich, Prague, Hamburg, Berlin, Cologne, Amsterdam, Rotterdam, Frankfurt – where he meets Alvar Aalto – and Basel. In this city, Neutra meets the industrialist and architecture enthusiast CH Van der Leeuw, who invites him to visit the Netherlands and give lectures there. Two years later, Leeuw would finance the construction of the architect's house – VDL House (1932) –, in Silverlake, Los Angeles. In Berlin, in addition to a reunion with Erich Mendelsohn – whom he worked with from October 1921 to October 1923, the period immediately before his departure for the United States –, he was invited by Ludwig Mies van der Rohe to teach at the Bauhaus, in Dessau, as a visiting professor, where he stayed for about a month.

Before leaving for Brussels to attend the International Congress of Modern Architecture as the North American representative, Richard Neutra discussed with Mies van der Rohe how could one introduce the system proposed by the Bauhaus School to the United States and how Neutra seemed to be the right man for propagating its ideals.[131] Commenting on this episode, Thomas Hines quotes a text by Mies, published in English, extolling the idea – "Richard J. Neutra, the progressive American architect who has taught Architecture both in European Bauhaus as in the U.S. was delegated to develop preliminary plans how to promote in America the idea of such cooperation" –, and then mentions the failure that followed it: "Yet despite Mies' endorsement and Neutra's subsequent efforts to effect the planned union, such developments were halted by the deepening economic crisis in both America and Germany and the rapidly deteriorating German political situation."[132]

In the midst of his journey as an architect of Austrian origin and training who sought to understand the climate and forms of construction in America,[133] adapting them to the concepts of modern European architecture he was familiar with, Richard Neutra designed important school and housing projects, thus becoming nationally and internationally known. To mention a few: the Corona (1935) and Emerson Junior (1938) schools; and the Avion Village (1941), Hacienda Village (1942), Pueblo del Rio (1942) and Channel Heights (1941-1942) public housing projects. Besides the social nature of these developments, all these projects have in common the attention to the relationship between architecture, climate and landscape.

At this point, it is important to clarify that two particular experiences in Richard Neutra's trajectory made him the ideal candidate for the diplomatic mission in Latin America. First, the issues directly related to his architecture, that is, the constant effort to improve the interplay between architecture, nature and local conditions – the local culture and its possibilities in terms of technology and building materials – as well as his interest in large-scale social projects, such as housing projects and schools. Secondly, his involvement with institutional promoters of architecture: in this case, the federal planning agencies. So far, our research has been able to identify four different agencies for which he developed specific projects or even operated as a hired employee. It's worth pointing out what was discussed above: to overcome the crisis generated by the crash of the New York Stock Exchange, Franklin Roosevelt was elected president in 1933 promising a more active approach to the economy on the part of the government. Thus, with the New Deal, the government set out to intervene in order to propel job creation, as well as access to housing and training for young people.

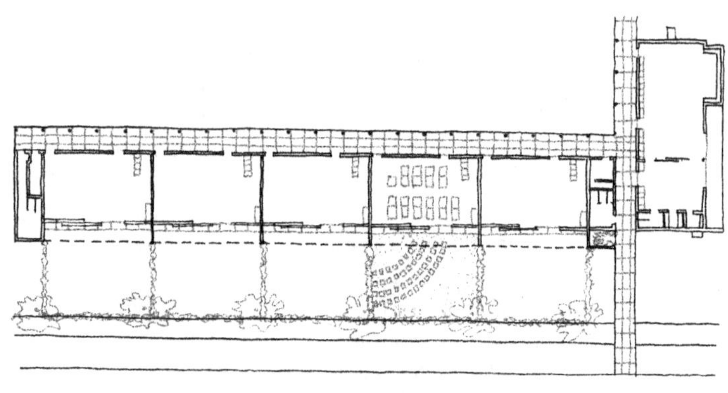

Corona School, ground floor plan,
classroom detail and section, Los
Angeles. Richard Neutra, 1935. Croquis
Fernanda Critelli

In 1935, Neutra was hired as assistant administrator
at Works Progress Administration – WPA,[134] a position he
held for only one year. After that, the architect remained
a member of the board, working as an entrepreneur and
consultant on social housing projects.[135] In the same period,
he was hired by the National Youth Administration – NYA,
where he developed a few isolated projects until he became
the consultant architect responsible for the entire western
region of the country from 1939 to 1940. Headed by Eleonor
Roosevelt, wife of President Roosevelt,[136] this federal agency
"provided young Americans with temporary jobs and with
training for more permanent ones. Neutra designed several
California training and activities centers."[137] His involvement in such agencies – mainly within the National Youth
Administration – and his insistence on ensuring architectural

96

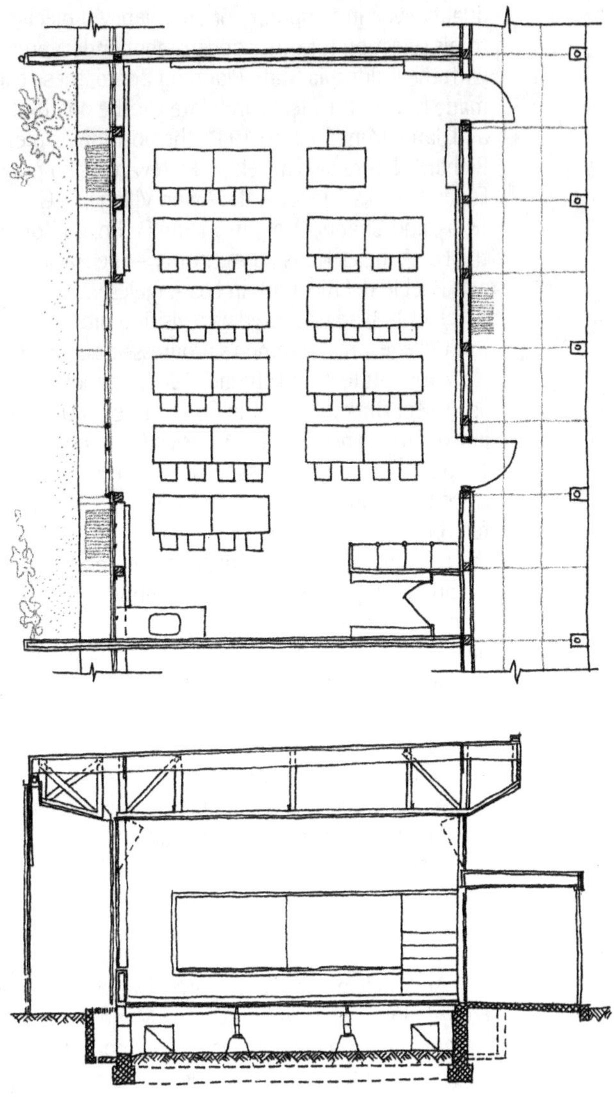

quality even in temporary or emergency projects were crucial to his selection for other government endeavours. Starting with the California State Planning Board, these experiences made Neutra the ideal candidate for the board of advisers and, later, from 1939 to 1941, the position as president.[138] Richard Neutra also developed a few housing projects for the Federal Works Agency – the Avion Village, in Grand Prairie, Texas, and Channel Heights in San Pedro, California – and for the Los Angeles Housing Authority – the Hacienda Village and Pueblo del Rio, both in Los Angeles.[139]

In 1943, he was hired as a visiting professor at Bennington College, an all-women's progressive school in Vermont, New York State.[140] In February 1944, he took on the position as Project Director[141] of the Committee on Design of Public Works organized by Puerto Rico Governor Rexford Guy Tugwell.[142] A free state associated with the United States since the Spanish-American War in 1898, Puerto Rico suffered from economic and social problems, largely ignored by the US government[143] – which, incidentally, was responsible for appointing the governor. The imminence of World War II made Puerto Rico a rather weak spot in the image of good neighbors that the North Americans were trying to project throughout Latin America.

> Obviously, Puerto Rico connoted the failure of US colonial administration. However, at war time, it was more important for the foreign policy focused on South America that the island demonstrated the benefits of US assistance. In this way, Puerto Rico became a laboratory, or in Tugwell's words: *[in] a good testing ground fo American intentions.*[144]

An article published in March 1945 in the *Architectural Forum magazine* corroborates Luz Marie Rodríguez López's statement, transcribed above. According to the report, the island of Puerto Rico is strategically located between the two hemispheres and, therefore, has become Latin American's guinea pig for the political, cultural, social and economic experiments of the United States. "What happens in Puerto Rico may answer the question of all Latin American countries surrounding the Caribbean as well as the British and Dutch colonies in the hemisphere."[145] Thus, in May 1943, Governor Tugwell passed the law establishing the creation of the Committee on Design of Public Works. Operating as an emergency agency, the Committee "would resort to modern processes and techniques to design – on mass scale – functional works emphasizing economy in design and space."[146]

The initial aim of this Committee was to create a typological system of architectural ideas, products and processes, such as a catalog of models to be developed on the island. It would also serve as a center for Puerto Ricans to acquire skills in modern techniques for designing and planning government buildings through processes already developed and tested abroad. In addition, the architect who took on the position of Project Director would be able to generate the preliminary drawings directly on the island or in the United States.[147]

In September 1943, the Committee members discussed the possibility of hiring Richard Neutra as Project Director for a period of twelve months, given his previous experiences with large-scale school and housing projects.[148] However, in December, a series of deadlocks during the negotiations led the Committee to consider the names of Eero Saarinen, Vernon DeMars, Walter Gropius and Eliel Saarinen for a position in design consultancy.[149] Neutra, however, was officially hired on February 18, 1944, through a letter sent by Rafael Picó, president of the Committee on Design of Public Works of Puerto Rico. Luz Marie Rodríguez points out that the official records covering the Committee's meetings attest to the architect's presence in Puerto Rico in November 1943, from February to March 1944, and then from May to June of that same year. According to her, "the Board of the Design

Committee decided to dismiss Neutra's services once his contract ended in February 1945,"[150] but his architectural studies continued to spread, mainly through his book *Architecture of Social Concern in Countries of Mild Climate* (1948) and the book *Tropical Architecture* (1956), written by the British Maxwell Fry and Jane Drew.

During the period in which he worked as Project Director – a position later renamed Architect and Consultant –, Richard Neutra developed a series of projects for schools, housing, health centers and hospitals for rural and urban areas. However, according to the architect's report to Governor Rexford Tugwell in April 1944, architects were not as receptive as engineers, "what is, after all, understandable if you consider their previous work and my approach with the designs problems."[151] Neutra also faced opposition from the College of Engineers and Architects of Puerto Rico, whose representatives met with members of the Committee on Design of Public Works to lay their case against hiring foreign professionals, stating that this went against the initial goal of generating jobs for the local community.[152] Despite these internal conflicts, historian Thomas Hines states that, throughout the 1940s, Neutra kept in touch with his former associates in order to learn about the development of the projects.

> Indeed, Despite the internal rivalries within his Puerto Rican office, the occasional native resentment of his outsider status, and the inevitable changes in his designs as they were built in succeeding years, Neutra had reason to feel good about his Puerto Rican achievements. Throughout the forties he kept in touch with old associates about the island's development.[153]

Regarding the projects developed by Neutra in Puerto Rico – and which would later make up the book *Architecture of Social Concern in Countries of Mild Climate*, published in

São Paulo –, little is known about those that would actually be built. In the book, there are photos of the Sabana Llana Model School, in Rio Piedras, with horizontal pivot doors,[154] the very same school that, in Thomas Hines' book, is seen in the background of a photo of Governor Tugwell; in this picture, one can spot a classroom opening to the patio, with students and teachers interacting.[155] Barbara Lamprecht's book *Richard Neutra: Complete Works*, besides this particular school, also presents a few pictures of an urban school in Paraíso.[156] In a travel account titled "Puerto Rican Encounters," Raymond Neutra, the youngest son of Richard and Dione Neutra, categorizes his father's works in Puerto Rico as follows: the Urban School in the city of Paraíso and other works designed by Neutra, but which have suffered changes over the years; works designed by Neutra and built after the publication of *Social Architecture*; and works not designed by Neutra, but influenced by him.[157]

The importance of this work by the architect in Puerto Rico in propping up the image of the United States internationally was, of course, crucial for choosing him as a representative/messenger of American good will. Richard Neutra's trajectory until that moment – and throughout his professional career – reveals an architect concerned with social, economic, technological and environmental issues in architecture, all central themes in political discussions at the time.

Taking up Ron Robin's analysis, the embassy building program, of which then-President Franklin Roosevelt was the main mentor, sought to express, through architecture, a modern society totally at ease with technology and mindful of the environment.[158] Obviously, this interest extended to all the foreign policy efforts of the time: among them, Richard Neutra's work as a public works consultant in Puerto Rico and his subsequent tour through South America.

However, the purpose of this book is to show that, although the main goal of the mission was to *teach* good architecture and modern urbanism, Neutra also *took* some lessons from Latin American architects. The short-sighted view in general canonical historiography – as well as in studies regarding Neutra's work – makes it difficult to grasp the network of relations developed by Neutra with Latin America. Furthermore, the reservations that the academy holds against the idea of influence propels the notion that only weaker, less original architects allow themselves to be influenced. Contrary to this understanding, our analysis intends to show that, as in any other kind of field, influences occur in multiple directions and imply a series of conscious acts of an ever-changing artist.

Richard Neutra, who, as Barbara Lamprecht aptly put it, "empirically observed all his life,"[159] was aware that an architect must be able to change when addressing the economic, environmental and technological demands either of a client, a particular historical moment or the space in which he operates. Thus, his relationship with Latin America, which began with his trip under the auspices of the Department of State, was very fruitful for him as well as for us.

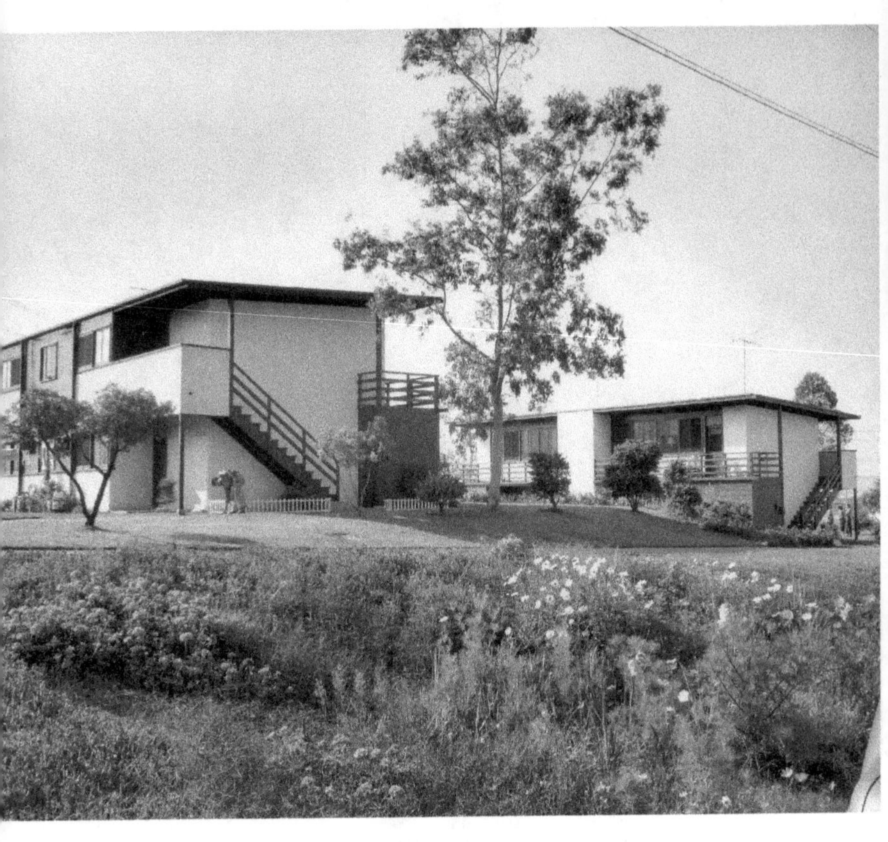

Channel Heights, San Pedro. Richard Neutra,
1941-1942. Photo Julius Shulman. © J. Paul
Getty Trust Archive. Getty Research Institute,
Los Angeles (2004.R.10)

Architect and Messenger of Good Will

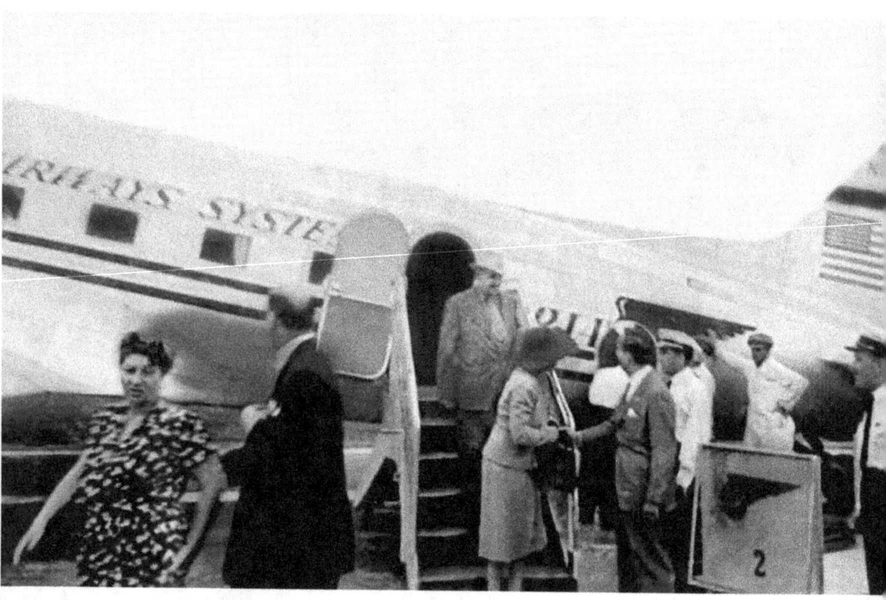

Richard and Dione Neutra disembarking at São Paulo airport, 1945. Photo Gregori Warchavchik. Warchavchik Family Archive

As seen earlier, the Division of Cultural Affairs of the US Department of State was responsible for coordinating long-term programs focusing on Latin America. These programs, which would continue well after World War II, were intended to project an image of the United States as a good neighbor – a political actor committed to promoting hemispheric solidarity. Such programs included the interchange of influential people and of ways of demonstrating interest in the well-being of the continent as a whole. It was in response to this policy and this department that Richard Neutra was summoned to undertake a recon trip to the "other American republics." Traveling by plane and, in some parts, by train, Neutra roamed through South America between October and November 1945.

The documents collected in UCLA's *Neutra Collection*, the article published in 1946 in the *Progressive Architecture* magazine, "Observations on Latin America," and our research in the main Brazilian newspapers of the time point out the countries and some of the cities and places Neutra visited, as well as the lectures, conferences and social events in which he participated. The purpose of the trip was to demonstrate cooperation with local authorities and architects, assisting them in matters concerning urban planning and projects for social housing, hospitals and schools.[161] It was a type of consultancy very similar to his work with the Puerto Rican government, only now he did not hold an official position, operating in a collaborative way. The historical fact that the Austrian architect living in the United States operated as an "agent of good will" in the post-war period is our starting point for the study of his relationship with Latin American architects and landscape architects; nevertheless, it is only the initial reason, not the final one. As will be seen throughout this book, the ties established at this time unfolded in different ways – publications, future visits, collaborative work – in the different countries he visited and were driven by mutual interest and admiration.

Just as Walt Disney had done three years earlier, Neutra toured the South American countries aboard a Pan American Airways plane, a company that, according to Jenifer Van Vleck, was the only US airline dedicated to international travel until 1945.[162] Disney's mission had a direct impact on US defense issues, as it was focused on propaganda and cultural rapprochement between countries on the continent in the midst of the war. As a result, it was managed directly by the Office of the Coordinator of Inter-American Affairs, unlike Neutra's mission, which took place under the auspices of the Department of State. It is important to keep in mind that, just as building new embassies was a way for Americans to project themselves as a global power, the consolidation and expansion of their international airlines guaranteed access to foreign markets and facilitated cultural influence as well as future military interventions. As Van Vleck states:

> Discourse on aviation thus framed the policies, strategies, and ideas that propelled the United States' ascendance as a global power. [...] As airplanes transported American people and products to places that were no longer distant, the logic of the air became the common-sense logic of a type of American empire – an empire based, primarily, not on the direct control of territory but on access to markets, on the influence of culture and

ideology, and on frequent military interventions in other countries, all of which the airplane facilitated. Aviation both created and legitimized a new international order in which power itself was increasingly defined in extraterritorial terms, consistent with U.S. foreign policy objectives.[163]

According to Dione Neutra, in an interview with Lawrence Weschler as part of the Oral History Program at the University of California, the Department of State invited Richard Neutra for a reconnaissance mission to South America in 1944,[164] but our research has not been able to identify the precise date yet. However, documents found in the *Neutra Collection* show that, as early as June 1945, the architect had a list with the names and addresses of people he would meet in Peru, Chile, Rio de Janeiro and São Paulo. Here's the list: Emilio Harth-Terré (1899-1983), Peruvian architect and urban planner based in Lima; Chilean architects Emilio Duhart (1917-2006) – active in Santiago and holding a Master's degree from Harvard Graduate School, where he was a student under Walter Gropius (1883-1969) – and Sergio Larraín García-Moreno (1905-1999); Brazilian architects Oscar Niemeyer (1907-2012), Marcelo Roberto (1908-1964), Milton Roberto (1914-1953), Maurício Roberto (1921 1996), Henrique Mindlin (1911-1971) and Rino Levi (1901-1965); and the Brazilian painter, writer and art critic Sérgio Milliet (1898-1966).[165] On September 12, 1945, the Consulate of Brazil in Los Angeles issued a visa so that Neutra could enter the country.[166]

These documents also reveal some of the process in preparation for the trip and the lectures that would be given here: in an undated correspondence, the Uruguayan architect Eduardo Barañano – who was then teaching at Princeton University – informed that he had already contacted architect Daniel Rocco, director of the Faculty of Architecture in Montevideo, and Mme. Muller, head of the Cultural

Division of the Education Department, requesting letters of invitation for Neutra to speak there.[167] Also, in a telegram sent on August 15, 1945, Ruben Saslavsky informed Neutra that he would soon receive a letter from the Architecture School at the University of Buenos Aires inviting him as a speaker.[168] In addition to these invitations, on September 9 of that same year, Richard Neutra sent a letter to Charles W. Collier, representative of the United Nations Relief and Rehabilitation Administration, in which he apparently asks for help and tips in organizing the trip, with a special focus on Bolivia.[169]

Collier, himself an architect, had also worked as a diplomat of Cultural Relations in La Paz and, therefore, had the knowledge and information necessary to give guidance for Neutra's lectures and travel itinerary in Bolivia. He also put Richard Neutra in touch with a former professor of architecture at the University of La Paz, so she could give him the names and addresses of the architects he was supposed to meet in the country. In the letter, Charles Collier adopted a stance of severe criticism regarding Bolivian architecture:

> In my opinion contemporary architecture in Bolivia has much more to learn from you than you have to learn from it. I frankly do not believe there is a single first-class Bolivian architect, nor have I seen any outstanding contemporary architecture in that country. Architects who have the right point of view have no ability and vice versa. [...]
>
> The great shame of it is that the revulsion against traditional methods of construction and design is so strong in these countries that they are in the process of tearing down the entire historical architectural settings, both good and bad, and are substituting for it shoddy, badly designed modernistic houses which add up to nothing at all. No doubt, in the course of the time the architects will evolve beyond their present state and

turn out better work, but by that time most of the beautiful old settings will be quite well ruined. You will see what I mean when you get to La Paz, a shining example of destruction with nothing substituted.[170]

The letter goes on to suggest that, for his lectures in Bolivia, Peru, Ecuador, the republics of Central America and Mexico – though not in Brazil, Uruguay, Chile or Argentina –, Neutra should address the differences between functional and *modernist* architecture and the use of traditional materials in modern architecture.[171] What is clear from reading these documents is that Richard Neutra spent months preparing himself for this trip: he sought information about which cities to visit and which architects to meet, and also organized as many lectures and conferences as possible. The scope and objectives of the diplomatic mission are quite evident: sending a well-respected architect from the United States to Latin America, one who showed genuine interest in social, climate and urban planning issues, to act as a consultant on public projects, share his knowledge and report back to the Department of State what he saw and with whom he spoke.

However, this was not all that Neutra did. While preparing for the trip in the United States, the architect expanded his range of contacts, finding interlocutors in Latin America to discuss the issues that interested him. This fact will become even clearer in the next chapters, when we explore the relations he established on the continent, but it is already possible to see that not one, but actually two Neutras came to visit us: the agent of good will on a diplomatic mission, promoting hemispheric solidarity through the social and functional issues of architecture and urbanism; but also the renowned and experienced architect, quite interested in exploring nature and local conditions (building materials and technology, climate and society's customs) in his works.

The 1945 South American recon trip was the first time Neutra had worked directly with the US Department of State. His previous experiences in federal agencies (Works Progress Administration, National Youth Administration, California State Planning Board and Federal Works Agency) and his work as a consultant on the Puerto Rico Committee on Design of Public Works – also a program under the auspices of the State Department – were crucial for his selection for this diplomatic mission. Dione Neutra, in the interview with Lawrence Weschler, noted that the trip quickly brought to the couple a perception of how the foreign policy of the country in which they lived at that time worked: "We noticed very soon that our State Department was interested to bolster the businessmen who were there, the business interests; but any movement where people tried to pull themselves up by their bootstraps was considered communist."[172]

That may have been the first time Richard Neutra worked directly with the US Department of State, but it seems that it was not the first time he was involved in programs led by the US government. In a letter dated back to December 9, 1941, Jacob Crane, Assistant Coordinator of the Defense Housing Coordination Division – within the Office for Emergency Administration of the Executive Office of the President – informed Neutra that, with the help of the Office of the Coordinator of Inter-American Affairs, he was arranging visits to the United States and Puerto Rico of one or more representatives from each of the "other American republics", where the group would participate on a tour dedicated to studying housing projects. The program was still in the making, but, according to Crane, Neutra would be notified when everything was set.

> We are trying to organize to bring one or more delegates from each of the other American republics to this country and to Puerto Rico in April on a sort of Housing Study Tour. The Office of the Coordinator of

Inter-American Affairs is considering the project and
will probably help to finance it. The official sponsors
at this end are Mrs. Dorothy Rosenman, Chairman of
the National Committee on the Housing Emergency,
Coleman Woodbury, Executive Director of the National
Association of Housing Officials, and Governor Tugwell
of Puerto Rico. [...]
The delegates would probably visit several cities in
the eastern United States. They will probably visit Puerto
Rico. I believe that some of them will want to make
more extensive tours of the States.[173]

The circumstances of this letter are curious: in the
Neutra Collection of the Special Collections Library at the
University of California, it is cataloged under the theme of
CIAM (Professional Papers, Congrès Internationaux d'Architecture Moderne); and, in the body of the letter, Jacob
Crane commented on the proposal of US government to
take the Latin American representatives to Puerto Rico for a
study trip regarding housing. The text of the letter mentions
a congress, but never specifies exactly which congress it
was – thus, it does not actually confirm whether or not this
correspondence was related to the group; nevertheless, it is
known that Neutra was listed as a North American representative in the CIAM since its founding in La Sarraz, in addition
to having been appointed in 1943 as president of the New
York Section of Post-War Rehabilitation and Planning – an
attempt initiated by Sigfried Giedion (1888-1968) in 1939 to
bring CIAM to America.[174] It is also curious that, as early as
1941, Crane, the architect responsible for the urban design
of Greendale, Wisconsin,[175] proposed Puerto Rico as one of
the sites on the route of this study tour. It is indeed curious,
because, according to a research developed by Luz Marie
Rodríguez, the Planning Board – which would constitute
the Committee on Design of Public Works in 1944 and
which was responsible for the modernizing wave as well as

for housing, schools and hospitals projects – was created
by Governor Rexford Guy Tugwell just the following year, in
1942.

So far, the research has not been able to clearly establish the real circumstances of this letter, but it is possible that new data will come up that may help to clarify this episode. What is known, however, and which may perhaps contribute to the understanding of the circumstances of this exchange between Jacob Crane and Richard Neutra even before the recon trip through South America, is that both Richard and Dione Neutra – possibly, in the same way as architects Wallace Harrison[176] and Buckminster Fuller[177] – actually believed in the Good Neighbor Policy as a way to strengthen the American continent and in the importance of the role of architects in this scenario. In response to Lawrence Weschler's question – "Politically, in terms of national politics, international politics, which of you was the person in the family that kept up?" –, Dione Neutra makes her political commitment clear:

> Oh, you know, I told you that I always marked his ballots.[178] And we were very enthusiastic about Roosevelt. And I joined the League of Women Voters and became very much interested, for instance, in the Negro community. [...] I think we were very enthusiastic Americans.[179]

After the recon trip to South America, the US Department of State hired Richard Neutra to develop two further projects: the US Embassy in Karachi (1955-1959), Pakistan, and the visitorcCenter of the Lincoln Memorial Museum (1958-1961), in Gettysburg. However, his involvement with government projects, especially those related to the development of low-cost housing and fast assembly, did not end there. Another curious document found in the *Neutra Collection* is a letter, dated February 4, 1943, from John B. Blandford Jr., manager of the National Housing Agency, to R.

J. Thomas, president of the International Union (UAW CIO). In it, Blandford mentions his interest in learning about Richard Neutra's experiences in the Diatom series.

> The suggestions of Mr. Neutra regarding Diatomaceous earth are very interesting. We are familiar with the use of Diatomaceous earth as a concrete aggregate but have not had experience with the "Diatom" composition to which Mr. Neutra refers.[180]

To understand the subject to which this letter refers, a parenthesis is needed. In the same way that Rush City Reformed was for Richard Neutra a theoretical exercise in urban planning as well as an experiment for his own designs, the Diatom houses were theoretical experiments in low-cost housing developed throughout the 1920s and 1930s.[181] According to historian Barbara Lamprecht, "Neutra came West to seek new technologies"[182] and, in a period of economic depression followed by war, this search aimed at creating quick and cheap ways to build social housing. Neutra would use a composition of folded metal sheets (for the foundation and structure as well as for the closings) and slabs of a mortar produced out of diatomaceous earth – a material similar to lightweight concrete mortar – for thermal insulation.[183]

The structure of the Diatom Houses followed a model that Richard Neutra described in a book published in Vienna in 1930 – *Amerika: Die Stilbildung des neuen Bauens in den Vereinigten* [America: the development of the style of modern construction in the United States] – as the main promise of a style of building construction peculiar to North America: the circus tent, which, according to him, "gathered all the requirements for lightness in construction."[184]

> The fact that most of the construction components, such as roofing and cables, appear in their mere traction

condition and therefore have minimal cross-sections,
gives the tent an example for our times in yet another
sense, which it really worries, which is to consider lightness as a commandment under construction.[185]

The use of the model of a circus tent is also present
in the work of Richard Buckminster Fuller. The Dymaxion
Deployment Unit – DDU project, developed between 1941
and 1944 – was part of a larger humanitarian project conceived by Fuller – Home for All – and was financed by the
United States Army. The American architect, who, according
to Roberto Segre, advocated for the use of technology and
scientific advances as a way to improve people's quality of
life,[186] assumed, during World War II, the position of Special Assistant to the Vice-Director of Foreign Economies
Administration. Regarding the prototype of his DDU houses,
he argued that, in addition to being tough, detachable and
mass-produced, they were bullet and fireproof, thermally
insulated, and economical in terms of he cost and the
application of the materials.[187] Fuller believed that the DDU
units were also of great value in the air bases that the United
States, at that time, was building in strategic points of the
American continent – as, for example, the air base in Natal –
Parnamirim Field, on the northeast coast of Brazil.

> It is my opinion that in building our air bases, Dymaxion
> Houses could be erected on the job and thereby con-
> serving rubber, gasoline, etc. in transportation. After the
> air base is completed, they could be used for housing
> the air base personnel. [...] After the war, the re-use of
> these houses by underprivileged civilian population is an
> important consideration.[188]

Neutra, as Buckminster Fuller and many others – such
as Charles (1907-1978) and Ray Eames (1912-1988), Eero
Saarinen (1910-1961), Julius Ralph Davidson (1889-1977),

Rodney Walker (1910-1986) and Ralph Rapson (1914-2008), to name just a few – believed in pre-fabrication as a logical response to the demand for architecture, especially at that time of economic crisis and world conflicts. In the case of diatomaceous earth plates, Neutra argued for them until the late 1950s as a cheap structural system, superior to concrete.[189] The development of these low-cost, prefabricated housing prototypes was not limited, however, to government programs. In 1945, John Entenza (1905-1984), editor of the magazine *Arts & Architecture*, from California, created the Case Study House program – a series of modern, experimental prototypes of low-cost housing.

First released in the February issue of the magazine with Julius Ralph Davidson's unbuilt design, the program was seen by Entenza as an effort to "provide the public and the construction industry with low-cost housing models in the modern language, based on a prediction of construction growth as an inevitable trend after the dramatic shortage in homes during the depression and war years."[190] Richard Neutra's participation in this program took place at three different times: in 1945, with the Case Study House – CSH #6, the Omega House, unbuilt; in 1946, with the CSH #13, the Alpha House, also unbuilt; and in 1947-1948, with the CSH #20, built on Chautauqua Boulevard, Pacific Palisades.[191]

Now, going back to the recon trip: with everything set in place, Richard Neutra embarks in October 1945 on the flight that would take him to the republics of South America. The first city visited was Guayaquil, Ecuador, but he could not linger there, given his priorities for the trip. Nevertheless, he was able to meet with Mr. Reed,[192] an official at the service of the OCIAA, with whom he visited the construction sites for the Stadium, the Assembly of the People and the Museum. He then left for Peru, where he was welcomed at the airport by architect Emilio Harth-Terré – who at the time was head of the Department of Urban Studies, associated with the Ministry of Development. Together they visited the metropolitan region of Lima, Callao, San Miguel, Madalena, San Isidro, Miraflores and Rimac. According to a comment present in the report, Richard Neutra believed that the measures adopted by Peruvian urban planners at the time did not seem adequate to the fast metropolitan growth, especially in terms of preservation of historical heritage.

In addition to dinner parties and social receptions, Neutra gave two lectures to students at the Universidad Nacional de Ingeniería and a more formal one, held at the Salão dos Artistas Afisionados. The theme was "the metropolitan future of a city with great historical heritage". Regarding this lecture, he stated:

> I proposed to preserve the true monuments of the past by all available means, but honor them by keeping them protected against badly imitative and falsifying neighbors, who only would cast a shadow of doubt over their own authenticity and genuineness.[193]

In Peru, Richard Neutra also visited the cities of Arequipa – where he met with architects and engineers from the Southern Peruvian Railroads company and OCIAA representatives – and Cuzco – where he met officials from the *Consejo Nacional de Conservación de Monumentos Historicos y Archeologicos*. From there, he traveled by train to Bolivia; on the border between the two countries, he was welcomed by a delegation led by Emilio Villanueva, director of the Faculty of Architecture at the University of La Paz; the delegation followed Neutra on the journey to the capital. There, he delivered two lectures to architecture students and professors – "Report on American Colleges of Architecture" – and another one for the general public, which took place at the Municipal Library, with the theme "Conflicts of tradition with modern development."

According to Neutra:

La Paz, partly due to its unique physiographic requirements of a narrow but most picturesque site, partly to
the special ability of at least three or four professionals
supported by useful others, may develop into one of the
very interesting cases of planning and designing. Not
least, the Park Department, whose ambitious projects
have taken a visible start, must be appreciated.[194]

From Bolivia, he flew to Argentina; in Buenos Aires, he
gave four lectures, all of which, according to him, had significant audiences, despite the unofficial nature of his visit,
which was due to the lack of political cooperation from the
Argentine government and the shutting of the University.
The first of the lectures took place at the Editora Sur office
and presented for discussion the topic "The Possible Values of
the Strange Visitor" – a subject that sparked controversy in
several newspapers. According to Richard Neutra's comments, constructive criticisms brought by local architects and
urban planners greatly inspired him.

The second lecture took place at the home of writer and
intellectual Victoria Ocampo. There, anchored by colorful
slides, Neutra discussed the issue of the conceivable "clients
of the planner and architect", including government agencies
and their demands for social housing. A third conference
took place at the headquarters of the Sociedad Central de
los Arquitectos: "The Materials of Today and Tomorrow" was
the theme. Finally, the fourth lecture, which took place in the
Sala de Francia de los Amigos del Arte, discussed the "socio-
economic determinants of design." In addition to these four
conferences and social gatherings, Richard Neutra met with
a group of approximately forty students with whom he spoke
about the "popular initiative in planning matters" and with a
similar group of young architects interested in international
cooperation in the field of professional planning.

Of Buenos Aires he wrote:

Among the impressive features of the capital and
provincial areas, I had the opportunity to visit, was the
near absence of slum sections, the visible orderliness of
the technical administration and obvious cooperation in
maintenance by the populace in the city and along the
well-kept highways as far as they are paved. I enumerate
well done modern projects: Hospital de la Policia, Municipal Hospital, Hospital of the War Ministry, Automobile
Club Downtown and highway dependencies of Auto
Club, housing project in the northern suburbs for 500
families, peripheral freeway, General Paz, Riverbank Park-
way Costanera, bridge approach to Avellaneda Industrial
zone south, project for development of southwest inun-
dation section Bajo de las Flores, the hippodrome and
the stadium, open air school for weak children, a retail
market of modern layout, several very advanced motion
picture houses and apartment buildings, a project for
the reconstruction of the earthquake-destroyed city of
San Juan, the recreational development of the "Tigre,"
roadside parks every driving hour along the principal
highway of the province of Buenos Aires.[195]

Richard Neutra then left for Uruguay; at the Montevideo
airport, he was received by Mauricio Gravotto, author of
the Master Plan for Montevideo, in 1930, and for Mendoza,
Argentina, in 1941, one of the main figures in Uruguayan
architecture, and also by Ms. De Muller, head of the Department of Art and Culture at the Ministry of Education. He
met with the team of the Institute of Urbanism and with the
Urban Planning Department in order to discuss the problems
of the city. He gave lectures for students and professors
at the University of Montevideo on the following themes:
"Contemporary Needs and Requirements of Tradition" and
"Architecture and Art for the People."

In his report he stated:
Especially impressive developments or projects were
the very well managed and appointed housing projects,
beaches inside the city and all along from Atlantida to
Punta del Vallena and Punta de l'Este, public parks, People's Hotel and recreation areas, children's playgrounds,
the new structures for the University Departments of
Architects and Engineers, the inauguration of the Spring
Salon by the President of the Republic, the work of the
Inter-American Cooperative Health Service, and the
huge modern hospitals.[196]

From Montevideo, Richard Neutra left for São Paulo,
making a stopover in Porto Alegre, where he visited a hospital designed by Jorge Machado Moreira. At the airport in
São Paulo, he was received by a large group – approximately
24 people, according to a report – of government officials,
architects and urban planners, as can be seen in photos from
the Warchavchik collection. The first big meeting took place
at Gregori Warchavchik's house. In addition to three press
conferences, he also met with architects interested in the
inter-American cooperation program and gave two lectures:
one together with Henrique Mindlin and Chilean architect
Enrique Gebhart; and another at the Faculty of Law, discussing the topic "Communal and Social Requirements Confront
the Designer."
The architect noted about São Paulo:

Impressive developments and projects: seaside
resorts Guaruja and Santos, with first rate design
of Warchavchik for resort home Conde Crespi; the
Hydro-Electric development of Sao Paulo; the skyscraper
Public Library; the University Hospital, nurses school and
a splendid project by Rino Levi for Maternity Hospital; the Entre-Lagos suburban subdivision; the motion
picture house Excelsior; various apartment, office and

residential buildings by Artigas, Rino Levi, Warchavchik, Rudofsky, Calabi.[197]

From São Paulo, he left for Rio de Janeiro, where he was welcomed by a group of architects and students. After a tour accompanied by the head of the Engineering Department – he visited the Gávea and Tijuca parks and the cities of Niterói and Petrópolis –, he joined a gathering at the house of mayor Filadelfo de Azevedo. He met with the Minister of Foreign Affairs, Pedro Leão Veloso, the director of the Foundation for Brazilian Internal Development, João Alberto, and the US ambassador. He also spoke with architects interested in the International Urban Planning and Architecture Congress and gave two lectures: one at the headquarters of the Institute of Architects of Brazil - IAB, with the theme "Architecture for the People at Large"; and another for the teachers and students of the Escola Nacional de Belas Artes, regarding "The Social Responsibility of the Architect."

From Rio he traveled to Minas Gerais, on a two-day visit to Belo Horizonte, Pampulha and Ouro Preto, places where Richard Neutra found other brilliant examples of modern Brazilian architecture:

Impressive developments and projects: Hospital by Moreira for Porto Alegre, Education Ministry, Resiguros Buildings, airport, theatre in Belo Horizonte, apartments Guinle, Botanical Garden, two residences, roof gardens, and garden projects by Burle Marx.[198]

During his stay in Brazil, Neutra received an invitation from Bahia government officials to visit the state – possibly Salvador, its capital – and learn about some of the projects that were being developed there. However, with no means of transportation, he was forced to follow through with the original plan and return to the United States.

Brazilian newspapers at the time reported the arrival of Richard Neutra with the following headline: "One of the most famous architects in the world arrives on Monday. Creator of a school of architecture attentive to the human experience, Mr. Richard J. Neutra is president of CIAM, which stands for the international conscience of contemporary architecture – in the opinion of his colleague Gregori Warchavchik, he is the greatest North American architect active today."[199] It is interesting to note that the vast majority of news published in newspapers at the time reported that Neutra was visiting Latin America as part of a cultural exchange trip. The architect's connection with CIAM also seemed to be of the utmost importance – he was appointed president of the New York Section of CIAM in 1943 – but not the fact that the trip was made under the auspices of the US Department of State. Only two articles, both from Rio de Janeiro newspapers, pointed out this connection: one in *A Manhã*, on the day of Neutra's arrival in Rio, and another in the *Diário Carioca*, reporting on his return to the United States.[200] It is also curious that Neutra stayed in Rio de Janeiro longer than originally planned: in a letter dated November 7, 1945, addressed to the US Embassy in Rio de Janeiro, Willian Griffith (special representative for the Inter-American Educational Foundation, connected to OCIAA) alludes to the mismatch in their correspondence – given that, according to the itinerary sent by the architect, he would already be back in Los Angeles on that date – and reiterates the invitation for Richard Neutra to visit Guatemala.[201]

Something similar happened in the visits of Walt Disney and Orson Welles to Brazil. Newspapers at the time announced that the visits were part of a cultural exchange effort– also mentioning personal interests –, but did not allude to the cultural rapprochement program carried by the Rockefeller Office. In a press interview held in Hollywood prior to the trip, Orson Welles said:

My trip to Brazil means the fulfillment of a long-held
desire to get to know this colossus of the South, often
mentioned, but little known. During my days in Rio de
Janeiro, I'll try to learn about Brazilian culture and its
historical bases, documenting some aspects of its people
– popular music, festivals, revelries and regional dances.
I'm interested in getting to know Brazilian rural types
and documenting the different phases of Brazilian life.[202]

When reporting on the upcoming arrival of Walt Disney
in Rio de Janeiro, the newspaper *Diário Carioca* transcribed a
correspondence received from the Office of the Coordinator
of Inter-American Affairs. Here, the message was clear: the
"ambassador" and "genius creator of Donald Duck" stood for
the "constitution of a state of mind capable of promoting
great change in the environment of a nation, a generation
or even a simple village. This is not just a bold statement, but
a proven reality."[203] Even though it did not openly express it,
both passages projected the image of a good neighbor who
held a genuine interest in the "other American republics."

Now, it is possible that the *seductive* feature, which
Antonio Pedro Tota mentions when exploring US imperialist
policies towards Latin America,[204] is more intrinsically related
to the programs developed by the Rockefeller's Office than
to those of the Department of State, maybe because of the
different nature of the programs: Disney and Welles' travels
involved cultural issues and cinema; Neutra, on the other
hand, focused on social housing and urban planning. In any
case, the fact is that the Brazilian media at the time was
heavily influenced by the message of good neighborliness.
On January 30, 1942, three articles published in the same
issue of *A Noite* caught our attention.

In the first of them, right at the top of the first page, the
departure speech of Under Secretary of State Sumner Welles:

I say goodbye to Rio with deep emotion, bringing back to my country the assurance that the spirit of solidarity in the Americas has given, at the Conference of Chancellors, the most decisive and robust proof of vitality, which we will not be lacking during our struggle in defense of the integrity of the continent and of human freedom. The gratitude of the American people will never forget the demonstrations of sympathy, trust, and value by free nations that strive, above all, to preserve themselves and defend their independence. We will never forget the cooperation and encouragement given to our work by President Getúlio Vargas and his loyal collaborator, Chancellor Oswaldo Aranha. I wish, using this column of *A Noite*, to express my deep gratitude for the appreciation and the applause with which the people of Brazil distinguished, in my person, the United States of North America.[205]

Right below this, we find a mention to the birthday of Franklin D. Roosevelt, a "great friend of Brazil and Brazilians."[206] Here, the US president is placed side by side with President Getúlio Vargas:

Incidentally, it is interesting to observe the simultaneity of the revolution that took place in Brazil, with the rise of President Getúlio Vargas to power, an equally redemptive mission, imbued with equal predestination. From the early days of his administration, Roosevelt abandoned all routine and sought to innovate and reform, fighting political prejudices and administrative nonsense. He faced the liveliest and fiercest opposition a president has ever encountered in the United States. However, he knew how to win it over, gallantly, and yesterday's opponents are now his collaborators, defeated by his sincerity of purpose and the strength of his patriotism.[207]

The third article, published more discreetly on the second page of the newspaper, reported on the trip of Dr. Lutero Vargas – the president's son – to the United States and his reception at the White House.[208] Even though he met with President Roosevelt, Luther and his wife Ingeborg Vargas were watched by the US intelligence service at the request of Rockefeller.[209] Despite facing strong opposition from the Department of State for wanting to "monitor the daughter-in-law of the president of a friendly nation,"[210] Nelson Rockefeller managed to keep the couple under "low-key surveillance."[211] The magnate's distrust was due not only to Ingeborg's German nationality, but mainly to Luther's behavior and relationships:

> While he was on the East Coast with his wife, he dated a showgirl suspected of being a spy in the service of enemy powers. Luther was drunk several times and could have passed on some information to the girl. Unwarranted paranoia from meticulous agents?[212]

Richard Neutra finishes his report to the US Department of State on his visit to South America stating that he believes that his experience in Latin America – the social meetings and lectures – were successful in terms of publicizing cultural cooperation efforts:

> In summing up my experience, I believe that apart from the customary social meetings, considered useful to make for good will, my procedure to make the problems of the visited city itself the subject of formal lectures, round table discussions and broadcasts, proved very satisfactory and was very well received. It naturally required a speedy way of gathering the necessary information, but in many cases it yielded, according to my local friends, truly constructive publicity and appreciation of the State Department's cultural cooperation effort.[213]

The architect's involvement in the efforts for cultural convergence and consolidation of North American hegemony did not occur only during his public works in Puerto Rico and the recognition trip through South America. In a letter to the United States delegate to Unesco, Richard K. Nobbe, dated May 1969, Dione Neutra confirmed her husband's role throughout his professional career as a volunteer in this publicity project:

> You have so devotedly aided our government and ourselves that we want to thank you cordially, while we are continuing to volunteer our own services as good will messengers![214]

Yet another interesting point is that, from the data collected in the report sent to the US Department of State as well as in other documents found in the UCLA's *Neutra Collection* and in the articles published in the *Progressive Architecture* magazine, it is possible to delineate Neutra's itinerary on his trip. Assuming that the meeting with Charles W. Collier in Washington actually took place – in a letter of September 14, 1945, the representative of the United Nations Relief and Rehabilitation Administration invites Richard Neutra to dinner before his trip –, it is consistent to state that, from Washington, Neutra left for Miami, Florida, thence flying to Ecuador, with stopovers in Cuba, Haiti and the Dominican Republic.[215] From the Ecuadorian city of Guayaquil, he traveled through Peru, Bolivia, Argentina and Uruguay. With a stopover in Porto Alegre he then arrived in São Paulo, later moving on to Rio de Janeiro and Belo Horizonte. The mission almost finished, Neutra would leave Brazil from the city of Belém, in the state of Pará. Thus, from Belo Horizonte, he returned to Rio de Janeiro[216] and took a plane to Barreiras, Bahia, passing through Carolina, Maranhão[217] before leaving by train to Belém,[218] following one last advice from Charles Collier: to visit the Amazon Forest.[219]

While still in Lima, Richard Neutra was commissioned by the US government to act as an adviser on projects for rural and urban schools in Guatemala,[220] a possibility that was enthusiastically accepted by William J. Griffith, special representative of the Inter-American Educational Foundation, under the auspices of the Office of Inter-American Affairs:

> I am very much interested in the possibility of your coming to Guatemala to consult on building plans. I am not entirely sure what administrative arrangements Washington may have had in mind when they wrote to you in Lima, but as I shall be leaving for the States within a week I shall have the opportunity to explore the matter thoroughly with the Central Office. When ways and means have been discussed I shall write to you again.[221]

In addition to Guatemala, Neutra made a second stopover – in San Juan, the capital of Puerto Rico –, where he met with Governor Tugwell and discussed the projects of hospitals and various schools which were either already built or almost finished.[222] From then on, our research has not been able to establish his route and point of entry into the United States. Frank McCann Jr., in his book on the relationship between Brazil and the United States, mentions that the flights between these two countries, operated by companies such as Pan-American and Panagra, departed "from Miami to Belém, near the mouth of the Amazon, thence to Rio de Janeiro via the coastal cities of Natal, Recife, and Salvador; from Rio its clippers flew to Porto Alegre in southern Brazil and on Buenos Aires."[223] On the other hand, in an article regarding the advance of Pan American Airlines in Brazil, Gianfranco Beting states that, as of 1945, the company had created an air route from New York to San Juan, in Puerto Rico, and Port of Spain, in Trinidad, reaching Belém, in Pará, and thence Rio de Janeiro.[224]

The analysis of this material exemplifies the various
layers of US foreign policy at that time of war: the effort
of rapprochement and collaboration as a way to guarantee
the integrity of the continent against the advance of enemy
powers, accompanied by close surveillance and use of media
and cinema as seductive forms of imperialism. The opening
years of the Cold War, however, brought obstacles at home
and abroad. According to historian Justin Hart, at that time,
"policymakers were heavily criticized for their methods,
their management, and their messages, as they struggled to
establish their legitimacy with skeptical colleagues."[225] In an
attempt to resolve this crisis, President Eisenhower created,
in 1953, the United States Information Agency – USIA,
responsible for controlling all cultural and propaganda programs developed abroad. "Although public diplomacy lived
on and continued to grow, the creation of the USIA marked
the conclusion of its first phase."[226]

Notwithstanding the intentions of the US government
behind these efforts to bring hemispheric solidarity and
approximation, and also the changes in the global landscape
after World War II, the fact is that this political game gave
an opportunity for Richard Neutra to establish personal
and professional contacts with Latin America, and that the
reciprocity of this dialogue and this influence – in terms of
architecture, urbanism and landscaping – benefited both
Latin American architecture as well as the works of Richard
Neutra, who would later draw on local ideas.

Notes

1. Edward W. Said, *Cultura e impe-rialismo*, 25. Free translation.
2. Gerson Moura, *Tio Sam chega ao Brasil: a penetração cultural Americana*; Gerson Moura, *Brazilian Foreign Relations 1939-1950: The Changing Nature of Brazil-United States Relations During and After the Second World War*.
3. Antonio Pedro Tota, *O imperial-ismo sedutor: a americanização do Brasil na época da Segunda Guerra*; Antonio Pedro Tota, *O amigo americano: Nelson Rockefeller e o Brasil*.
4. Luiz Alberto Moniz Bandeira, *Presença dos Estados Unidos no Brasil*.
5. Fernando Atique, *Arquitetando a "Boa Vizinhança": arquite-tura, cidade e cultura nas relações Brasil-Estados Unidos 1876-1945*.
6. Lauro Cavalcanti, *Moderno e brasileiro: a história de uma nova linguagem na arquitetura (1930-60)*.
7. Carlos Minchillo, *Erico Verissimo, escritor do mundo: circulação literária, cosmopolitismo e relações interamericanas*.
8. Jorge Francisco Liernur, "Latin America: The Places of the "Other;" Jorge Francisco Liernur, "'The South american way'. O milagre brasileiro, os Estados Unidos e a Segunda Guerra Mundial – 1939-1943."
9. Anaioly Glinkin, *Inter-American Relations: From Bolívar to the Present.*
10. Michael D. Blumenthal, "The Economic Good Neighbor Aspects of United States Economic Policy Toward Latin America in the Early 1940s as Revealed by the Activities of the Office of Inter-American Affairs."
11. Patrício Del Real, "Building a Continent: The Idea of Latin American Architecture in the Early Postwar."
12. Thomas M. Leonard, *United States-Latin American Relations, 1850-1903*.
13. Justin Hart, *Empire of Ideas. The Origins of Public Diplomacy and the Transformation of U.S. Foreign Policy*.
14. Jenifer Van Vleck, *Empire of the Air: Aviation and the American Ascendancy*.
15. Gisela Cramer and Ursula Prutsch, ¡Américas Unidas! *Nelson A. Rockefeller's Office of Inter-American Affairs (1940-46)*.
16. Thomas S. Hines and Arthur Drexler, *The Architecture of Rich-ard Neutra: From International Style to California Modern*, 20.
17. See: *Josep Lluís Sert: A Nomadic Dream*.
18. Alcilia Afonso de Albuquer-que Costa, "As contribuições arquitetônicas habitacionais propostas na Cidade dos Motores (1945-46). Town Plan-nings Associates. Xerém, RJ."
19. Costa, "As contribuições arquitetônicas habitacionais propostas na Cidade dos Motores (1945-46)."
20. Josep M. Rovira, *José Luis Sert: 1901-1983*, 113.

21. One of North America's main rivers, the Rio Grande begins in south-center Colorado, in the United States, and flows to the Gulf of Mexico. On this route, it forms part of the border between Mexico and the United States.

22. Rovira, *José Luis Sert*, 114.

23. Leonard, *United States-Latin American relations*, 2. Regarding the theme of the US monopoly over Latin America, I suggest reading the interesting debate brought by Russian researcher Anaioly Glinkin in his doctoral dissertation.

24. Tota, *O amigo americano*, 82. Free translation.

25. Alan Brinkley explains in detail the New Deal politics in his book *Franklin Delano Roosevelt: o presidente que tirou os Estados Unidos do buraco*.

26. Alan Brinkley, *Franklin Delano Roosevelt: o presidente que tirou os Estados Unidos do buraco*, 77. Free translation.

27. Frank D. Mccann JR., *The Brazilian-American Alliance, 1937-1945*, 7.

28. Moura, *Brazilian Foreign Relations 1939-1950*, 53.

29. Hart, *Empire of Ideas*.

30. Uwe Lübken, "Playing the Cultural Game: The United States and the Nazi Threat to Latin America," 63.

31. Hart, *Empire of Ideas*.

32. Atique, *Arquitetanto a "Boa Vizinhança,"* 25-26.

33. Donald W. Rowland, ed., *History of the Office of the Coordinator of Inter-American Affairs: Historical Reports on War Administration*.

34. Atique, *Arquitetanto a "Boa Vizinhança,"* 26-27.

35. Cf. Rowland, ed., *History of the Office*, 4; Moura, *Brazilian Foreign Relations 1939-1950*, 53-59.

36. Catha Paquette, "Soft Power: The Art of Diplomacy in US-Mexican Relations, 1940-1946," 145.

37. Mccann JR., *The Brazilian-American Alliance*, 7.

38. Mccann JR., *The Brazilian-American Alliance*, 213.

39. Rowland, ed., *History of the Office*, 5.

40. Gisela Cramer and Ursula Prutsch, "Nelson A. Rockefeller's Office of Inter-American Affairs and the Quest for Pan-American Union: An Introductory Essay." In ¡Américas *Unidas!*, by Gisela Cramer and Ursula Prutsch, 15.

41. Moura, *Brazilian Foreign Relations*, 68.

42. Bandeira, *Presença dos Estados Unidos*, 250-251.

43. Tota, *O amigo americano*, 79.

44. Mccann JR., *The Brazilian-American Alliance*, 8.

45. Rowland, *History of the Office*, 3; Moura, *Brazilian Foreign Relations*, 53-54.

46. Cf. Rowland, *History of the Office*, 7-8; Lübken, "Playing the Cultural Game," 63-67.

47. The agency has received the following names throughout its existence: Office for Coordination of Commercial and Cultural Relations between the American Republics from August 16, 1940 to July 30, 1941; Office of the Coordinator of Inter-American Affairs from July 30 to 1941 to March 23, 1945; and Office of Inter-American Affairs from March 23, 1945 to its extinction on May 20, 1946.

48. US National Archives and Records Center. *Records of the Office of Inter-American Affairs.* *Washington*, 1973, quoted in Moura, *Brazilian Foreign Relations*, 79.
49. Tota, *O amigo americano*, 25.
50. Rowland, *History of the Office*, 6; Tota, *O imperialismo*, 45.
51. Rowland, *History of the Office*, 6.
52. Cf. Tota, *O amigo americano*, 64-72.
53. Tota, *O imperialismo*, 46.
54. Tota, *O amigo americano*, 68. Free translation.
55. Rowland, *History of the Office*, 8.
56. Ibid., 7-8.
57. Ibid.
58. Ibid., 181 (note 3).
59. Franklin D. Roosevelt to Nelson A. Rockefeller, April 22, 1941, quoted in Rowland, *History of the Office*, 183. In the digital file made available online by the US government, some words appear partially or totally cut off; in this selected excerpt, one of them appears marked as "[illegible]".
60. Minutes of Executive (or Policy) Committee Meeting, December 9, quoted in Rowland, *History of the Office*, 92.
61. Cf. Minutes of Executive (or Policy) Committee Meeting, December 9, quoted in Rowland, *History of the Office*.
62. Cf. Ibid.
63. Statement on the Division of Responsibility between the Division of Cultural Relations of the Department of State and the Division of Science and Education of the CIAA (no date), quoted in Rowland, *History of the Office*, 198. It is worth noting that cultural relationship issues were under the responsibility of the Division of Science and Education of the Office.
64. Cf. Hart, *Empire of Ideas*.
65. Certainly, Veríssimo was not the only Latin American writer to participate in this cultural transit established by the good neighbor policy; however, as stated by Kátia Baggio, professor of history of the Americas at the Federal University of Minas Gerais, he "played – especially in the case of the United States, but also in relation to Hispanic America – a role of cultural mediator between Brazil and most of the countries on the continent". Kátia Gerab Baggio, "Prefácio." In *Erico Verissimo*, by Carlos Minchillo, 12.
66. Cf. Rowland, *History of the Office*, 271.
67. Ibid., 275-276.
68. Hart, *Empire of Ideas*.
69. Ibid.
70. Del Real, *Building a Continent*, 14-15.
71. Ibid., 11-12.
72. Regarding the exhibition, see: Ricardo Rocha, "Resenhar Brazil Builds."
73. Del Real, *Building a Continent*, 141.
74. Ibid., 24.

75. Ibid., 5-6. Assistant curator of architecture and design at MoMA, Patricio del Real is responsible, along with Barry Bergdoll, chief curator, for the exhibition *Latin American in Construction: Architecture 1955-1980*, regional curators being Carlos Eduardo Comas (Brazil) and Jorge Francisco Liernur (Hispanic countries). New York Museum of Modern Art – MoMA, from March 29th to July 19th, 2015. More than seventy years after the mythical *Brazil Builds* exhibition and precisely half a century after the *Latin American Architecture since 1945* exhibition, both held by MoMA, the institution still takes on the mission of bringing the countries of the continent closer together and disseminating qualified Latin American architecture to the North American citizen. See Luis Salvador Gnoato, "O Brasil novamente no MoMA de Nova York. Latin American in Construction: Architecture 1955-1980."

76. Ron Robin, E*nclaves of America: The Rhetoric of American Political Architecture Abroad, 1900-1965*, 5.

77. Ibid., 4.

78. Ibid., 92-93.

79. Jane C. Loeffler, *The Architecture of Diplomacy: Building America's Embassies*, 3.

80. Robin, E*nclaves of America*, 102.

81. Passed on May 7, 1926, the Foreign Service Buildings Act had the power to oversee the purchase and construction of buildings around the world for diplomatic and consular use. And, for this task, it received an initial fund of $10 million to be spent over a 5 year period. Loeffler, *The Architecture of Diplomacy*, 19.

82. Ibid., 37-38.

83. Ibid., 49.

84. Cf. Ibid., 37.

85. Cf. Ibid., 57.

86. Ibid., 58.

87. Garry Stevens, *O círculo privilegiado: fundamentos sociais da distinção arquitetônica*, 76-77. Free translation.

88. Pierre Bourdieu, *O poder simbólico*, 28-29. Free translation.

89. Paul Goldberger, "Wallace Harrison Dead at 86; Rockefeller Center Architect."

90. Richard Guy Wilson, "Reflections on Modernism and World's Fairs," 198.

91. Loeffler, *The Architecture of Diplomacy*, 79.

92. United Nations Member States, www.un.org/en/members/, quoted in Arif Belgaumi, "Legacy of the Cold War: Richard Neutra in Pakistan," 83.

93. Belgaumi, "Legacy of the Cold War," 83.

94. Loeffler, *The Architecture of Diplomacy*, 41.

95. House Appropriations Subcommittee, *Department of State, Justice, and Commerce Appropriations for 1955*, 29 January 1954, p. 326, quoted in Loeffler, *The Architecture of Diplomacy*, 41.

96. In 1952, a fire destroyed part of the building for the US Embassy in Rio de Janeiro, which was still under construction, starting a discussion among Federal Building Operations – FBO agents about fire prevention measures in the new projects. Cf. Loeffler, *The Architecture of Diplomacy*, 61.

97. The first terrorist attack on US embassies took place in Saigon, Vietnam, in 1965, an incident that marked the rise of anti-American sentiment and threats. The need to change and improve security measures had a direct consequence in the architecture of embassies: they went from prominent and accessible public buildings designed to be seen, visited and admired to closed and inaccessible buildings, with bars, walls and bulletproof glasses. Cf. Ibid., 236-259.

98. Ibid., 41.

99. Thomas S. Hines, *Richard Neutra and the Search for Modern Architecture*, 266.

100. Cf. Barbara Mac Lamprecht, "The Obsolescence of Optimism? Neutra and Alexander's U.S. Embassy, Karachi, Pakistan," 174.

101. Fernanda Critelli, "Richard Neutra e o Brasil," 105-110.

102. Gregori Warchavchik, "Introduction." In *Architecture of Social Concern in Regions of Mild Climate*, by Richard Joseph Neutra, 30.

103. We will discuss here just a few issues in the trajectory of Richard Neutra. For a broader view of his biography, see: Hines, *Richard Neutra and the Search*; Hines and Drexler, *The Architecture of Richard Neutra*; Esther Mccoy, *Richard Neutra*; Barbara Mac Lamprecht, *Richard Neutra: Complete Works*; Critelli, "Richard Neutra e o Brasil."

104. Richard Joseph Neutra, *Life and Shape*, 128.

105. Hines, *Richard Neutra and the Search*, 59.

106. Ibid., 70.

107. Raymond Richard Neutra, *Cheap and Thin: Neutra and Frank Lloyd Wright*.

108. Neutra, *Life and Shape*, 209.

109. The couple's first child was named after Frank Lloyd Wright. Hines, *Richard Neutra and the Search*, 66.

110. Neutra, *Cheap and Thin*.

111. Dione Neutra, *Richard Neutra: Promise and Fulfillment, 1919-1932*, 125-128; Neutra, *Cheap and Thin*.

112. Neutra, *Richard Neutra: Promise and Fulfillment*, 129; Neutra, *Cheap and Thin*.

113. Dione Neutra, *To Tell the Truth: Interviewed by Lawrence Weschler*, 100-101.

114. Hines, *Richard Neutra and the Search*, 75; Neutra, *Life and Shape*, 207; Neutra, *Cheap and Thin*.

115. The professional and friendly
     relationship between Neutra
     and Schindler – who shared an
     apartment at some point – is a
     theme present in several discus-
     sions about architects and even
     about the status quo of modern
     architecture in California. To
     mention just a few examples:
     José María Lapuerta, "Casas de
     maestros / House of Masters;"
     Lyra Kilston, *Sun Seekers.
     The Cure of California*; Hines,
     Richard Neutra and the Search;
     Judith Sheine, *R. M. Schindler*.
116. Hines, *Richard Neutra and the
     Search*, 78.
117. Kilston, *Sun Seekers*, 76-78,
     87-88.
118. Sheine, *R. M. Schindler*, 66-67;
     Kilston, *Sun Seekers*, 88.
119. Kilston, *Sun Seekers*, 80.
120. Willy Boesiger, *Buildings and
     Projects: Richard Neutra, 1927-
     1950*, 18.
121. Kilston, *Sun Seekers*, 93.
122. Neutra, *Life and Shape*, 218.
123. The Fellows Logo & The Frank
     Lloyd Wright Foundation. Avail-
     able in <https://bit.ly/3A4Hfks>.
124. Frank Lloyd Wright to Richard
     and Dione Neutra, August 1929,
     quoted in Neutra, *Richard
     Neutra: Promise and Fulfillment*,
     179; Neutra, *Cheap and Thin*.
125. Mccoy, *Richard Neutra*, 24.
126. In the volume concerning Rich-
     ard Neutra in the *Masters of the
     World Architecture* collection,
     Esther McCoy dedicates only
     one paragraph to this subject,
     mentioning the project for the
     utopian city Rush City Reformed
     and implying that the school
     only operated between 1928
     and 1929. Thomas Hines cites
     the school on two occasions: in
     the caption of a photo showing
     Neutra and his students inspect-
     ing Lovell House's construction
     in 1928, and later on identifying
     Harwell Harris and Gregory Ain
     as students of the "short-lived
     Los Angeles Academy of Modern
     Art". Mccoy, *Richard Neutra*, 24;
     Hines, *Richard Neutra and the
     Search*, 104 and 122. Barbara
     Lamprecht doesn't mention
     the school in her books about
     Neutra.
127. Stevens, *O círculo privilegiado*,
     76. Free translation.
128. Hines, *Richard Neutra and the
     Search*, 82.
129. Neutra, *Life and Shape*, 219-220.
130. Harold Bloom, *The Anxiety of
     Influence: A Theory of Poetry*,
     xxxiii.
131. Hines, *Richard Neutra and the
     Search*, 113-117.
132. Ibid., 117.
133. In 1927, Richard Neutra
     published the book *Wie baut
     Amerika?* ("How does America
     build?", in direct translation) in
     Stuttgart, Germany.

134. According to Alan Brinkley, the WPA "built hospitals, schools, airports, theaters, roads, hotels in national parks, monuments, post offices and other federal buildings across the country." Its efforts to create as many jobs as possible and inject funds into the economy "also raised people's expectations of the government and helped give legitimacy to the idea of public assistance to the poor." Free translation. Brinkley, *Franklin Delano Roosevelt*, 65.

135. Hines, *Richard Neutra and the Search*, 188.

136. Raymond Richard Neutra, "Encontros porto-riquenhos."

137. Hines, *Richard Neutra and the Search*, 191-192.

138. Ibid., 193.

139. Lamprecht, *Richard Neutra*, 160-176.

140. Hines, *Richard Neutra and the Search*, 212.

141. According to research developed by Luz Marie Rodríguez, in June 1944, it was decided that the position of Project Director would be abolished in favor of the position of Architect and Consultant. Luz Marie Rodríguez López, "¡Vuelo al porvenir! Henry Klumb y Toro-Ferrer: proyecto moderno y arquitectura como vitrina de la democracia – Puerto Rico, 1944-1958," 210.

142. The last Puerto Rican governor to be appointed by the President of the United States, Tugwell took over the island government from 1941 to 1946. Previously, he had been one of Roosevelt's advisors on the Brain Trust committee, Undersecretary of Agriculture and director of the Resettlement Administration responsible for construction of the Greenbelt cities. Rodríguez López, "¡Vuelo al porvenir!" 200. In this book, we will deal only with some aspects of the Committee on Design of Public Works of Puerto Rico and the work of Richard Neutra as a consultant. For more detailed information on the subject, see: Leonardo Santana Rabell, *Planificación y Política Durante la Administración de Luis Muñoz Marin: Un Análisis Crítico*; Rodríguez López, "¡Vuelo al porvenir!;" Neutra, "Encontros porto-riquenhos;" Critelli, "Richard Neutra e o Brasil."

143. Rexford Guy Tugwell, *The Stricken Land: The Story of Puerto Rico*, 70-71, quoted in Rodríguez López, "¡Vuelo al porvenir!" 205.

144. Ibid., 206. Free translation.

145. Puerto Rico. *Architectural Forum*, n. 82, mar. 1945, p.119-120, quoted in Hines, *Richard Neutra and the Search*, 212.

146. Rodríguez López, "¡Vuelo al porvenir!" 207. Free translation.

147. Ibid., 209-210.

148. Besides Neutra, another four architects were hired: Henry Klumb, Isadore Rosenfield, Simon Brienes and Joseph Blumenkranz. Santiago Iglesias Filho, *Futurama de Puerto Rico. Planificando Alrededor del Mundo*, 60, quoted in Rodríguez López, "¡Vuelo al porvenir!" 210.

149. Rodríguez López, "¡Vuelo al porvenir!" 210 (note 19).

150. Ibid., 218. Free translation.
151. Letter from Richard Neutra to Rexford Tugwell (April 3, 1944), Henry Klumb Collection, box 3.1, AACUPR, quoted in Rodríguez López, "¡Vuelo al porvenir!," 216. Free translation.
152. Rodríguez López, "¡Vuelo al porvenir!," 215.
153. Hines, *Richard Neutra and the Search*, 214.
154. Richard Joseph Neutra, *Arquitetura social em países de clima quente*, 51; "Escuéla modelo de Sabana Llana está operando", October 08 (1944). Folder 29. Box 1419. Office Records, Publicity. Neutra Collection, UCLA Library Special Collections.
155. Hines, *Richard Neutra and the Search*, 214.
156. Lamprecht, *Richard Neutra*, 178.
157. Neutra, "Encontros porto-riquenhos."
158. Robin, E*nclaves of America*, 92, 93 and 145.
159. Lamprecht, "The Obsolescence of Optimism?"
160. "Neutra in Latin America. Raw Material for Editorial Introductory Remarks". Folder 8. Box 167. Professional Papers, Ideas. Neutra Collection. UCLA Library of Special Collections.
161. Richard Joseph Neutra, "Observations on Latin America," *Progressive Architecture*, no. 5, May 1946, 67.
162. Vleck, *Empire of the Air*.
163. Ibid.
164. Neutra, *To Tell the Truth*, 282.
165. Latin America. Folder 8. Box 1429. Office Records, Correspondence. Neutra Collection. UCLA Library of Special Collections.
166. According to data from the Consular Qualification Form made available on the internet by Dion Neutra.
167. Letter from Eduardo Barañano to Richard Neutra. Folder 8. Box 1429. Office Records, Correspondence. Neutra Collection. UCLA Library of Special Collections.
168. Telegram from Ruben Saslavsky to Richard Neutra, August 15, 1945. Folder 29. Box 1419. Office Records, Publicity. Neutra Collection. UCLA Library of Special Collections.
169. I say *apparently* because no records were found of this letter, just Collier's reply, sent five days later. Letter from Charles W. Collier to Richard Neutra, September 14, 1945. Folder 8. Box 1429. Office Records, Correspondence. Neutra Collection. UCLA Library of Special Collections.
170. Ibid.
171. Ibid.
172. Neutra, *To Tell the Truth*, 282.
173. Letter from Jacob Crane to Richard Neutra. Folder 1. Box 233. Professional Papers, CIAM. Neutra Collection. UCLA Library of Special Collections.
174. Eric Munford, "The CIAM Discourse on Urbanism, 1928-1959," 80, 234 and 154.
175. Ibid., 195.
176. Wallace K. Harrison worked as Vice Coordinator for Inter-American Affairs in the Rockefeller Office. Ibid., 195.

177. From 1941 to 1944, Richard Buckminster Fuller took over as Special Assistant to the Deputy Director of Foreign Economies Administration in Washington. Yunn Chii Wong, "Fuller's DDU Project (1941-1944): Instrument, Art or Architecture? (Heroic Design versus ad hoc Pragmatism)." In *Transportable Environments: Theory, Context, Design and Technology*, edited by Robert Kronenburg, 59.

178. During the interview, Dione Neutra says that Richard Neutra was apolitical and that, since the time he lived in Germany, he distrusted all politicians and all newspapers. Thus, on voting days, it was Dione Neutra who filled out the ballot. Neutra, *To Tell the Truth*, 159.

179. Ibid., 238-239.

180. Letter from John B. Blandford JR. to R.J. Thomas. Folder 7. Box 1985. Office Records, Correspondence. Neutra Collection. UCLA Library of Special Collections.

181. Lamprecht, *Richard Neutra*, 28.

182. Ibid., 26.

183. Barbara Mac Lamprecht, *Richard Neutra 1892-1970: formas criadoras para uma vida melhor*, 17.

184. Ibid. Free translation.

185. Richard Joseph Neutra, *Amerika. Die Stilbildung des neuen Bauens in den Vereinigten*. Viena, Verlag Anton Schroll, 1930, p. 76, quoted in Lamprecht, *Richard Neutra 1892-1970*, 17. Free translation.

186. Roberto Segre, "Ideias e invenções de Buckminster Fuller são analisadas por Roberto Segre."

187. Wong, "Fuller's DDU Project," 62.

188. Ibid.

189. However, this material turned out to be too soft and not at all competitive against concrete in terms of cost. Lamprecht, *Richard Neutra 1892-1970*, 28.

190. Elizabeth A. T. Smith, *Case Study Houses*, 6. Free translation.

191. Ibid., 19, 35 and 43.

192. No further references were found concerning Mr. Reed.

193. "Report on visit South American Republics, by Richard Neutra, architect and President, US Chapter of Congres Internationeaux d'Architecture Moderne". 1946. Folder 8. Box 1429. Office Records, Correspondence. Neutra Collection. UCLA Library Special Collections, 2.

194. Ibid., 3.

195. Ibid., 4-5.

196. Ibid., 5.

197. Ibid., 6.

198. Ibid., 7.

199. "Chega 2a- feira um dos mais famosos arquitetos do mundo." *Diário da noite*, November 10, 1945. Folder 29. Box 1419. Office Records, Publicity. Neutra Collection. UCLA Library of Special Collections. Free translation.

200. "Visita o Rio destacado arquiteto norte-americano." *A Manhã*, November 18, 1945, 7; "Sociais." *Diário Carioca*, November 30, 1945, 8.

201. Letter from Willian Griffith to Richard Neutra, November 07, 1945. Folder 8. Box 1429. Office Records, Correspondence. Neutra Collection. UCLA Library of Special Collections.

202. Dante Orgolini, "O interesse de Orson Welles pelo Brasil." *A Noite*, January 30, 1942, 2. Free translation.

203. "As fábulas do Brasil nos desen-
hos animados de Walt Disney."
Diário Carioca, August 17, 1941,
5. Free translation.
204. Cf. Tota, *O imperialismo*.
205. "Sumner Welles despede-se do
povo brasileiro por intermédio
de 'A Noite.'" *A Noite*, January 30,
1942, 1. Free translation.
206. "Um grande amigo do Brasil
e dos brasileiros: o aniversário
do presidente Roosevelt." *A
Noite*, January 30, 1942, 1. Free
translation.
207. Ibid., 3. Free translation.
208. "Recebido pelo presidente Roosevelt: o Dr. Lutero Vargas em
viagem de estudos nos Estados
Unidos." *A Noite*, January 30,
1942, 2.
209. Tota, *O amigo americano*, 152.
210. Ibid., 153. Free translation.
211. Ibid. Free translation.
212. Ibid. Free translation.
213. "Report on visit South American
Republics, by Richard Neutra,
architect and President, U.S.
Chapter of Congres Internationeaux d'Architecture Moderne". 1946. Folder 8. Box 1429.
Office Records, Correspondence.
Neutra Collection. UCLA Library
Special Collections, 7.
214. Letter from Dione Neutra to
Richard K. Nobbe. May 12,
1969. Folder 19. Box 230. Office
Records, Correspondence. Neutra
Collection. UCLA Library Special
Collections.
215. Neutra, "Observations on Latin
America," 67.
216. "Conferências." *Correio da
Manhã*, November 28, 1945.
Digital Archive, Biblioteca
Nacional.

217. Letter from Richard Neutra to
Mario Leal Ferreira. February 18,
1946. Folder 8. Box 1429. Office
Records, Correspondence. Neutra
Collection. UCLA Library Special
Collections.
218. "Carolina, Maranhão," November
1945. Folder 13. Box 1. Profes-
sional Papers, Travel Sketches.
Neutra Collection. UCLA Library
Special Collections.
219. Letter from Charles W. Collier to
Richard Neutra. September 14,
1945. Folder 8. Box 1429. Office
Records, Correspondence. Neutra
Collection. UCLA Library Special
Collections, p. 3.
220. Letter from Richard Neutra to
Willian J. Griffith. October 05,
1945. Folder 8. Box 1429. Office
Records, Correspondence. Neutra
Collection. UCLA Library Special
Collections.
221. Letter from William J. Griffith to
Richard Neutra. November 02,
1945. Folder 8. Box 1429. Office
Records, Correspondence. Neutra
Collection. UCLA Library Special
Collections.
222. Letter from Richard and Dione
Neutra to Henrique e Helena
Mindlin. December 18, 1945.
Folder 8. Box 1985. Office
Records, Correspondence. Neutra
Collection. UCLA Library Special
Collections.
223. Mccann JR., *The Brazilian-Amer-
ican Alliance*, 214.
224. Gianfranco Beting, "Pan Am: a
pioneira mundial no Brasil."
225. Hart, *Empire of Ideas*.
226. Ibid.

Brazilian and Latin American Connections

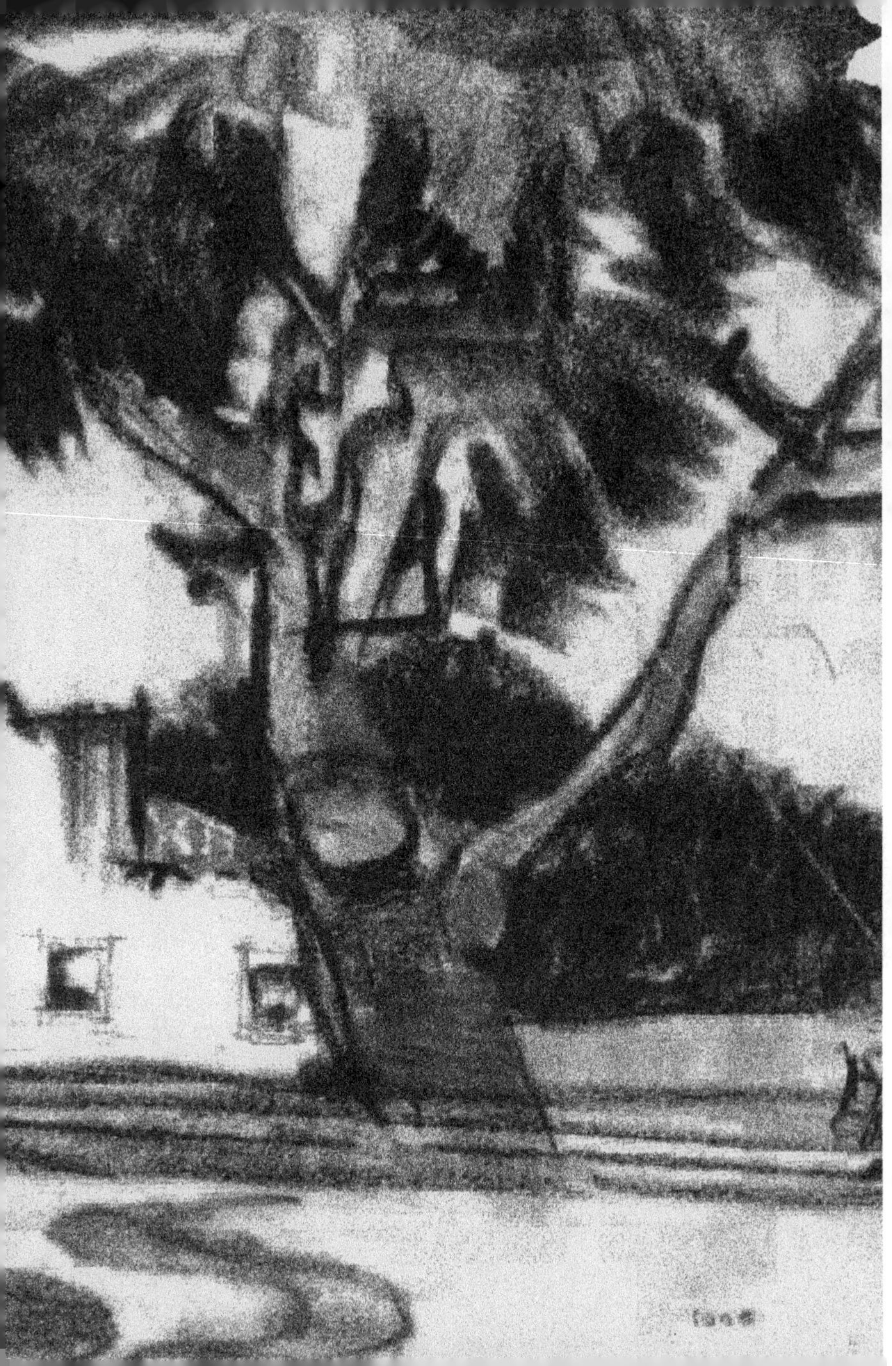

Preamble

The same facts – the documents – when observed from other angles, can give way to other assumptions and distinct consequences and may display some potential to undermine, even if partially, what seems to be quite well-established. Perhaps that is the reason why new (and apparently outrageous) interpretations, even then they were born from careful reflection over documentation, have such a difficult time in achieving credibility. It is not because they are unreasonable, but because they are overcast by the previously accepted theoretical constructions that are surreptitiously hindering the field.
Ruth Verde Zein, When Documenting is not Enough. *Critical Readings*[1]

The process of understanding Richard Neutra, the character (his educational background, his move to the United States, his works, particularly in relation to Latin America), and the historical panorama of the time (the political, economic and cultural exchanges between the United States and Latin America and the conflict in Europe) – that is, the articulation between micro and macro histories – provides the necessary foundation for a new look at the architect's

works. Identifying the "uncanny" in the speech of main-
stream historians – starting with Thomas Hines, via Barbara
Lamprecht reaching, more recently, José Vela Castillo and
Catherine Ettinger –, new connections and new understand-
ings of these works will be proposed, in an attempt to tackle
them from an inverse perspective – from the periphery to the
center –, an approach quite familiar to the pluralism of Latin
America.

Despite the mention of the terms "center" and "periphery", we shall follow Marina Waisman's observation on the
need to replace the "(totalitarian) idea of a superior culture"
– "center" – with a "cultural pluralism" – "regions".[2] According
to the author, this shift in point of view allowed for a new
look at history and the understanding of the specificity and,
consequently, of the architectural responses of each region:

> The replacement of the concepts of periphery or margin
> with that of region, the radical shift in point of view
> – entailing almost a Copernican revolution – made it
> possible for architects, critics and historians to direct a
> new, more constructive and original look to history itself,
> resituating episodes in this new historiography, as well
> as to architectural praxis, laying the foundations of a
> theory.[3]

As Marina Waisman suggests, the objective here is to
resituate "episodes in this new historiography". For this, the
first step is to define the concept of the "uncanny", which we
will make use of:

> The German word *unheimlich* is obviously the oppo-
> site of *heimlich, heimisch*, meaning "familiar," "native,"
> "belonging to the home"; and we are tempted to
> conclude that what is "uncanny" is frightening precisely
> because it is *not* known and familiar. Naturally not
> everything which is new and unfamiliar is frightening,

however; the relation *cannot* be inverted. We can only say that what is novel can easily become frightening and uncanny; some new things are frightening but not by any means all. Something has to be added to what is novel and unfamiliar to make it uncanny.[4]

The definition elaborated by Sigmund Freud when studying cases of psychoanalysis through literature can be adapted to the analysis of historian' discourses when dealing with certain works by Neutra. The "new" element proposed by him in some projects brought "something" that made it, at the eyes of these historians, "uncanny" or "unfamiliar." This "things," as will be seen below, has to do with Richard Neutra's relationship with Latin America. This manifestation caused discomfort and strangeness because it did not fit the mold of what was understood to be the exceptional works of the architect. Again, according to Freud, *"unheimlich is the name of everything that ought to have remained hidden and secret and has become visible."*[5]

Before moving on, it is important to clarify here that our intention is not to point out a simple influence and/or mimicry of Latin American projects in Neutra's work. From his very first trip, in 1945, Richard Neutra was already an internationally renowned architect with an established work. Thus, our focus here is to identify, through architecture, the points of convergence between him and his Latin American colleagues, and also to single out the elements of Latin American architecture studied by Neutra which he incorporated in later works.

According to Harold Bloom,

Poetic Influence – when it involves two strong, authentic poets –, always proceeds by a misreading of the prior poet, an act of creative correction that is actually and necessarily a misinterpretation.[6]

The concept of "poetic misprision" developed by Bloom can be easily applied in the context of the relationship between architects and particularly in the exchange between Richard Neutra and Latin American colleagues. Having already completed his education at the time of the 1945 trip makes Neutra a "strong poet;" as such, he carefully observed the solutions found in Latin America regarding control over heat and sunlight, as well as the plastic applications projected to reinforced concrete, which he would then develop in his own unique way. That is, he made a "misreading of the prior poet," resulting in a "misinterpretation." The very fact of *observing, reading* and *interpreting* gives Neutra a status as an active agent that consciously chooses the influence that best matches his needs at the time.[7] And it is precisely this response as expressed through his architecture – the "something," mentioned by Freud – that generates the uncanniness observable in the discourses of historians.

This shift in the scale of analysis from the general to the more specific – from macro to micro-history – brings to light some facts that the more panoramic take of previous historiography on Richard Neutra has not bothered to observe. In addition to demystifying ideological issues that spread automatically in the narratives, understanding seemingly specific and unimportant facts can be useful in understanding a broader phenomenon.[8] According to Italian historian Giovanni Levi: "The reduction of scale [...] assumes that the delineations of context and its coherence are apparent, revealing those contradictions that only show up when the scale of the reference is altered."[9]

From Puerto Rico to São Paulo

Typical classroom, section, ground floor plan and detail of swing up patio door, Puerto Rico. Richard Neutra, 1943-1945. Croquis Fernanda Critelli

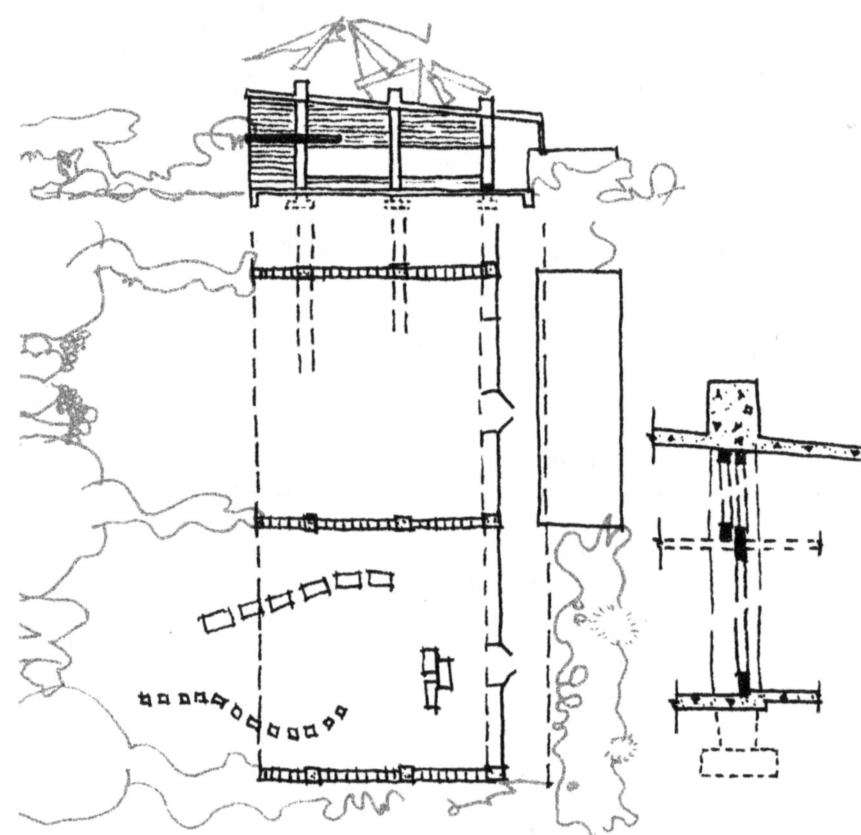

For countries as for men to stimulate and be stimulated may mean much needed creative and peaceful collaboration.
Richard Neutra, letter to Gerth Todtman[10]

That Richard Neutra visited Brazil for the first time in November 1945 and that, on this trip under the auspices of the US Department of State, he played the role of a messenger of good will – with the mission of giving lectures, offering consultancy in public works, meeting local authorities and architects and learning about modern Latin American architecture –, it is already a well-established fact. Not that new evidence cannot emerge – which is very likely to happen with new research. However, to fulfill our goal in this book – that is, to understand the connections established in Latin America, especially in Brazil –, one must focus on a succession of events that begins with the hiring of Neutra as a consultant to the Committee on Design of Public Works of Puerto Rico.

As previously studied,[11] Neutra's designation to this position was not random. His previous experience – design and construction of Emerson Junior and Corona schools and Avion Village and Channel Heights housing de velopments; his work as a consultant to the government's National Youth Administration program, created by President Franklin Roosevelt and coordinated by the First Lady;[12] and his research on adapting architecture to local conditions – made Neutra the appropriate choice. Then, the experience and knowledge accumulated during this period of just over a year (1943-1945) developing model projects for hospitals, health centers, housing for doctors and schools in this Latin American territory of the United States made Neutra, yet again, the best choice for the new mission required by the Department of State: the recon trip through South America countries (1945).

During the two-month trip, Richard Neutra was expected to engage with local authorities, give lectures and conferences on modern architecture in relation to local circumstances and constraints, as well as to provide advice on public projects of each government. The architect was also asked to survey modern works produced by Brazilians, Argentines and Uruguayans.[13] But, in addition to fulfilling his mission and following social etiquette, Neutra – who believed in mutual creative stimulation through collaboration and contact between people/architects[14] – took particular interest in the architecture he found and established personal and professional relationships with the Latin American colleagues.

Neutra sought to understand the cultural and landscape aspects of each location and their correspondent architectures. He took photographs and made drawings and notes of what interested him. This material was eventually presented in two articles published in the May and October issues of the American *Progressive Architecture* magazine in 1946. "Observations on Latin America" and "Sun Control Devices" are accounts of his experience among Latin Americans, concerning local landscape and climate, the historical heritage of these countries, their urban planning issues and their successes in terms of architectural solutions. In the first article, Neutra presents general comments about Latin America, and then, based on his drawings, describes his impressions of each country.

Starting from the initial idea that, in certain historical periods, foreign architectural procedures, once imported, overlooked local differences,[15] Neutra sought to understand issues such as the indigenous cultural heritage of each nation and their rise to political power:

Millions of the descendants of original, native Americans [Peruvians], representatives of past great cultures, have now become voters and a political force. Increasingly, they will become consumers of our technological civilization. They need schools, health centers, hospitals, housing; they present urgent problems to planners, designers, and architects.[16]

The tension between preserving architectural heritage and modernization is also addressed:

Many Latin American countries, from Santo Domingo to Peru, have a rich architectural heritage. In some cases, city planners are puzzled how to preserve these monuments without impairing the desirable growth of their communities. Old Havana, for example, lies directly between the Cuban Republic's most important port facilities and the main highway outlots to the 800-miles stretch of an increasingly active hinterland.[17]

On the urban planning challenges, faced by public authorities, architects and engineers in São Paulo, Richard Neutra commented:

The Mayor of the past regime, Prestes Maia, was an engineer with a strong planning instinct. His administration produced ring and arterial avenues, river regulations, bridges, and tunnels. But Sao Paulo, the capital city of a state with an immense future, still lacks a planning department, still has no zoning laws. For their efforts toward rectifying these limitations, congratulations must go to such incipient civic organizations as the Citizens Housing Committee and to the chapter of the Brazilian Institute of Architects of which Eduardo Kneese de Mello is president and Gregori Warchavchik, the pioneer of contemporary architecture in Brazil, Rino Levi, and many others studious and capable professionals are active members.[18]

As for the issue of industrialization, particularly its underdevelopment, and how architects tried to circumvent this problem, he said:

> As the populations and purchasing power continue to grow during the coming decades, these countries will become a vast market for mass-produced items for the construction and equipment of buildings. The current lack of certain materials and equipment has made Mexican, Argentinian, and Brazilian manufactures inventive; their avant-garde architects, experimental; their engineers, daring; and their building ordinances (in some cases), very open-minded. Much has been gained; their industry adds considerably to the diversity of world production.[19]

In the article "Sun Control Devices," Richard Neutra goes on to survey the solutions applied by Latin American architects in order to tackle the issue of sunlight and heat, quite inevitable in a tropical region. Relying on photographs taken mostly during the trip through South America – it is worth noting that some of the photographs used in this article were taken by Kidder Smith, originally to illustrate the exhibition and catalog *Brazil Builds* by MoMA, in 1943 –, Neutra presents a series of procedures for the US public: canopies with ventilation openings, such as those developed with the Committee on Design of Public Works of Puerto Rico; balconies functioning as peripheral circulation, as is the case of a school in Bahia and the Excelsior Hotel designed by Rino Levi in São Paulo; pierced canopies, with projects by North American Raphael Soriano and Gregori Warchavchik; exterior blinds used by Álvaro Vital Brazil for the Esther Building in São Paulo as well as by Gregori Warchavchik for his residence in Guarujá; the *cobogós* ("egg-crates") used by Lúcio Costa and Oscar Niemeyer in the Brazilian Pavilion at the New York International Fair, in 1939; fixed vertical louvers in the Ministry of Education and Health building, in Rio de Janeiro; the operable louvers in the Leonidas Moreira building, designed by Eduardo Kneese de Mello, and in the boat passenger station designed by Atílio Corrêa Lima, as well as an apartment building in Buenos Aires;[20] at last, the pivoting wall sections – windows and doors – on the facade of an unidentified building.

According to Neutra, "No other single feature of South American architecture has excited as much attention as the conspicuous means of controlling sunlight which characterize the buildings."[21] He also claims to have found such cultural and architectural diversity and richness that he was amazed that no book had been published yet to show the world the production of these countries.[22]

Now, going back to his steps during the journey through South America, it is worth mentioning that Richard Neutra visited Guarujá, staying at Gregori Warchavchik's house; he was accompanied by a large group of Brazilian architects. It is quite likely that, on that occasion, the colleagues started to envision the book *Architecture of Social Concern in Regions of Mild Climate*. The Warchavchik family was very much involved in the edition: the translation to Portuguese was carried out by Minna Klabin Warchavchik, Gregori's wife, and Carmen de Almeida; the paper used in the printing was provided by Klabin Irmãos & Co. New evidence strengthens this hypothesis: a 1946 letter – no particular date has been established, but it is most likely from early January – from Richard Neutra to Walter Hylton Scott, editor of the Argentine magazine *Nuestra Arquitectura*. In the letter, Neutra announces the release of *Architecture of Social Concern* and inquiries about a possible Spanish edition, which never happened.

We have safely reached Los Angeles again after a most interesting time in Sao Paulo and Rio. Remembering your interest in my Puerto Rico designs I thought you

might like to know that Mr. Gregori Warchavchik, 120
Barão de Itapetininga Street, Sao Paulo, intends to bring
out in bookform some of my work and especially that
concerned with non-metropolitan architecture for mild
climates. He would probably be interested to cooperate
with you for a Spanish edition in case you would like to
contact him.[23]

The web of relationships also extends to the choice of
the publisher responsible for the book. The partners at Todtmann & Cia. Ltda. at the time were Gerth Todtmann – after
whom the company was named –, Renato Cintra Pimentel,
Alexandre Pelosi, Gabriel Pelosi and Duilio Marone.[24] Engineer
graduated from the Polytechnic School of the University
of São Paulo in 1936, Marone worked with Vilanova Artigas between 1937 and 1944 at the construction company
Artigas & Marone Engenheiros.[25] In June 1946, Artigas was
awarded a John Simon Guggenheim Memorial Foundation
Fellowship to study American modern architecture for twelve
months, beginning in October of that year.[26] During this trip,
Artigas writes a letter to Richard Neutra on March 5, 1947,
letting him know that he would arrive in Los Angeles in five
days and that he would like to visit him: "I expect to be in Los
Angeles at the 10th, and I hope I can visit you; I have a list of
your houses which I suspect is incomplete, and I would like
to spend as much time as I have studying very closely your
works."[27] Adriana Irigoyen confirms that this meeting actually
took place, according to evidence she found in a letter from
Artigas to Charles Wagley.[28] It is possible that Duilio Marone
– Artigas' former partner and now also partner at Editora
Todtmann – was not directly implicated in the encounter
between Vilanova Artigas and Richard Neutra; nevertheless,
it is symptomatic that the same characters keep showing up
in the same narrative plot.
Apparently, the book was not a Department of State
requirement: although, obviously, the program of cultural

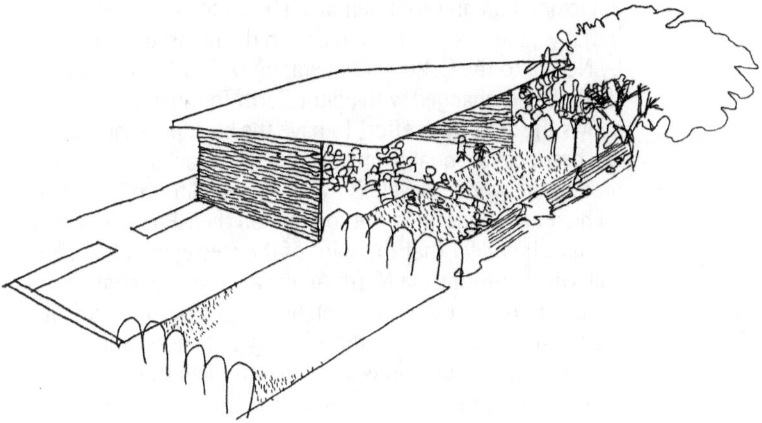

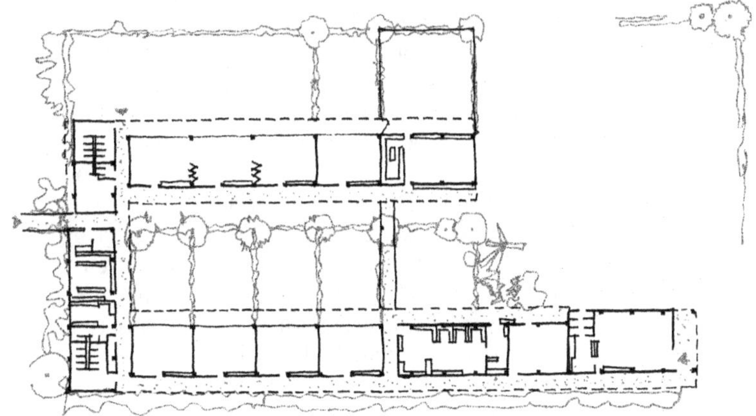

Perspective of a classroom open to
the patio and ground floor plan of an
eight classroom school, Puerto Rico.
Richard Neutra, 1943-1945. Croquis
Fernanda Critelli

approximation and continental aid benefited from the initiative, there is no mention of it in the report delivered by Neutra to the Cultural Cooperation Division. In any case, the letters exchanged with editor Gerth Todtmann clearly shows the architect's effort to have the book published with the best possible quality and also for it to reach bookstores around the world, as well as the hands of editors of the main architecture magazines, not to mention then-President Harry Truman. It is clear that the spirit of the messenger of good will, which informs the North American effort for continental cooperation, is present in the architect's discourse: "Brazilian readers and government officials are glad to acknowledge constructive stimulation which come to them from United States."[29] But this *mission* taken up by Neutra goes well beyond politics; it points to his desire to energize and be creatively energized.[30]

At this point, it would be interesting to resume the discussion on influence brought by Michael Baxandall. If we reverse our point of view and focus on the one who receives the influence, rather than on the influence itself, it is possible to attribute him a lot of agency: aligning himself with this or that; opposing this or that; opening himself up to be creatively stimulated etc. That is, this inversion allows us to understand that the agent of the action, "Y", does it consciously. He selects this influence, "X", from a range of options that one might align with, oppose, interpret, etc. And the roles of "X" and "Y" can be swapped, depending on each situation: the agent who chooses a certain influence can also have been chosen as a stimulus by "X" in the past and even by another agent.[31] When Richard Neutra says that, for men/architects, "inspiring and being inspired implicate a much needed creative and peaceful collaboration", he makes it clear that he's aware of this give and take between influence and agent of the action that selects it. And, despite the political interests of the United States behind his relationship with Latin America, the architect did not intend to impose his architecture as a sole, overwhelming truth, his major goal being exchange and contact with his colleagues.

One would imagine that, for someone like Neutra, who sought to establish a legacy for future generations – as Robert Alexander informs us, Richard and Dione Neutra were always involved in the publication of some new book[32] –, the success of *Architecture of Social Concern* was very important. Hence his insistence for editor Gerth Todtmann to send copies of the book to President Truman and editors of international architecture journals.

A composition with 16 photographs, taken by Julius Shulman and Arthur Luckhaus, of "largely non-metropolitan" works[33] by Richard Neutra ignites the discussion in the book, which aims to address the social aspects, methods and processes of developing an architecture particularly focused on undeveloped areas: "we have in this volume and in the following condensed review of Neutra's work in three decades, tried to stress the stimulating generic, the broad, the supra-individual aspect, which is perhaps most fertile and most deeply instructive to our generation, ready to act on a widened world's stage."[34]

Thus, drawing from the projects developed along with the Committee on Design of Public Works of Puerto Rico, Neutra discusses the need for architects to work in rural areas and points out to the reader several ways to deal with the matter. The book, therefore, presents itself almost as a guiding manual for young professionals – with plans, cuts, perspectives and details of possible furnishings for the design of schools, hospitals and health centers, rural and urban, with different capacities. All this with an architecture that respects climatic conditions and technological possibilities in each location:

During my various trips and periods of work in Latin American countries, I have found them closer relatives to California than other parts of Northen Union. There has altogether been a large zone of our world rather misguided in taking *cold Europe* and *cold America* as their example to follow in design. It is a mental colonialism that no longer fits the day.[35]

Gregori Warchavchik wrote the preface, highlighting Neutra's efforts in the search for more efficient materials and methods, suited to the specificities of each location. That is, his search for a functional architecture designed to meet human needs.[36] Warchavchik comments on Neutra's education background as an architect and his professional career after migrating to the United States in 1923. He concludes by saying that "he is also a sociologist and psychologist who is profoundly attracted by the intrinsic and the essential requirements of the groups and individuals for whom he builds, and whom he serves in love and care from the programming and preliminaries, to furnishing and management of maintenance."[37]

In December 1948, amidst the turmoil during the preparations for the release, Neutra received a letter from the director of the recently opened Museum of Art of São Paulo – Masp, Pietro Maria Bardi, inviting him to exhibit his works at the museum.

I received from Rome the notice that you were supposed to get in touch with my friends of the Studio d'Arte Palma which I own; it seems that the office of the public instruction of Italy was interested in this reception. But you were forced to leave home and unfortunately you weren't able to meet my friends. / I am director of the new museum of arts of S. Paulo. You know this town, in part because one of your books is being published here. By the other side, in our didactic section your name is quite popular.

I write you know, to ask you to hold a complete
exhibition of your works at our museum. Thus, we would
be happy of presenting your work to Brazil.[38]

The origin of this invitation is not clear, but it is evident
that the ties between Bardi and Assis Chateaubriand to
Nelson Rockefeller was a determining factor. It is true that
Neutra accepted the invitation because of the prospect of
exhibiting more of his works in Brazil; but also because he
saw it as an opportunity to promote his new release and
increase its sales.[39] The first edition of the *Neutra: Residên-
cias/Residences* catalog was published in 1950, coinciden-
tally – or not – by Todtmann & Cia. Ltda. publishing house;
despite being announced in newspapers in January 1949,[40]
and also to the editors of foreign magazines – *The Architectural Forum*,[41] *L'Architecture d'Aujourd'Hui*[42] and *Progressive
Architecture*[43] – in July of the same year, the exhibition was
nevertheless postponed several times due to lack of space at
the Museum of Art of São Paulo. Finally, on May 7, 1951, the
exhibition *Neutra: Residência/Residence* was inaugurated
at the São Paulo headquarters of the Brazilian Institute of
Architects.

The Museum could not realize the exhibition in its own
rooms this year. This occurred because of the reconstruction and its enlargement to another floor. We therefore
wanted to have this exhibition in collaboration with
the Institute of Architects of São Paulo. This, however,
cause some delay. We will inform you soon about the
definite dates, which we will got from the Institute of
Architects.[44]

On November 29, 1952, a letter from Francisco
Matarazzo Sobrinho – dated the 10th of that same month
– reached Richard Neutra's office, announcing the 2nd
International Exhibition of Architecture as part of 2nd

Biennial of the Museum of Modern Art of São Paulo – MAM.
Matarazzo mentions that the opening of the exhibition
would mark the beginning of the celebrations for the IV
Centenary of São Paulo, in December 1953, and says that
Sigfried Giedion – president of the jury at the I International
Exhibition of Architecture – had suggested they invite Neutra
to participate.

> It was exactly professor Giedion who gave us the good
> advice of requesting your valorous collaboration in order
> to obtain immediate and profitable divulgation amongst
> the professional Architects, the Students and, as well
> through the wide publication in specialized informa-
> tive newspapers with reference to material and norms
> concerning our initiative, which only can be successfully
> realized with your indispensable help.[45]

Neutra seems to have been interested in the invitation:
on January 2, 1953, his secretary, Régula Thorston, replied
to the letter requesting further information about the São
Paulo Award, an international architecture competition that
would pay CR$ 300,000.00 to the winner.[46] Moreover, in
the various letters exchanged with Lucian Korngold during
this period – which have not yet been fully translated –, it is
understood that one of the subjects discussed is precisely the
2nd Biennial de São Paulo.[47]

However, there seems to have been some confusion.
In an undated letter to Pietro Maria Bardi – which, judging
from its content, is most likely from July 1953 –, Dione Neutra sends the application forms regarding three projects for
the International Exhibition. According to her, these forms
had reached her hands earlier that year, but Richard Neutra
had suddenly become very ill and they could not manage to
send the documents sooner. At that time, MAM and Masp
shared the same address, on Rua 7 de Abril, and Pietro Bardi,
in a reply dated July 24, 1953, explains the misunderstanding

and assures that the material, once received, would be for-
warded to the director of II Biennial.

> I suppose you know, the 2nd Biennial is organized by the
> Museum of Modern Art of São Paulo, which is entirely
> independent from ours: at any rate do not be anxious
> about the material, I shall ask them to handle it with the
> utmost care.[48]

A few days earlier, Arturo Porfili, secretary of the
2nd Biennial, wrote to Dione saying that Pietro Bardi had
informed him of the confusion regarding the address and
that he had also received a visit from Lucian Korngold to
discuss the same matter. Another concern for the Neutra
couple was a possible delay in the arrival of the material to
be exhibited in São Paulo, despite the fact that US mail had
set the deadline for August 15, 1953.[49] On this issue, Porfili
stated that the organizers of the exhibition would be willing
to make an exception, as they believed that the participation of Richard Neutra would be of great value for the 2nd
Biennial.

> We should like to let you know that even if the entry
> forms and the exhibition material should have to arrive
> with a slight delay – in any case not more than the one
> or two weeks you mentioned – the participation of
> the architect Neutra would mean such an interesting
> element for the International Exhibition of Architecture
> that we feel the exception we are prepared to grant in
> his case, would be justified.[50]

Dione sent to MAM-SP five enlarged photographs of
the two most important projects of Richard Neutra: three
from the Warren Tremaine house and another two from
the Edgar Kaufman House[51] (these were received on August
10th).[52] However, the remainder of the material – which had

ended up in the care of Pietro Bardi –, had yet to reach its final destination. Concerned about the excessive delay, Dione turned to the Brazilian Consulate in Los Angeles to have them intercept the documents and guarantee that it would continue on its journey to its proper end.[53] She also sent a letter to Lucian Korngold, dated November 13, asking for help and mentioning that she did not tell any of this to Richard Neutra: his health was very poor and the matter would only make it worse.[54]

The search for the lost shipment continued until May 10, 1954, when Wolfgang Pfeiffer, director of the Museum of Modern Art in São Paulo, informed that the material had been mistakenly delivered to Masp and, given that Pietro Bardi had been traveling, the routing to the correct destination took too long, arriving only when the 2nd Biennial had already ended. Pfeiffer, however, suggested organizing a new exhibition with this material.

> We would like to make some use of it anyway and to exhibit it in our museum at a time in which we have some space available and some other objects in exhibition which combine with your architecture. We would be glad to have a notice from you that you agree with this plan.[55]

Quite dissatisfied with what had happened, Dione Neutra wrote to Bardi, on May 15, 1954, saying she could not understand how Masp had kept hold of the material, while the next door museum was setting up an international exhibition: "Would not have a simple telephone call of inquiry whether they expected any material from Mr. Neutra have solved the problem?"[56] Then, Dione asked Wolfgang Pfeiffer that, if the exhibition suggested did not materialize, the material be returned, as these were photographs and drawings of the three biggest projects of Richard Neutra.[57] However, on June 7, 1954, Pfeiffer informed the Neutras that the exhibition of their works at MAM-SP would indeed take place the following July and that the material would be returned soon after.[58] The exhibition was announced by the newspaper *O Estado de S. Paulo.*[59]

According to Pfeiffer, in a letter dated August 30, 1954, Neutra's projects received great attention among museum visitors.[60] Dante Paglia, from American Editions of Art and Architecture – EDIAM publishing house, responsible the Biennial's catalogue, expressed interest in including such projects in his next book about the international exhibition. According to Paglia, this catalogue, which would be published in Portuguese, English and French and distributed around the world, would consist of a compilation of the most expressive works exhibited at the 2nd International Exhibition of Architecture.

> Among the names who honored us with their work, at the 2nd Biennial, yours enjoys a particular place. Your work House for Warren Tremaine, 1949, having been a subject of extensive divulgation in technical reviews, we would very much like to offer you something special, by inserting in our publication, some of your unpublished works.[61]

These were not the sole immediate developments in Richard Neutra's relationship with Latin America, nor was São Paulo the only city in which they occurred. The Argentinean magazine *Nuestra Arquitectura*, for example, published a great number of his projects. As for Brazil, in 1946, Neutra sent the students of the Escola Nacional de Belas Artes material about some of his works and a short text to be published in a magazine organized by them.[62] The same was done for Mackenzie students: in response to a request from Jorge Wilheim in 1949, Neutra sent material to be published in the *Pilotis* magazine.[63] This thesis, however, seeks to highlight the direct connection between two episodes in Neutra's life, related to the US Department of State – his projects in

Puerto Rico and the recognition trip through South America – and the publication of a book that later functioned as a guide for countless generations of architects.

Richard Neutra's relationship with Latin America extended well beyond these initial fruits. In 1957, three years after the original publication in English, the Fund for Economic Culture of Mexico published the first edition in Spanish of *Survival Through Design*.[64] In a preface written especially for the Mexican edition, Neutra mentions his transit through Latin American countries (through conferences and lectures), his familiarity with the Spanish language and culture, and also his idea of cultural influence.

> Not long ago, when I was invited to give a conference in Mexico City, a very generous person asked me to go to Acapulco, to spend a few days at his house on the seafront. Culturally, I felt very familiar with these people who thought in Spanish, just as I felt when I was in Argentina and Peru, perhaps because, of course, in another time their history had been guided and shaped by the Spanish attitude towards life, as well as in my homeland, Vienna, during the post-renaissance. [...]
>
> This afternoon I left Acapulco, only in the opposite direction. I had to give lectures at Harvard and a plane took me directly to Boston. Two days later, professional obligations detained me in my current urban domicile, which, however controversial it may be – given the powerful reason for its origins – will always retain its Spanish name and heritage: Los Angeles. And then, [...] I arrived at the University of Manila, after a period of several days on the Guam Island, where I inspected the works being carried out there, very similar to the tropical schools I built in Puerto Rico.[65]

The following year, in 1958, the Editorial Nueva Visión, based in Buenos Aires, published *Realismo Biológico – Un*

Nuevo Renacimiento Humanístico en Arquitectura. Published only in Spanish, this book consists of a translation of Neutra's speech at a congress organized by the Association of Architects of Alberta, Canada.[66] In the preface, the editor dwells on the relative isolation of the architect and puts forth his opinion that Neutra transcends the recurrent label of representative of an international style.

> For quite some time, Neutra was an isolated figure in the Western Hemisphere, from Montreal to Buenos Aires. In order to acknowledge this loneliness, it suffices to take a look at architectural magazines from 1920 to 1930. The Los Angeles house presented itself as an original work that synthesized the shaping forces of the new architecture; it has often been said, quite superficially, that it represented the intersection of the European 'International Style' with the work of Frank Lloyd Wright, which alone constituted the ingenious and confusing synthesis of the prairies and the Far East. But this encounter did not constitute a middle ground or a happy compromise: its integral physiological attitude gave it a distinct stamp, surpassing the mere stylistic display which borrows from a variety of sources. Considered retrospectively and as a whole, his works show an unmistakable mark, revealing the vigorous personality of their creator.[67]

In 1972, two years after his death, another book was published in Argentina, this time by Editorial Marymar: *Vida y forma*, a translation of Richard Neutra's autobiography originally published in 1962. In the prologue to the Spanish edition, Dion Neutra comments about his father's relationship with Latin America and Spain:

> I remember how happy and proud my father felt when we had the privilege of carrying out our first work on

Spanish-speaking soil: a residence in Havana (Cuba),
completed in 1956. A contract for the construction of
a series of houses on a Spanish air base took me and
my father to Madrid for a month in early 1955. On this
occasion, we made many good friends.[68]

Besides books, two works mark the continuity of his
relationship with Latin America: the Schulthess House
(1956), in Havana, and the Gorrondona House (1958-1965),
in Caracas. Both built for quite influential people in a period
when the United States maintained good relations with the
governments of these countries, these houses pay tribute to
the entire trajectory of Richard Neutra's involvement with
his Latin American colleagues. Coincidently or not, both are
completely ignored by the main books on the architect's
work, i.e. those by Thomas Hines and Barbara Lamprecht.
In *Richard Neutra and the Search for Modern Architecture*,
the only time they are mentioned is to exemplify what the
historian considers to be bad (Schulthess House) and good
(Gorrondona House) in the architect's large-scale residential
projects.[69] Already in the first edition of the compendium
organized by Lamprecht, the lack of emphasis given to the
houses is crowned by a confusion in the images: in place of
what should have been a photo of Casa Gorrondona, a photo
of Casa Schulthess appears.[70]
Both houses will be presented from a historiographic
point of view – or from the point of view of their exclusion
from historiography, rather –, together with four other
works: three on North American soil (Los Angeles Hall of
Records and the VDL II houses, Kaufmann and Tremaine) and
one in Pakistan (US Embassy in Karachi). The objective here is
to propose new readings and interpretations regarding these
works from the point of view of Richard Neutra's relationship
with Latin America.

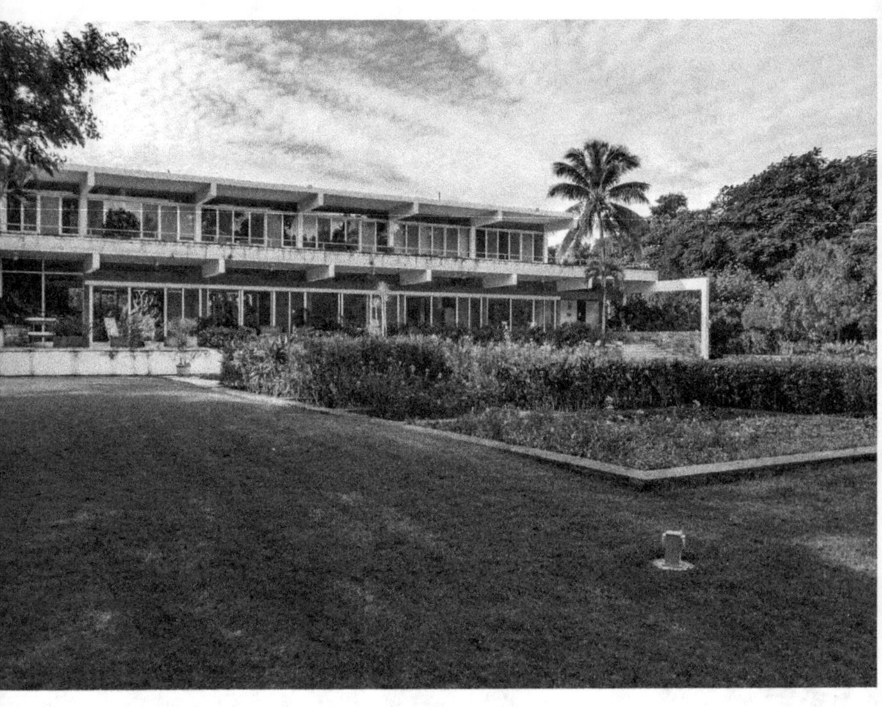

Alfred De Schulthess House, Havana,
Cuba. Richard Neutra, 1956. Photo
André Marques

Three Other Visits to Brazil

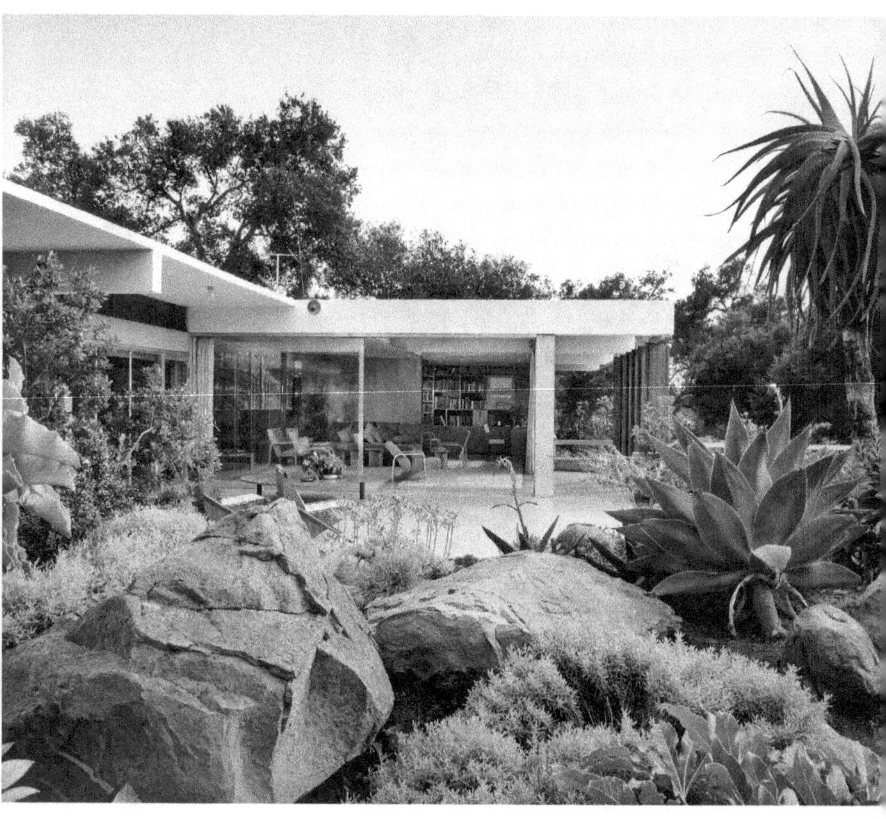

Tremaine House, Santa Barbara. Richard Neutra, 1948. Photo Julius Shulman.

© J. Paul Getty Trust Archive. Getty Research Institute, Los Angeles (2004.R.10)

*Although Neutra has designed for many countries and
many climates, his architecture is an eternal search
for the southland, cradle of civilization. Man 'loves to
immigrate to the South, or to conquer it,' he wrote. 'Like
all Nordic barbarians we want to go to sunny Hellas, or
to the land where the lemon blooms and no icy storms
trouble us.'*
Esther McCoy, *Richard Neutra*[71]

After 1945, Richard Neutra visited Brazil three more times: in
1957, 1958 and 1959. In the case of this last visit, he came
for the International Congress of Art Critics, organized by
the Brazilian Section of the International Association of Art
Critics – ABCA-AICA[72] – a subject that will be discussed later.
However, to understand the reasons and circumstances of
the two previous trips, it will first be necessary to linger on
Neutra's involvement with the Congrès Internationaux d'Architecture Moderne – CIAM group and with the constitution
of the United Nations.

Created in Switzerland in 1928, CIAM represented a
group of architects concerned with establishing a unified sense of what they believed to be a new architectural
possibility – what is now known as the Modern Movement
in architecture.[73] Initially linked only to housing initiatives in
Europe, their members had very little involvement in North
America.[74] The first effort to promote a discussion regarding
urbanism in the United States consisted of the publication of
the book *Can our cities survive? An abc of urban problems,
their analyses, their solutions: based on the proposals by
CIAM*, written by José Luis Sert in 1942.

Once the book finally appeared the Harvard University
Press reported to Sert that it was selling well. Copies

were distributed to members of the National Resources
Planning Board, the Federal Housing Administration, the
National Housing Agency (successor to the United States
Housing Authority), and selected government officials,
including Wallace K. Harrison, then serving as Depu-
ty-Coordinator for Inter-American Affairs.[75]

After the publication of the book, CIAM focused on
the post-war reconstruction efforts in Europe and, to this
end, created, in 1943, the New York Chapter for Relief and
Postwar Planning.[76] Richard Neutra operated as chairman;
Longberg-Holm, José Luis Sert and Paul Nelson as vice pres-
idents; and Harwell Hamilton Harris as secretary-treasurer.[77]
At this time, the real concern of the group, according to Eric
Munford, seems to have been to secure commissions for its
members. "As Gropius has put it, their intention was perhaps
more going towards the practical effects than building a new
philosophic movement."[78]
The search for a more effective involvement of CIAM in
post-war reconstruction led the group to seek participation
in bodies such as the United Nations. Thus, in 1945, the CIAM
executive committee determined that Richard Neutra should
take part, as the group's representative, in the San Francisco
Conference – which would go on to consolidate the United
Nations. It was up to Stamo Papadaki – an architect who
would later also establish strong ties with Brazil by participating in the Brasília competition jury and writing a book
about Oscar Niemeyer – inform Neutra of the decision:

The New York Executive Committee of the CIAM Chapter
for Relief and Post War Planning, has entrusted me
to inform you the following: that they convey to you
their decision to have you represent the Chapter at the
San Francisco Conference, and that they express to you
their thanks for your effort in carrying out the above
responsibility.[79]

Neutra's relationship with CIAM, however, grew distant over time. Historian Eric Munford – in a statement given by email to the researcher in December 2014 – puts forward some possible reasons. First, the seemingly distant relationship with Walter Gropius, an influential member of the group. Second, Neutra's office and design practice were located in Los Angeles at a time when business travel in the United States was done almost entirely by train. In other words, Neutra's location was, at the time, remote. And finally, it was possible that CIAM's socialist past would negatively affect the postwar career of American architects. This reason could also justify the non-involvement of architects such as George Howe, Wallace Harrison and Eero Saarinen, who, according to Munford, were repeatedly invited to join the group, choosing to remain distant.

> My sense from close study of many of the relevant documents is that Sigfried Giedion, then in the United States, was the key organizer of the NY Chapter, continuing the role that he had played in CIAM since 1929. As far as I can tell, the goal of the group was to influence postwar reconstruction planning in Europe, and its main outcome seems to have been the creation of the American Society of Architects and Planners – ASPA – which I have written about in my *Defining Urban Design* —which then invited Le Corbusier to present his *St Die* project for French reconstruction (and by extension, world reconstruction) in New York immediately after the war. Given Neutra's remote (at the time) location and by necessity largely suburban sort of work, he was not seen as an important an urban design figure in CIAM as Le Corbusier.
>
> Had American CIAM remained viable, he may have continued to be the leader of it—he was invited by CIAM President Josep Lluis Sert to speak at the First Harvard Urban Design Conference in 1956, for example. But

the leaders of CIAM (Gropus, Sert, Giedion) in the US
had decided by the late 1940s that the US was not a
very receptive environment for CIAM, perhaps based in
part on Gropius's professional experiences and also on
the unwillingness to be much involved with CIAM by
American architects like George Howe, Wallace Harrison
and Eero Saarinen, who had all been approached to join
CIAM but stayed at some distance from it, like Mies van
der Rohe (though Mies continued to pay CIAM dues
down to 1956). This may well have been from a realistic
sense that CIAM's socialist past might negatively affect
their careers in the postwar US, as in fact happened to
many figures in the arts once McCarthyism got underway in the late 1940s in trying to root Communists out
of the State Dept. the military, Hollywood etc.[80]

Despite this apparent cooling off of Richard Neutra's
relations with CIAM, those established with the United
Nations group seem to have persisted. In the *Neutra Collection* of UCLA, letters were found revealing an ongoing
relationship with representatives of this group since the San
Francisco Conference, in 1945, up until a few months before
his death. And it is from these data that our assumption –
considered plausible by historian Thomas Hines in an interview given to the researcher in December 2014 – is based,
justifying the consecutive trips in 1957 and 1958.

Reading the book published by the United Nations
Department of Information in 1961 – *The United Nations
and Latin America: the collection of basic information material on the work of the United Nations and related agencies
in Latin America* – allows us to understand the interest of
the United Nations group and other allied agencies, such as
the Economic Commission for Latin America – ECLA, regarding issues of development and urbanization in Latin American countries.

ECLA has studied the problems of urbanization, particularly those associated with the large-scale migratory
movement from rural to urban areas which is greatly
affecting the majority of the large cities of Latin
America.[81]

In this context, several conferences and gatherings were
organized, taking place in Latin American countries, in order
to discuss issues such as financing for social housing – in
1957[82] – and the problems of architecture and urbanism in
new towns – in 1958, in Rio de Janeiro and Brasília.[83] Thus,
given Richard Neutra's interest in these matters, I believe it
is plausible to say that these meetings were the reasons that
brought him back to Brazil during those years.

These visits were covered by Rio de Janeiro newspapers,
such as *Diário de Notícias* and *Correio da Manhã*. In the first
case, the article mentioned a visit of approximately six days
in Rio de Janeiro – between June 15 and 21, 1957 –, when
Neutra gave lectures at the Escola Nacional de Belas Artes.[84]
In the second case, the report concerned a letter written by
Neutra and sent to President Juscelino Kubitschek – "Neutra to JK: Brasília, the wondrously work of Niemeyer" – in
July 1958, where the architect mentions, besides his visit to
Brasília while the new capital was still undergoing construc-
tion, his stop in Rio de Janeiro.

Richard Neutra's enthusiasm for Oscar Niemeyer's works
and for the construction of Brasília is very clearly expressed
in the letter sent to Juscelino. Therefore, we believed that the
integral reproduction here is of great value:

My dear Mr. President,

Back in Washington, I keep evoking, in my conversations,
the deep impression I gathered from the new Capital
of Brazil and the wondrous work planned by Oscar
Niemeyer and Lúcio Costa. I hope that the presidential
palace is completed, in all its beauty and splendor, illus-
trating Brazil's leadership in the architectural projects of

the contemporary world, to which architects of many countries I visited, on all continents, owe.

Allow me to thank you again for the meeting you conceded me upon my return from Brasilia. I am very interested in the book that Your Excellency mentioned, which provides an historical study of a dozen capitals founded and developed by man throughout the ages. Your Excellency was, as I said, reading this book at the time of our visit, and I would like to know its title.

Allow me to reiterate to you that it was an immense pleasure to meet Niemeyer, whose genius I have admired since I visited Belo Horizonte more than twelve years ago. Oscar Niemeyer created a masterpiece, prompted by a client with a fascinating vision such as Your Excellency. I hope that this admirable work in Brasilia, under the civic and artistic leadership of Your Excellency, will continue to be victorious till it reaches a happy conclusion.

As we are currently building the American embassy in Karachi, Pakistan, I had the opportunity to visit, in our State Department, Mr. Hughes, head of the Construction Division, and I was pleased to see that he is equally enthusiastic about Brazil.
Sincerely,
Richard Neutra.[85]

The following year, in September 1959, Richard Neutra returned to Brazil, accompanied by important figures such as Giulio Carlo Argan, Bruno Zevi, Eero Saarinen and Jean Prouvé, among others, to participate in the Extraordinary International Congress of Art Critics in Brasília, São Paulo and Rio de Janeiro. Structured by the International Association of Art Critics – AICA – a non-governmental organization created between 1949 and 1950, bearing some similarities, given its cultural focus, with Unesco (United Nations Educational, Scientific and Cultural Organization)[86] – , the central theme of the congress – the city as a new synthesis of the arts – was based on the construction of Brasília[87] and its place in the architecture and urbanism of the time.[88]

Henry Meyric Hughes, honorary president of AICA and head of the Construction Division of the US Department of State (mentioned by Neutra in his letter to Juscelino), said that Brasília represented the progressive efforts for the country's economic development.

> For many war-weary Europeans, underdeveloped Latin American countries like Argentina and Venezuela, as well as Brazil, offered the hope of economic regeneration and new ideas, while in the case of the US, there was the further lure of a last frontier, associated with its own founding myths. Thus, the construction of Brasília, on a broader and more ambitious scale than in other new capitals, such as Canberra and Chandigard, were seen by all involved as a gesture of great symbolic force.[89]

The objective of this work is not to discuss criticisms and defenses surrounding the construction of Brasília put forward in the debates of the congress, but rather to highlight the participation of Richard Neutra and his enthusiasm for the new Brazilian capital. The conferences took place in Brasília, between the 17th and 19th of September; in São Paulo, on the 21st and 22nd, coinciding with the opening of the 5th Biennial – now in its new home, the Palace of Industries, designed by Oscar Niemeyer –; and, finally, in Rio de Janeiro, from the 23th to the 25th. According to the documents of que congress, published by Docomomo do Rio in 2009, Richard Neutra participated in the Second Session on Urbanism held in the afternoon of September 18, 1959, at the Palace of Justice in Brasília. Accompanied by Giulio Carlo Argan, Mário Pedrosa, Bruno Zevi and Eero Saarinen, among others, Neutra discussed efforts to boost development while not losing sight of the needs of individuals.

We are living in an era of mass achievement, and President Kubitschek was able to carry that out. [...] In the midst of all these mass achievements, Oscar Niemeyer and Lúcio Costa managed not to get lost, and knew how to value the individual. Perhaps this is the most important lesson to be taken from Brasília. And it has been like this during all this time of three-shift, uninterrupted work in Brasília – fifty thousand people working at the same time.[90]

Brazilian newspapers at the time covered the preparations and the congress itself, reporting on the activities and opinions of the participants regarding Brasília.[91] In its September 25, 1959 issue, *Correio da Manhã*, a Rio de Janeiro newspaper, covered the lunch organized for critics which took place the day before at the Esquilos restaurant in Floresta da Tijuca. In the photos, it is possible to recognize Richard Neutra sitting next to Niomar Moniz Sodré, Executive Director of the Museum of Modern Art in Rio de Janeiro, with whom he was talking to at the time the photo was taken.[92] The next day the same newspaper covered the closing dinner of the International Congress of Art Critics, which took place in the gardens – designed by Roberto Burle Marx – of Museum of Modern Art of Rio de Janeiro and in which the president Juscelino Kubitschek was also present.[93]

The two visits to Brasília, in 1958 and 1959, seem to have really impressed Richard Neutra. Several copies – in English and Portuguese – of an article he wrote about the new Brazilian capital were found in the *Neutra Collection* at UCLA (there seems to be no evidence that it was ever published): *Brasília: A Peak of Initiative Revisited*. Honoring the creators, it reveals the architect's enthusiasm for the efforts in the development of this new city.

Cities are not compositions in plan and on paper. They
are three dimensional and they play in space and time.
Brasília especially is a time phenomenon. It changes and
fulfills its shape while you watch! The red iron oxyde soil
shows where the track of progress has been ploughed
by the miracle machines of our time. Huge and towering
structures cast their shadows over roads, built since I
admired this gigantic effort last year.

I am glad to have neglected all my obligations as an
architect and my clients in several continents gave me
leave to see Brasília again which means so much more
on our shrunken crowed globe than Brazilians themselves may know.

They know of course what it means to their own
current politics and economy. It is much harder for those
close by to judge its future significance when roads and
air routes, full of carriers and vehicles in all directions
juncture point, with rocket engines reaching it in short
hours from many parts of the planetary scene.[94]

Reading all the correspondence, articles and newspaper
clippings that make up the narrative of this chapter lead
to the conclusion that the measures adopted by the US
regarding inter-American relations were essential to bring
Richard Neutra closer to Latin America, but it was his personal interest in these countries and their architectures that
led to so many further developments – contacts and lectures,
as well as articles written and published both among North
Americans and Latin Americans. As for the relationship with
Brazilians, the main focus of our work, the attention given
to students from the National School of Fine Arts and the
Faculty of Architecture at Mackenzie University, as well as his
interest in publishing here in Brazil a book about his Puerto
Rico experiences – which counted on the collaboration
of Brazilians for the organization and translation – and in
participating in exhibitions in the country – as in the case of

the Masp exhibition and the São Paulo Biennial – points out
to a mixture between his role played as a messenger at the
service of the United States government and his actual and
personal interest for our architecture and for the Brazilian
modern scene.

Kaufmann House, detail of the opening
mechanism of the brise-soleil, Palm
Springs. Richard Neutra, 1946-1947.
Photo Julius Shulman. © J. Paul Getty
Trust Archive. Getty Research Institute,
Los Angeles (2004.R.10)

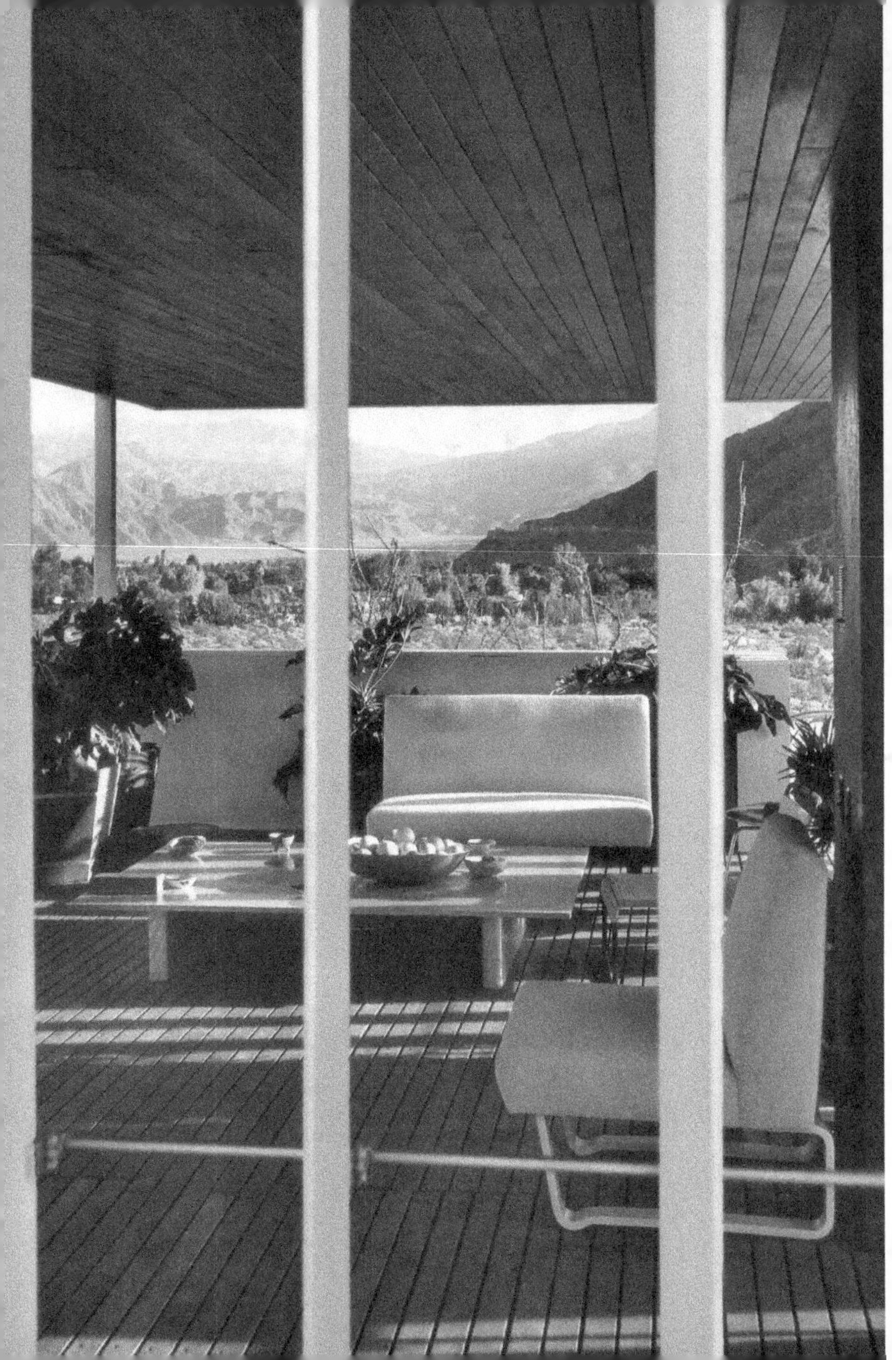

Relationship with Burle Marx

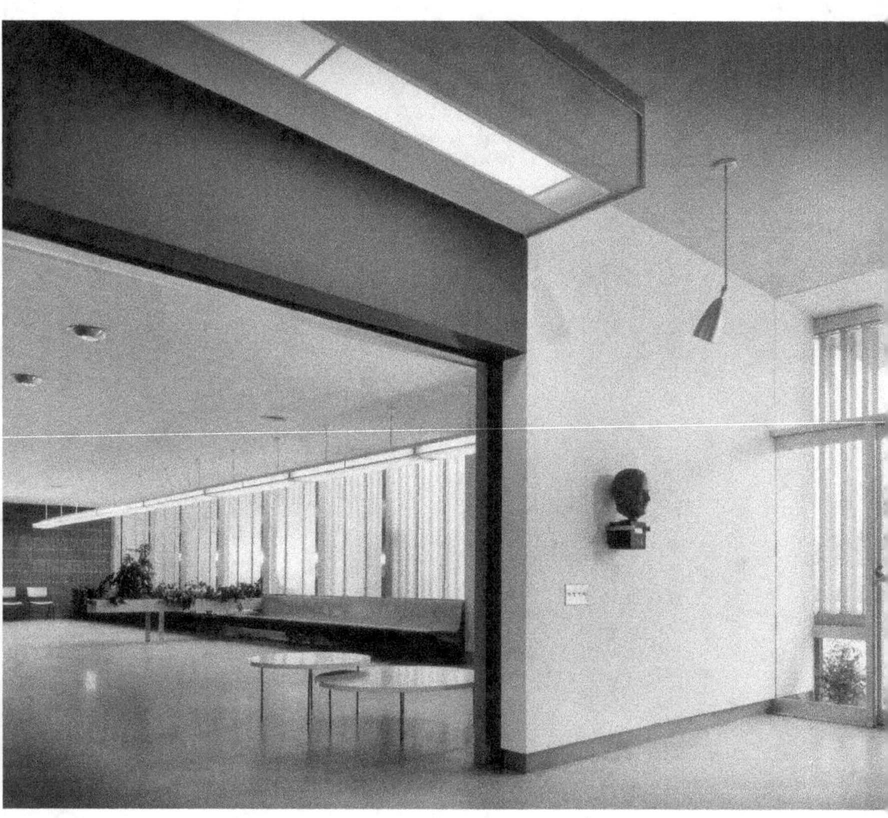

Amalgamated Clothing Workers of America, Los Angeles EUA. Richard Neutra, 1956. Foto Julius Shulman.

Acervo © J. Paul Getty Trust. Getty Research Institute, Los Angeles (2004.R.10)

The first document alluding to Roberto Burle Marx in
the *Neutra Collection* at UCLA is a montage of the article
Aspen Conference on Design, published by *Fortune* magazine
in September 1952. Among the selected clippings of this
article are a drawing by Neutra picturing the amphitheater
tent designed by Eero Saarinen and two photographs: one of
Richard Neutra next to Buckminster Fuller and Herbert Bayer
– Austrian architect, graduated from Bauhaus and also based
in the United States – and another with Neutra drawing with
his son Raymond (who, at the time, was 14 years old). At a
first glance, this document bears no relationship to the Brazilian landscape artist. However, in an email statement to the
researcher, Raymond Neutra says that he remembers a picnic
with Burle Marx taking place during the congress meetings.
Moreover, in the film *International Design Conference in
Aspen: The First Decade*, released in 1960 and which is now
part of the online collection of the *Chicago Film Archive*,[96]
the presence of the Brazilian artist is confirmed.

Richard Neutra and Roberto Burle Marx met during the
architect's visit to Brazil, in November 1945. A few years later,
in 1954 – right after the *Correio da Manhã* newspaper published a report on the success of the landscape artist among
North Americans[97] – and 1956, an extensive exchange of
correspondence between the two began. The reading of

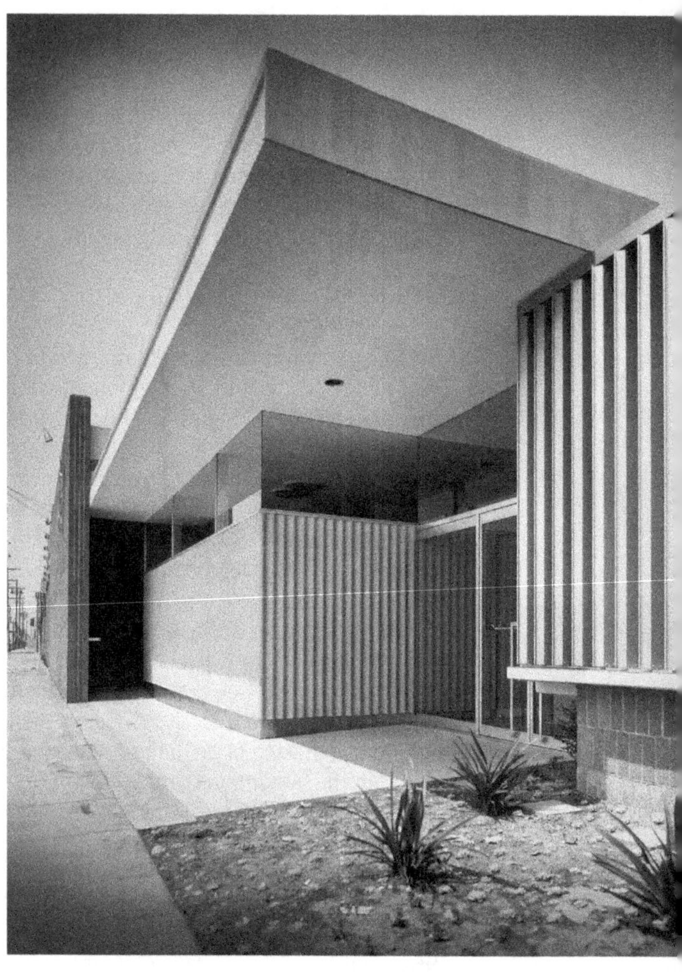

Amalgamated Clothing Workers of
America, Los Angeles. Richard Neutra,
1956. Photo Julius Shulman.

© J. Paul Getty Trust Archive. Getty
Research Institute, Los Angeles
(2004.R.10)

these documents reveal not only the bonds of friendship between the two, but mainly an effort on the part of Richard Neutra to establish partnerships with Burle Marx, as we can see in the letter written by the Brazilian:

> It was a great experience, to be with you, and the conversations we had and the days we passed together will be rich and fertile in their lessons for me, listening to your wonderful and lucid ideas. I hope that I may be able to live up the trust and confidence you've placed on me.[98]

Our research, however, was not able to specify what meeting Roberto Burle Marx refers to in his letter to Richard Neutra. Chronologically, this letter of August 18, 1954 is the first to be exchanged between them, judging by the correspondence available in the *Neutra Collection*. But it would be plausible to say that this meeting took place during the Design Conference in Aspen, in 1952. It is worth remembering that, on March 21, 1963, Neutra's house, VDL Research House I, caught fire and several documents got lost on the occasion. This is just speculation, but perhaps previous correspondence – and also documents from the period after 1956 up to 1963 – were lost in the incident.

Apparently, the first offer to Roberto Burle Marx consisted of the mural for the headquarters of Amalgamated Clothing Workers of America, in Los Angeles. In the letter of August 18, 1954, Burle Marx accepted the offer with great enthusiasm.[99] Neutra, in addition to the panel, had suggested to his clients that the landscaping should also be assigned to the Brazilian; however, for financial reasons, this possibility remained uncertain for a few months.[100] Then, on May 11, 1955, Neutra wrote to his friend saying there might be a possibility that the clients would accept the two projects.

As to the Labor Temple [Amalgamated Clothing Workers of America], we have started construction but are
still in the desperate process of trying to cut down
costs. A number of reduction lists have been prepared
and we are continuing to try to reduce the expense
because these labor people are not blessed with very
ample funds, but start with more enthusiasm than
money. I shall certainly let you know about this. Would
you perhaps consider a fee of some $250 for making a
sketch design for the small garden and the mural? I have
no idea how I can at present approach them for more
funds. However, they have listened with more than ordi-
nary interest to my many tales about the significance of
your contribution.[101]

In February 1955, Richard Neutra mentioned that he was
working on a project for a large residence in Havana, Cuba,
and said he strongly recommended that his client commission Roberto Burle Marx for the landscaping project.[102] A
few months later, two other opportunities emerged in the
conversation in which Neutra was again trying to secure
a partnership with Burle Marx: the Hammerman house
(1954) and the Brown house (1955). In the first case, Marx's
contribution would be a panel with dimensions 7.6m x 1.5m
x 0.25m (25 feet x 5 feet x 10 inches); as for the second, it
would be a landscaping project.[103]
Burle Marx actually started drawing the two new projects, but in a letter sent by Neutra in May 1955, the architect
requested that the work be suspended. In the case of the
Brown residence, the family was not yet fully resolved to
hire the Brazilian and, therefore, Neutra suggested that Burle
Marx send the project at its current stage, for he would use
the material as an argument. According to him, "it has really
come out to be a very satisfying job and the owners have
been very cooperative."[104] As for the Hammerman residence,
the situation seemed a bit more complicated. The client's

financial resources had come to an end, and the project was
now proceeding very slowly. Neutra suggests that no further
effort be expended on this work, but states that "they are
considerably receptive to the idea that landscaping advice or

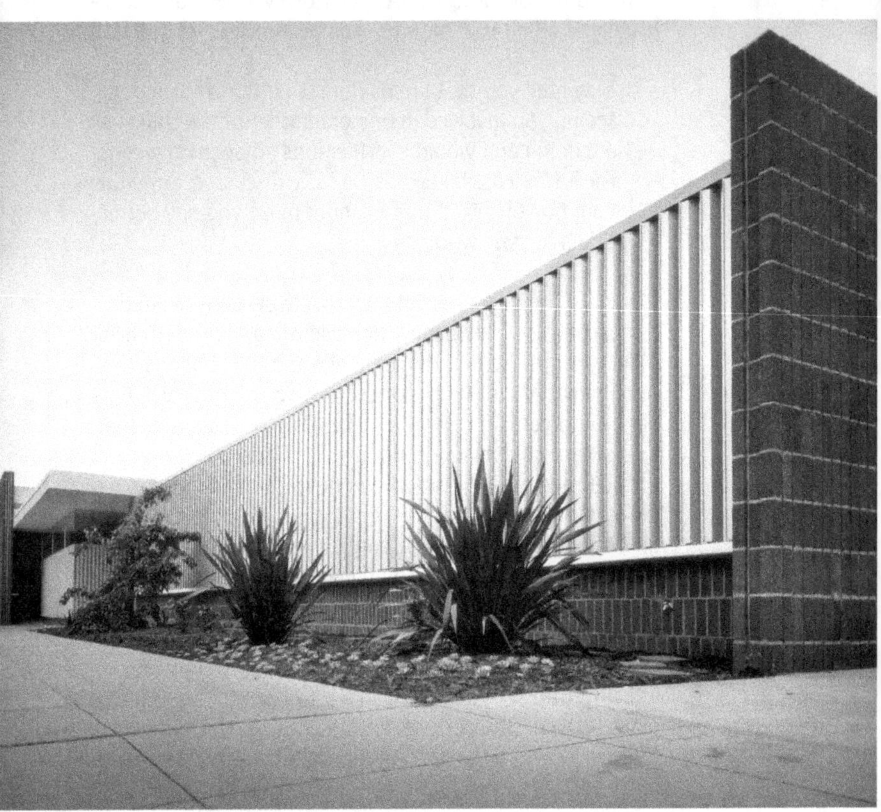

Amalgamated Clothing Workers of
America, Los Angeles. Richard Neutra,
1956. Photo Julius Shulman.

© J. Paul Getty Trust Archive. Getty
Research Institute, Los Angeles
(2004.R.10)

any other advice from you would be very valuable for their lives."[105]

In his letters, Richard Neutra was very enthusiastic about the possibility of working in partnership with Burle Marx and was committed to convincing his clients of the importance of hiring the Brazilian landscaper. However, several issues – usually of a financial nature – hampered these attempts.

> May I tell you that I remain most enthusiastic about seeing you involved in one or another of the things we are doing and would consider it as an opening wedge for future possibilities, as we have discussed. Sometimes I am downhearted that I cannot make you any better offers to start with.[106]

Thus, the only projects that effectively consolidated the partnership between Richard Neutra and Roberto Burle Marx were the Schulthess residence and the headquarters of Amalgamated Clothing Workers of America. However, Barbara Lamprecht, in her book on Neutra's works, states that Burle Marx offered suggestions for the landscaping project of the Brown house, "including one rhythm but with many different heights and colors in massing he wrote to Neutra on 14 July 1955."[107] Unfortunately, our research could not find the letter quoted by Lamprecht in the *Neutra Collection*.

Regardless of the number of partnerships, the fact is that Burle Marx seems to have really caught the attention of the Austrian architect. In a letter dated February 16, 1955, Neutra sent the Brazilian a list of photographs and plans – there is no clear specification as to which project Richard Neutra was referring to, as the drawings and images could not identified, but it is believed to be the headquarters building of Amalgamated Clothing Workers of America –, together with the text about Roberto Burle Marx written by Neutra.[108] It is possible that this material was sent for publication in Brazil.

Notes

1. Ruth Verde Zein, "When Documenting is not Enough. Buildings, Dates, Reflections, and Theoretical Constructions," 115-116.
2. Marina Waisman, *O interior da história: historiografia arquitetônica para uso de latino-americanos*, 96. Free translation.
3. Ibid., 97. Free translation.
4. Sigmund Freud (1919), "The Uncanny," 2.
5. Ibid., 3-4.
6. Harold Bloom, *The Anxiety of Influence: A Theory of Poetry*, 30. Italics in the original.
7. See: Michael Baxandall, *Patterns of Intention. On the Historical Explanation of Pictures.*
8. Giovanni Levi, "Sobre a micro-história," 158.
9. Ibid., 155. Free translation.
10. Letter from Richard Neutra to Gerth Todtman, November 29, 1948. Folder 5, Box 186. Professional Papers, Correspondence. Neutra Collection, UCLA Library of Special Collections.
11. To mention just a few: Fernanda Critelli, "Richard Neutra e o Brasil;" Fernanda Critelli, "Richard Neutra: conexões latino-americanas;" Luz Marie Rodríguez López, "¡Vuelo al porvenir! Henry Klumb y Toro-Ferrer: Proyecto Moderno y Arquitectura como Vitrina de la Democracia – Puerto Rico, 1944-1958;" Leonardo Santana Rabell, *Planificación y Política Durante la Administración de Luis Muñoz Marin: Un Análisis Crítico*; Catherine R. Ettinger, *Richard Neutra en América Latina: Una Mirada desde el Sur.*
12. Raymond Richard Neutra, "Encontros porto-riquenhos."
13. Letter from Charles W. Collier to Richard Neutra, September 14, 1945. Folder 8. Box 1429. Office Records, Correspondence. Neutra Collection. UCLA Library of Special Collections.
14. Letter from Richard Neutra to Gerth Todtmann, November 29, 1948. Folder 5, Box 186. Professional Papers, Correspondence. Neutra Collection, UCLA Library of Special Collections.
15. Richard Joseph Neutra, "Observations on Latin America," 68.
16. Ibid., 67.
17. Ibid., 70.
18. Ibid., 69.
19. Ibid., 72.
20. In a statement to the researcher, Raymond Neutra said that the movable louvers studied by Richard Neutra in Latin American buildings were incorporated into his architecture as early as 1946 with the Kauffman house, as well as in the reconstruction project for his own house, VDL II, in 1965.
21. Richard Joseph Neutra, "Sun Control Devices," 88.
22. Neutra, "Observations on Latin America," 71.
23. Letter from Richard Neutra to Walter Hylton Scott, 1946. Folder 8, Box 1429. Office Records, Correspondence. Neutra Collection, UCLA Library of Special Collections.
24. Letter from Editora Todtmann & Cia Ltda. to Richard Neutra, July 15, 1949. Folder 5, Box 186. Professional Papers, Correspondence. Neutra Collection, UCLA Library of Special Collections.

25. Adriana Marta Irigoyen Touceda, *Wright e Artigas: duas viagens*, 128.

26. Ibid., 147. For more specific info regarding dates, duration and figures, see note number 60.

27. Letter from João Vilanova Artigas to Richard Neutra, March 5, 1947. Folder 8, Box 1429. Office Records, Correspondence. Neutra Collection, UCLA Library of Special Collections.

28. Letter from Artigas to Wagley (24.3.47), quoted in Irigoyen Touceda, *Wright e Artigas*, 156.

29. Letter from Richard Neutra to Gerth Todtman, November 29, 1948.

30. Letter from Richard Neutra to Gerth Todtman, November 29, 1948. Excerpt highlighted in the epigraph.

31. Michael Baxandall. *Patterns of Intention. On the Historical Explanation of Pictures*, 58-62.

32. Robert E. Alexander, "Unpublished Memoirs." Alexander Papers, Cornell University, quoted in Thomas S. Hines, *Richard Neutra and the Search for Modern Architecture*, 268.

33. Richard Joseph Neutra, *Architecture of Social Concern in Regions of Mild Climate*, 8.

34. Gerth Todtmann, "Preface of the Publishers," in: Neutra, *Architecture of Social Concern*, 7.

35. Neutra, *Architecture of Social Concern*, 40.

36. Gregori Warchavchik, "Introduction." In *Architecture of Social Concern*, by Richard Joseph Neutra, 10.

37. Ibid., 30.

38. Letter from Pietro Maria Bardi to Richard Neutra, December 7, 1948. Folder "Richard Neutra." Biblioteca de Documentos Históricos, Masp.

39. Letter from Richard Neutra to Gerth Todtmann, February 4, 1949. Folder 5, Box 186. Professional Papers, Correspondence. Neutra Collection, UCLA Library of Special Collections.

40. "O Museu de Arte de São Paulo." *Correio da Manhã*, January 19, 1949. Fundação Biblioteca Nacional (digital archive).

41. Letter from Pietro Maria Bardi to the editors of magazine *The Architectural Forum*. Folder "Richard Neutra." Biblioteca de Documentos Históricos, Masp.

42. Letter from Pietro Maria Bardi to the editors of magazine *L'Architecture d'Aujourd'hui*. Folder "Richard Neutra." Biblioteca de Documentos Históricos, Masp.

43. Letter from Pietro Maria Bardi to the editors of magazine *Progressive Architecture*. Folder "Richard Neutra." Biblioteca de Documentos Históricos, Masp.

44. Letter from Pietro Maria Bardi to Dione Neutra. Folder "Richard Neutra." Biblioteca de Documentos Históricos, Masp.

45. Letter from Francisco Matarazzo Sobrinho to Richard Neutra. Folder 7. Box 187. Personal Papers, Public Relation Material. Neutra Collection. UCLA Library Special Collections.

46. Letter from Régula Thorston to Francisco Matarazzo Sobrinho. Folder 7. Box 187. Personal Papers, Public Relation Material. Neutra Collection. UCLA Library Special Collections.

47. Letter from Dione Neutra to Lucian Konrgold. Folder 23. Box 1972. Office Records, Correspondence. Neutra Collection. UCLA Library Special Collections.
48. Letter from Pietro Maria Bardi to Dione Neutra. Folder 7. Box 187. Personal Papers, Public Relation Material. Neutra Collection. UCLA Library Special Collections.
49. Letter from Dione Neutra to Pietro Maria Bardi. Folder 7. Box 187. Personal Papers, Public Relation Material. Neutra Collection. UCLA Library Special Collections.
50. Letter from Arturo Porfili to Dione Neutra. Folder 7. Box 187. Personal Papers, Public Relation Material. Neutra Collection. UCLA Library Special Collections.
51. Letter from Dione Neutra to Arturo Porfili. Folder 7. Box 187. Personal Papers, Public Relation Material. Neutra Collection. UCLA Library Special Collections.
52. Letter from Arturo Porfili to Dione Neutra. Folder 7. Box 187. Personal Papers, Public Relation Material. Neutra Collection. UCLA Library Special Collections.
53. Letter from Dione Neutra to Brazilian Consulate. Folder 7. Box 187. Personal Papers, Public Relation Material. Neutra Collection. UCLA Library Special Collections.
54. Letter from Dione Neutra to Lucian Korngold. Folder 7. Box 187. Personal Papers, Public Relation Material. Neutra Collection. UCLA Library Special Collections.
55. Letter from Wolfgang Pfeiffer to Richard Neutra. Folder 8. Box 187. Personal Papers, Public Relation Material. Neutra Collection. UCLA Library Special Collections.
56. Letter from Dione Neutra to Pietro Maria Bardi. Folder 8. Box 187. Personal Papers, Public Relation Material. Neutra Collection. UCLA Library Special Collections.
57. Letter from Dione Neutra to Wolfgang Pfeiffer. Folder 8. Box 187. Personal Papers, Public Relation Material. Neutra Collection. UCLA Library Special Collections.
58. Letter from Wolfgang Pfeiffer to Dione Neutra. Folder 8. Box 187. Personal Papers, Public Relation Material. Neutra Collection. UCLA Library Special Collections.
59. "Museu de Arte Moderna." *O Estado de S. Paulo*. July 7, 1954, and July 22, 1954. Estadão Archive (digital archive).
60. Letter from Wolfgang Pfeiffer to Dione Neutra. Folder 8. Box 187. Personal Papers, Public Relation Material. Neutra Collection. UCLA Library Special Collections.
61. Letter from Dante Paglia to Richard Neutra. Folder 8. Box 187. Personal Papers, Public Relation Material. Neutra Collection. UCLA Library Special Collections.
62. Letter from Richard Neutra to Diretório Acadêmico da Escola Nacional de Belas Artes, January 28, 1946. Folder 8, Box 1429. Office Records, Correspondence. Neutra Collection, UCLA Library of Special Collections.

63. Letter from Jorge Wilheim to Richard Neutra, November 10, 1949. Folder "Richard Neutra." Biblioteca de Documentos Históricos, Masp; Richard Joseph Neutra, "Uma casa inédita de Neutra," 4-9; Critelli, "Richard Neutra e o Brasil," 190-192. In his master's thesis on the work of Salvador Candia, Eduardo Ferroni lingers on the publication of the fourth issue of *Pilotis* magazine and the impact that the book *Architecture of Social Concern* had on the students who organized it. See: Eduardo Rocha Ferroni, "Aproximações sobre a obra de Salvador Candia," 29-37.

64. Richard Joseph Neutra, *Planificar para sobrevivir.*

65. Neutra, *Planificar para sobrevivir*, 9-10. Free translation.

66. Richard Joseph Neutra, *Realismo Biológico. Un Nuevo Renacimiento Humanístico en Arquitectura*, 12.

67. Ibid., 8. Free translation.

68. Dion Neutra, "Prólogo para la Edición em Español," in: Richard Joseph Neutra, *Vida y Forma*, 5. Free translation.

69. Hines, *Richard Neutra and the Search*, 303.

70. Barbara Mac Lamprecht, *Richard Neutra: Complete Works*, 415.

71. Richard Joseph Neutra. "Unpublished Autobiography," quoted in Esther McCoy, *Richard Neutra*, 7-8.

72. Henry Meyric Hughes, "A crítica de arte amadurece: Brasília, AICA e o Congresso Extraordinário de 1959," in: *Congresso Internacional Extraordinário de Críticos de Arte. Cidade nova: síntese das artes*, 6.

73. Eric Munford, *The CIAM discourse on urbanism*, 1.

74. Ibid.

75. Ibid., 134.

76. Ibid., 142.

77. Ibid., 147.

78. Gropius to Sert, February 21, 1944 (JLS), quoted in Munford, *The CIAM discourse on urbanism*, 145.

79. Letter from Stamo Papadaki to Richard Neutra. Folder 2. Box 233. Professional Papers, CIAM. Neutra Collection. UCLA Library Special Collections.

80. Email interview from Eric Munford to Fernanda Critelli, December 08, 2014.

81. United Nations, *The United Nations and Latin America: A Collection of Basic Information Material about the Work of the United Nations and the Related Agencies in Latin America*, 19-20.

82. Ibid.

83. Ibid., 163.

84. "Notas e comentários." *Diário de Notícias*, June 22, 1957. Fundação Biblioteca Nacional (digital archive).

85. "Neutra à JK: Brasília, maravilhosa obra de Niemeyer." *Correio da Manhã*, July 31, 1958. Fundação Biblioteca Nacional (digital archive). Free translation.

86. Hughes, "A crítica de arte amadurece," 7.

87. Ibid., 6.

88. Roberto Segre, "A espiral da história: 1959-2009." In *Congresso Internacional Extraordinário de Críticos de Arte*, 12.

89. Hughes, "A crítica de arte amadurece," 6. Free tranlation.

90. *Congresso Internacional Extraordinário de Críticos de Arte*, 40. Free translation.

91. "Opiniões sobre Brasília por membros da Associação de Críticos de Arte, no Congresso Internacional Extraordinário de Críticos de Arte." *Correio da Manhã*, September 27, 1959. Fundação Biblioteca Nacional (digital archive).

92. "Almoço." *Correio da Manhã*, September 25, 1959. Fundação Biblioteca Nacional (digital archive).

93. "JK confraternizou com a crítica, estrelas, arquitetos e artistas internacionais." *Correio da Manhã*, September 26, 1959. Fundação Biblioteca Nacional (digital archive).

94. "Brasília: A Peak of Initiative Revisited. In honor of its Great Form Givers." Folder 30. Box 161. Professional Papers, Articles. Neutra Collection. UCLA Library Special Collections. Free translation.

95. "Roberto Burle Marx." Folder 12. Box 132. Office Records, Correspondence. Neutra Collection. UCLA Library Special Collections.

96. "International Design Conference in Aspen: The First Decade." Available in <https://bit.ly/3xPBq9M>.

97. "Aspen Conference on Design." Folder 55. Box 1399. Office Records, Publicity. Neutra Collection. UCLA Library Special Collections.

98. Letter from Roberto Burle Marx to Richard Neutra. Folder 12. Box 132. Office Records, Correspondence. Neutra Collection. UCLA Library Special Collections.

99. Ibid.

100. Letter from Richard Neutra to Roberto Burle Marx. Folder 12. Box 132. Office Records, Correspondence. Neutra Collection. UCLA Library Special Collections.

101. Letter from Richard Neutra to Roberto Burle Marx. Folder 12. Box 132. Office Records, Correspondence. Neutra Collection. UCLA Library Special Collections, 1.

102. Letter from Richard Neutra to Roberto Burle Marx. Folder 12. Box 132. Office Records, Correspondence. Neutra Collection. UCLA Library Special Collections.

103. Letter from Roberto Burle Marx to Richard Neutra. Folder 12. Box 132. Office Records, Correspondence. Neutra Collection. UCLA Library Special Collections, 2.

104. Letter from Richard Neutra to Roberto Burle Marx. Folder 12. Box 132. Office Records, Correspondence. Neutra Collection. UCLA Library Special Collections, 1.

105. Ibid.

106. Letter from Richard Neutra to Roberto Burle Marx. Folder 12. Box 132. Office Records, Correspondence. Neutra Collection. UCLA Library Special Collections, 2.

107. Lamprecht, *Richard Neutra: Complete Works*, 280.

108. "Roberto Burle Marx." Folder 12. Box 132. Office Records, Correspondence. Neutra Collection. UCLA Library Special Collections.

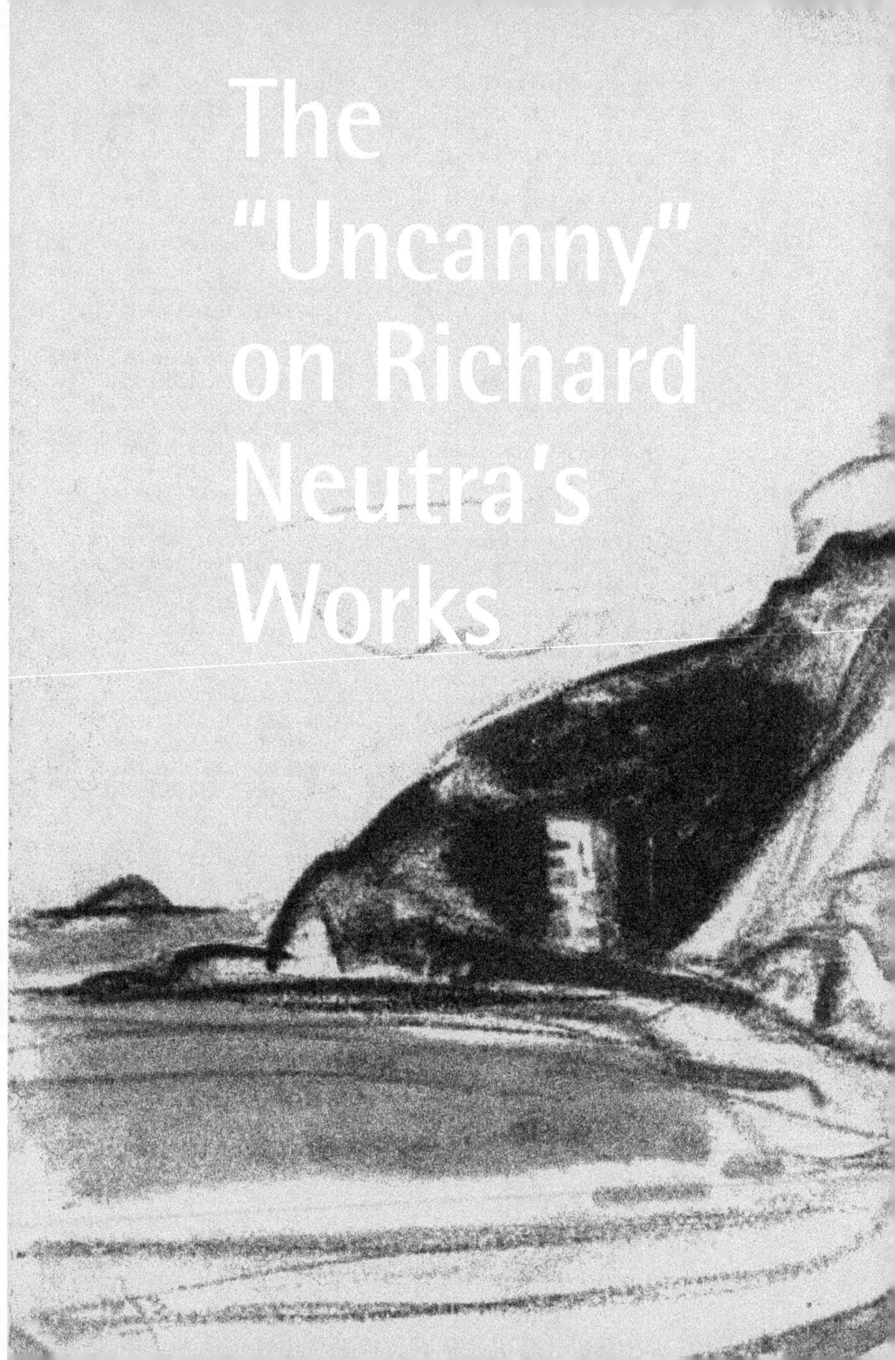

The "Uncanny" on Richard Neutra's Works

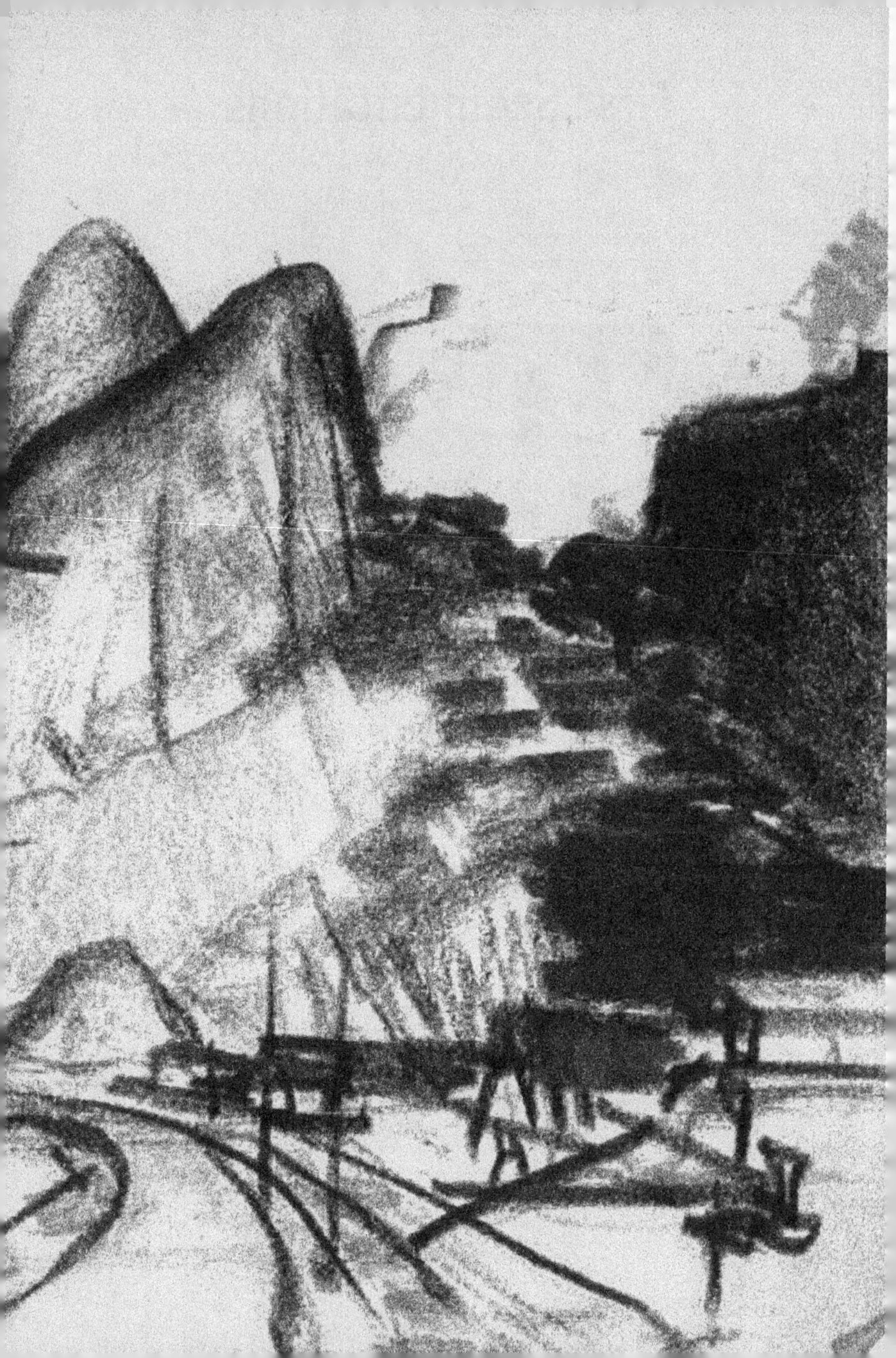

First Sedimentations

Article "Sun Control Devices",
published at *Progressive Architecture*
magazine in October 1946

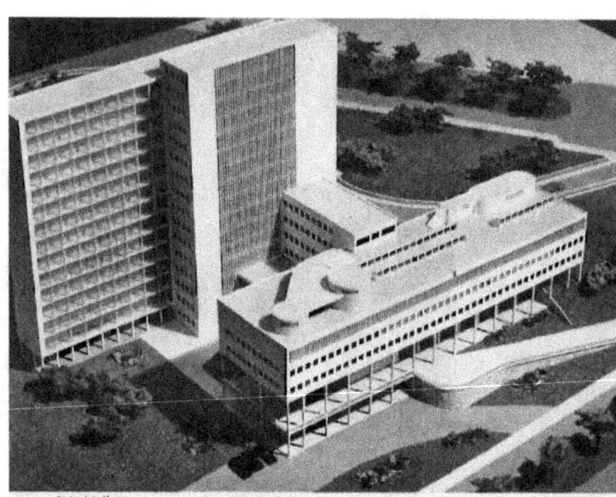

Richard J. Neutra

SUN CONTROL DEVICES

A presentation based primarily on examples collected in South America by RICHARD J. NEUTRA.

EDITOR'S NOTE: The earliest modern attempts at architectural integration of sun control devices to come to our attention were Le Corbusier's, exemplified in his apartment house for Algiers. Since then the architects of much of the literate world have continued to formalize devices which have grown up informally in regions where the sun is strong. Lighting engineers, in experiments in Texas, Massachusetts, and our Middle West, have investigated the scientific control of natural light in order to offset its ill effects. Manufacturers have brought products for the purpose to our attention: a patented, adjustable exterior Venetian blind from France, sent to us with word of the interest expressed by American G.I.'s; a slotted aluminum awning produced in the U. S. A.; polarized, anti-glare, and anti-heat glass; and others. Meanwhile traditional methods of excluding unwanted sun have continued in use, some of them more successful than certain highly rational formal attempts. Most of the successful devices, formal or naive, have a common principle: they stop the sun before it hits the glazing. The problem is of course acute in most of Latin America. We are indeed grateful to Mr. Neutra for assembling the majority of the accompanying illustrations and furnishing the incentive for this presentation.

No other single feature of South American architecture has excited as much attention as the conspicuous means of controlling sunlight which characterize the buildings. Vertical, movable louvers are particularly intriguing to me because a decade ago I experimented with this type of device, although I did not pursue my ideas to an ultimate conclusion. At the time we sketched various solutions for execution in different materials, some simple and some increasingly complex and mechanical.

Later I learned of the patents held by architect and city-planner Julio Villalobos of Buenos Aires, covering vertical blinds, of which he has shown me many examples. Good use has been made of this device by Hardoy, and Kurchan in elaborate apartment build Buenos Aires; by Roberto Brothers in their R Building and others in Rio de Janeiro; by Kneese in Sao Paulo; by Oscar Niemeyer, who has used great freedom in his church and yacht club at Pa Le Corbusier has suggested *bris soleil* of a simila Gropius has experimented with projected trellises are only a few examples. Other remarkable pieces c ment, such as glass louvers operated by concealed ca shutters, and mechanized, custom-built, metal sash an have been splendidly used by Gregor Warchavchik, V Acosta, and other Latin American architects.

Rather early, I started to use polarized, glare-resista especially when a building had to face both the beaut western ocean and the setting sun's reflection in it. I that no blind could compete with such a simple However— and quite apart from the high cost of South America and other places—there are two when some sort of blind would appear to be the best first, when there is no glass at all, as in tropical where local breezes must be turned to advantage; when there is no view from a window, and blinds c to exclude the undesirable sight as well as unwan

Many of the accompanying illustrations, in contras own designs (which utilize thin aluminum blades), asbestos-cement and fiber boards, or vanes prefabri reinforced concrete, which I assume should be vibi subjected to vacuum when manufactured.

—RICHARD J. N

Ultimately Alexander perceived Neutra as 'a veritable tyrant in his own home office', where he had several secretaries, 'including his long-suffering wife, Dione, working around the clock on worldwide correspondence, publications, and an always current book, calculated to make him immortal.'
Thomas S. Hines, *Richard Neutra and the Search for Modern Architecture*[1]

In his narrative of the life and work of Richard Neutra – the first truly dense and comprehensive biography published on the architect[2] –, Thomas Hines often draws from the memoirs of Robert Alexander,[3] Neutra's partner in the 1950s. Setting aside the issue of source liability, what calls for discussion is the emotional charge that contaminates Alexander's testimony and, consequently, the veracity of the historical facts. As the author himself notes at a certain point in his account, the personal and professional tensions between the two architects was there in the very beginning of the partnership and only intensified over the years, until the breakup.[4]

The quote highlighted above is a clear example of this conflict. In Robert Alexander's view, the incessant correspondence and international publications pursued by Richard Neutra represented nothing more than his ambition to immortalize himself in the history of world architecture. Obviously, this statement is credible and could also be directed at other architects who struggled for immortal fame – for example, Frank Lloyd Wright and Le Corbusier. However, it is not reasonable to ignore the fact that, as an innovative architect in a continuous search for the improvement of the interplay between architecture and landscape, Neutra also cultivated such contacts as a way to keep himself updated about the output of his colleagues.

A similar situation can be identified in the statements of Thomas Hines when examining works developed during the period of the Neutra & Alexander partnership. Aware of the conflict between the architects and armed with Alexander's memoirs – written after Neutra's death –, the historian goes on to attribute to Neutra's partner those elements in the works he considered "uncanny." Disentangling the characteristics of one architect or the other in projects developed through co-authorship can be quite complex. However, some facts will be addressed here in an attempt to establish certain outlines and, consequently, facilitate the analysis of the works in question. The first fact concerns the role played by each personality within the office.

> As a team, Neutra and Alexander were probably at their best on these planning projects of the early 1950s [designs for Guam Island]. In formulating the plans, each made basic conceptual contributions, with Neutra taking chief responsibility for architectural design and Alexander assuming control of planning organization and logistics.[5]

After graduating in architecture from Cornell University in the early 1930s, Robert Alexander, together with Lewis Wilson and Edwin Merril – his partners at the time (1935-1941)[6] developed the urban social housing project Baldwin Hill Village (Los Angeles, California), who secured him a seat on the Los Angeles City Planning Commission (1945) – later on, in 1948, he would become president of such Commission.[7] Although he soon achieved prestige as a city planner, he needed to partner up with a more established architect to secure commissions for building projects (either residential or commercial).[8] Richard Neutra, on the other hand, saw in the young architect the opportunity to land commissions on urban scales that he alone could not secure.[9] Their interests in the partnership were quite clear, and their obvious ambitions make it possible to state that, as in the projects for the Island of Guam – developed at the beginning of the partnership –, Neutra was responsible for the architectural projects, while Robert Alexander took care of the urban ones.[10]

Although the partnership seemed solid, Thomas Hines points out that the constant (and increasing) misunderstandings ended up disappointing both architects.[11] From then on, what is observed in the historian's account is that the features of the projects developed through partnership that, in Hines' view, did not correspond to Neutra's pure and simple style were, therefore, attributed to Alexander. The existence of a conflict between the two is not disputed here: if that were not the case, it is possible that the society would not have been dissolved. What is debatable is the imposing presence of memories loaded with personal impressions in the analysis of the works. As the historian himself pointed out, Alexander saw Neutra as a "tyrant," and it is natural that he injected this feeling into his recollections of the projects developed in partnership. Thus, conflicts gain relevance in the analysis, casting doubts on the reliability of the current interpretations of facts.

Relocating the question makes it possible to cast a new look at previous readings, in the search for a new explanation for the sense of "uncanniness" observed in the discourse regarding some of these works developed in partnership. The contrasts understood as evidence of conflict between the partners take on new meanings when one considers Neutra's professional trajectory, especially with regard to his relationship with Latin American architects and architecture. From this new perspective, instead of being disastrous, these works reveal the artistic coherence of an architect who incorporates, reinterprets and adapts new references to make them his own. The "uncanny" thus appears to be an obliterated connection between Richard Neutra and Latin America.

Los Angeles Hall of Records

Los Angeles Hall of Records, Los Angeles. Neutra and Alexander, 1962. Photo Julius Shulman. © J. Paul Getty Trust Archive. Getty Research Institute, Los Angeles (2004.R.10)

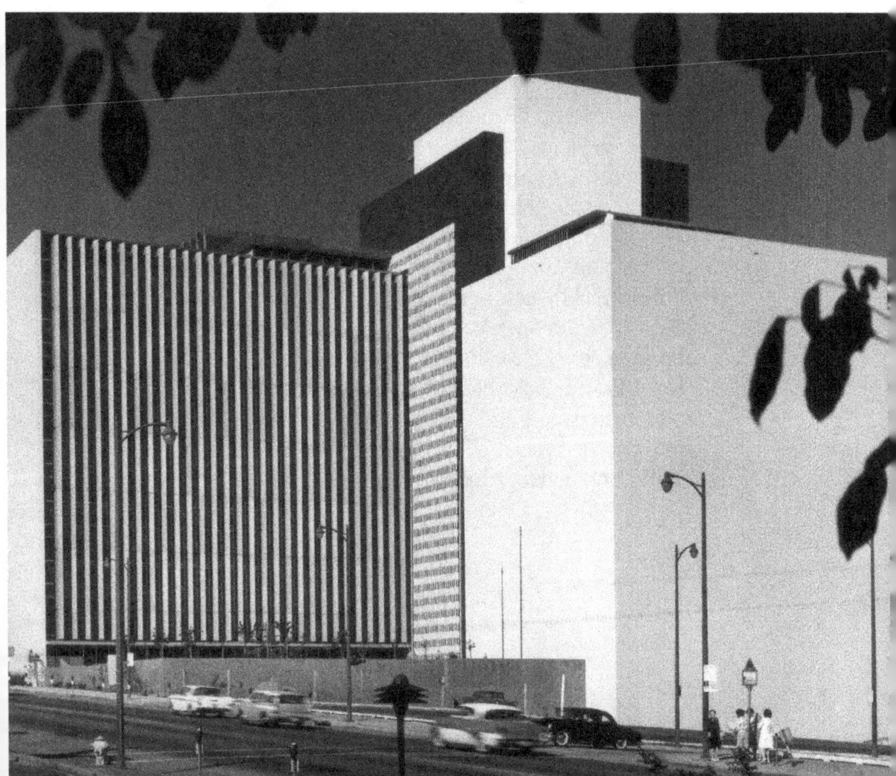

*Alexander's penchant for warming Neutra's stark
modernity with 'colorful, organic' artwork led to cacoph-
ony on the building's North façade and to mixtures
of too many competing and incompatible materials
elsewhere.*
Thomas S. Hines, *Richard Neutra and the Search for
Modern Architecture*[12]

Upon examining – in a few quick paragraphs – the design
for the Los Angeles Hall of Records (1962), Thomas Hines
starts off pointing to the obsolescence of the interior spaces,
originally designed to store public paper files which soon
after were largely replaced by microfilm. In addition to the
"interior programmatic problems,"[13] the historian brings up a
dispute over the authorship of the work, referring to a comment made by Robert Alexander.[14] The latter stated that, due
to Richard Neutra's lack of effort in developing the project,
he himself "produced schematic sketches substantially iden-
tical to the final design and completed building."[15] Given this,
Hines concludes that the final aesthetic result of the work
expresses the power struggle and the differences in style
between the partners. Regardless of who was responsible for
the initial sketch, the fact is that, as the historian himself had
already pointed out, it was Neutra who had the final say in
architectural projects.

The project's relevance, particularly its concern with the
environmental aspect, is highlighted in the dense monographic publication on the architect's works developed
between 1951 and 1960 by Willy Boesiger. The book devotes
two pages to an extensive and in-depth study of the solar
orientation on the building's facades and on the most appropriate louvers for each configuration – not to mention a first
page with the implantation, perspective and explanatory text
about the work, which at the time was still under construction.[16] In the following volume, dedicated to the works from
1961 to 1966, eleven pages are dedicated to the project, with

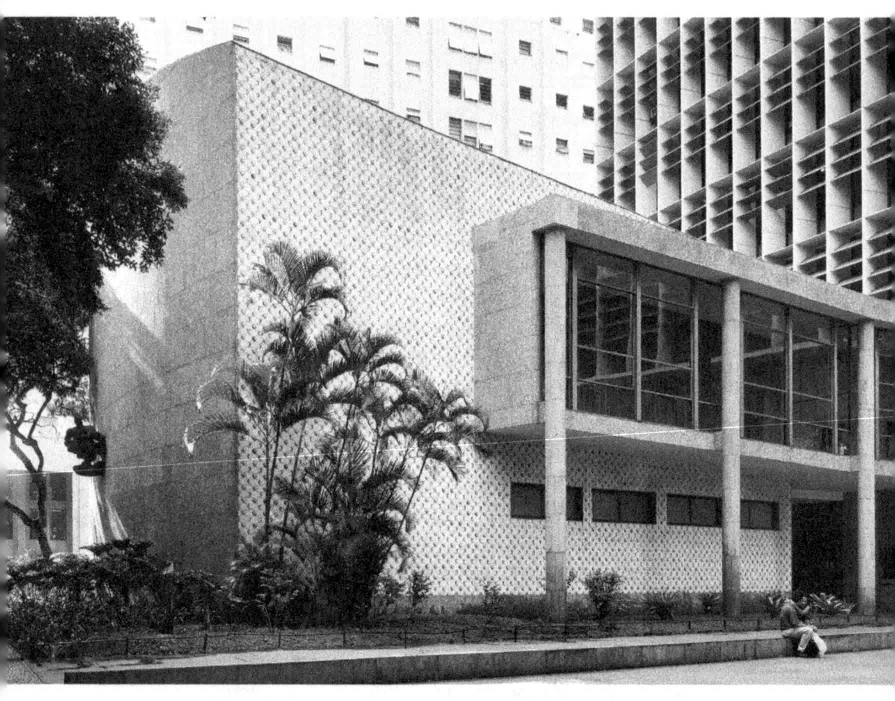

Ministry of Education and Health, Rio
de Janeiro, Brazil. Lúcio Costa, Oscar
Niemeyer, Affonso Eduardo Reidy, Jorge
Machado Moreira, Ernani Vasconcellos and
Carlos Leão, 1935-1945. Photo Nelson Kon

Los Angeles Hall of Records, Los
Angeles. Neutra and Alexander, 1962.
Photo Julius Shulman. © J. Paul Getty
Trust Archive. Getty Research Institute,
Los Angeles (2004.R.10)

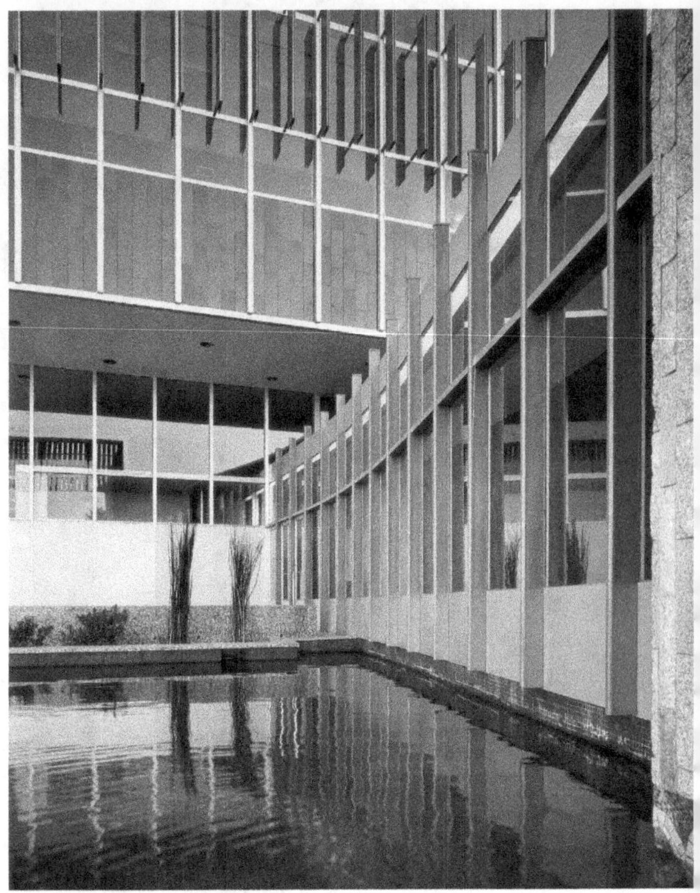

Los Angeles Hall of Records, northwest view and ground floor plan, Los Angeles. Neutra and Alexander, 1962. Photo Julius Shulman. © J. Paul Getty Trust Archive. Getty Research Institute, Los Angeles (2004.R.10). Croqui Fernanda Critelli

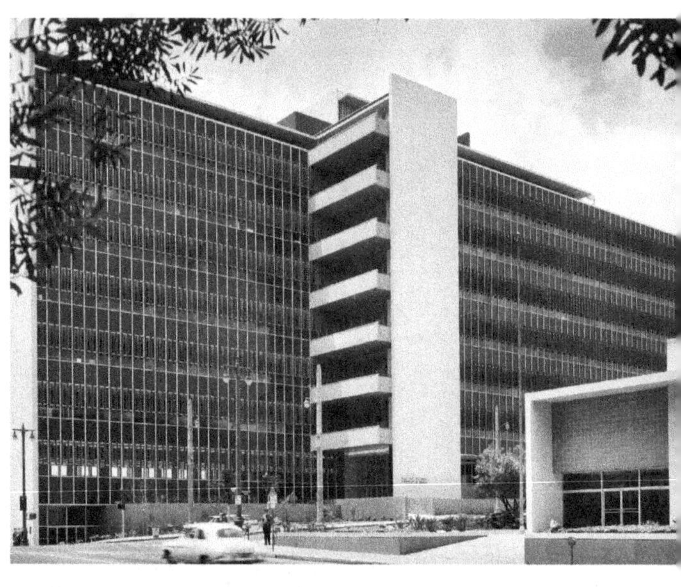

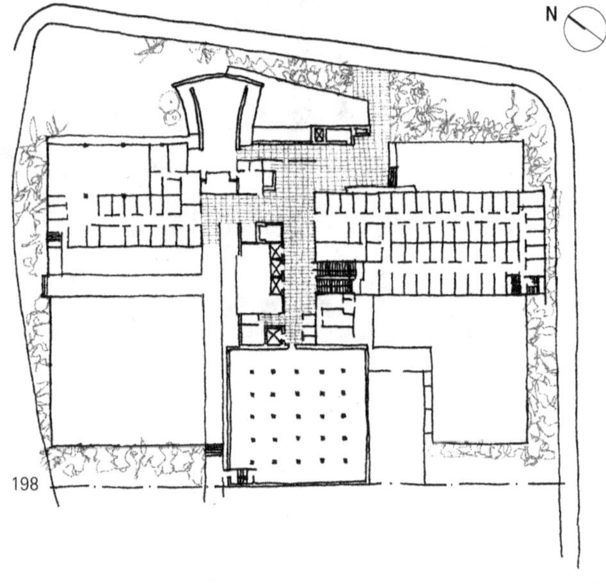

photos of the work already finished, several details and an excerpt from the January 11, 1962 issue of the *Los Angeles Times* commenting on the building.[17]

Going back to the epigraph above, Thomas Hines ends his brief analysis of the Los Angeles Hall of Records by stating that the art panel placed on a section of the North façade was part of Robert Alexander's effort to bring color and life to the overly austere style of Neutra, which ultimately resulted in a mix of competitive and incompatible materials. In the statement, the historian overlooks two relevant issues: first, the "tyrant" behavior of Neutra pointed out by Alexander is incompatible with the idea of a large-scale work being approved and built regardless of the architect's full endorsement; secondly – and this is even more relevant –, Hines refrains from any comment on Neutra's relationship with Latin America as well as on the presence of Latin American influences in his works.

As discussed in our master's thesis[18] and in some passages of our doctoral research, the efforts for cultural exchange in order to establish better relations with the countries south of Rio Grande – in response to the escalation of the conflict in Europe –, brought to North America works such as those by artists and muralists Cândido Portinari and Diego Rivera.[19] Both artists were familiar to Neutra. During his first trip to Brazil, in 1945, he visited the building of the Ministry of Education and Health – MES (1939-1945), featured in the exhibition and catalog *Brazil Builds* (1942), for which Portinari designed the tile murals. As for the Mexicans, Richard and Dione Neutra met Rivera and Frida Kahlo in 1937 during the American couple's first visit to Mexico.[20]

However, it is not just Neutra's familiarity with these artists that casts some doubt on Thomas Hines' analysis. Even more important is the architect's interest and involvement with Latin American architecture, as well as the fact that artistic panels were a recurring presence in major modern works produced here.

Reflecting on the Brazilian case, Roberto Segre wrote:

the 'Brazilian' expression of the heritage of European
rationalism [...] is the presence of chromatic or figura-
tive panels on the walls at the base of the buildings:
they appear on the tiles by Cândido Portinari at MES;
or in the persistent collaboration of Athos Bulcão in the
projects carried out at the beginning of the construction
of the capital: for example, at the Brasília Palace Hotel
(1957).[21]

As a means to attest to the great importance of the
panels in Neutra's work, it is necessary to refer once again
to his professional relationship with Roberto Burle Marx. As
our previous chapter points out, there were four partnership proposals offered to the Brazilian landscaper: two for
landscape projects – the Brown (1955, not executed) and
Schulthess (1956) houses – and two for artistic panels – the
Hammerman House (1954, panel not executed) and the
headquarters building of Amalgamated Clothing Workers of
America (1956).[22] This last project, of a commercial nature,
was in fact developed through the Neutra & Alexander office,
on Glendale Boulevard, and most likely suffered Alexander's
interference – with the final word belonging to Neutra. However, the design for the Hammerman house was developed
in the office on Silverlake Boulevard, where Richard Neutra
single-handedly managed his employees and residential
projects.
Regardless of the reasons why Burle Marx's panel did
not materialize – financial impossibilities, clients' personal
taste etc. – the fact is that Neutra argued with clients for the
panels and landscape projects and, more specifically, insisted
that Burle Marx design them.[23] Now, if this occurred during
the same period – inside and outside the partnership –, it is
conceivable that the same happened with the Los Angeles
Hall of Records. Neutra was interested in and made an effort

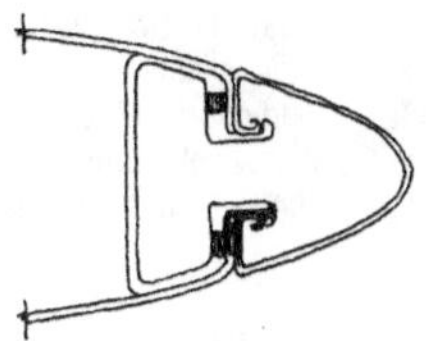

Los Angeles Hall of Records, detail and section of the brise-soleil and south-west view, Los Angeles. Neutra and Alexander, 1962. Croquis Fernanda Critelli. Photo Julius Shulman. © J. Paul Getty Trust Archive. Getty Research Institute, Los Angeles (2004.R.10)

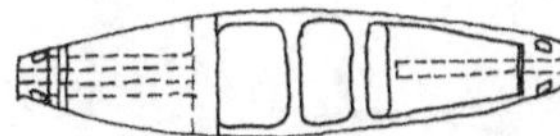

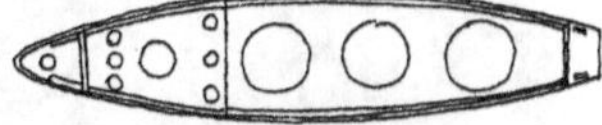

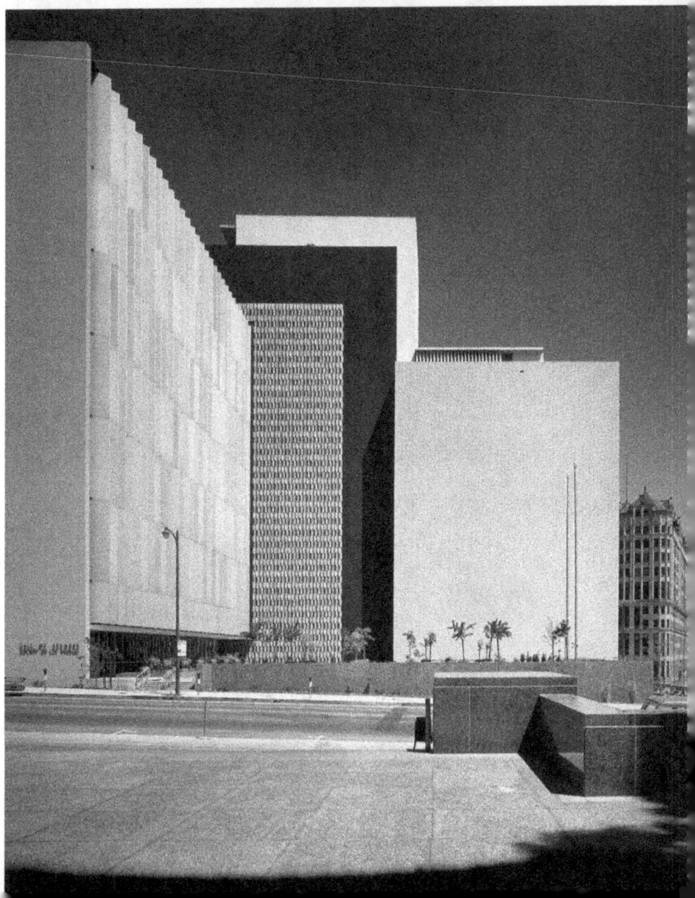

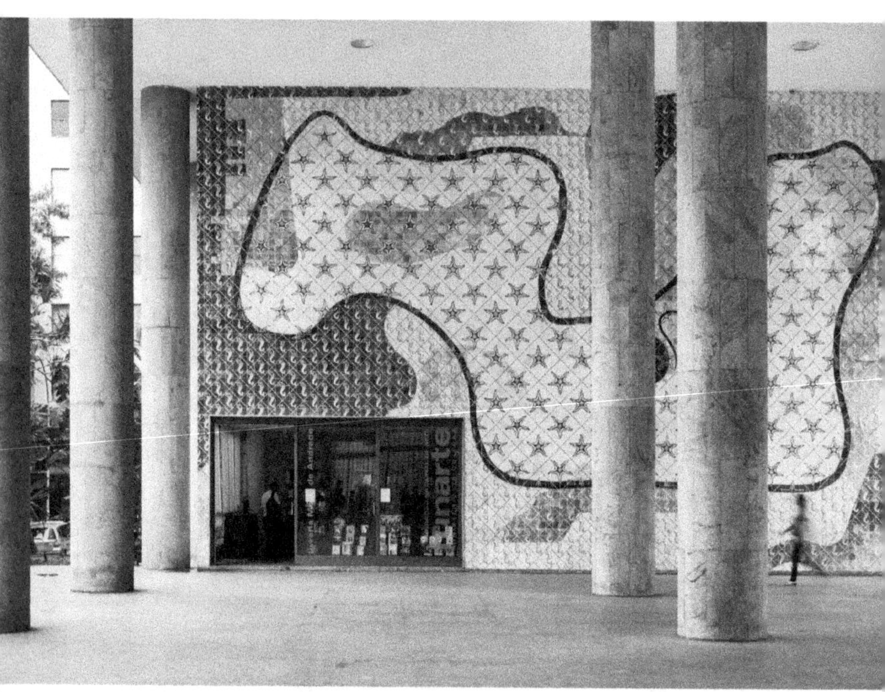

Ministry of Education and Health, Rio de Janeiro, Brazil. Lúcio Costa, Oscar Niemeyer, Affonso Eduardo Reidy, Jorge Machado Moreira, Ernani Vasconcellos and Carlos Leão, 1935-1945. Photo Nelson Kon

to integrate the other arts into his works, so there is no reason to doubt that the mosaic mural, more than 24 meters long, designed by artist Joseph Young (1919-2007), was indeed part of his designing decisions.

As there is no mention of the panel on the pages dedicated to the project in Boesiger's book, it is likely that it was not part of the initial plan.[24] But it is quite likely that the work emerged as a response to Neutra's concerns. In contrast, Thomas Hines – who adopted the discourse of Robert Alexander's memoirs and the conflict between the partners as an explanation for certain aspects of Neutra's work that seemed strange to him – disregarded the possibility that the presence of the mural represented a decision by the architect that he was analyzing. Reinforcing his position even further, he chose for his book a photo of the building without the panel, taken from the same angle represented in a hand-drawn perspective sketched by Neutra, which appears in the second volume of Boesiger's collection. It reiterates, therefore, this version as the only façade designed by the architect; consequently, the only one that presented his pure and austere style.

Thus, it is possible to suppose that the uncanniness related to Joseph Young's artistic panel on the facade of the headquarters building of the Los Angeles Hall of Records signals the hidden – and unfamiliar – presence of a buried connection. Unequipped to grasp the situation, Hines feels more comfortable in explaining away the fact with trite motivations, ignoring a presence that expresses Neutra's close relationship with and great admiration for Latin American architecture.

VDL House 2

VDL House 2, Los Angeles. Richard
Neutra, 1965-1966. Photo Julius
Shulman. © J. Paul Getty Trust Archive.
Getty Research Institute, Los Angeles
(2004.R.10)

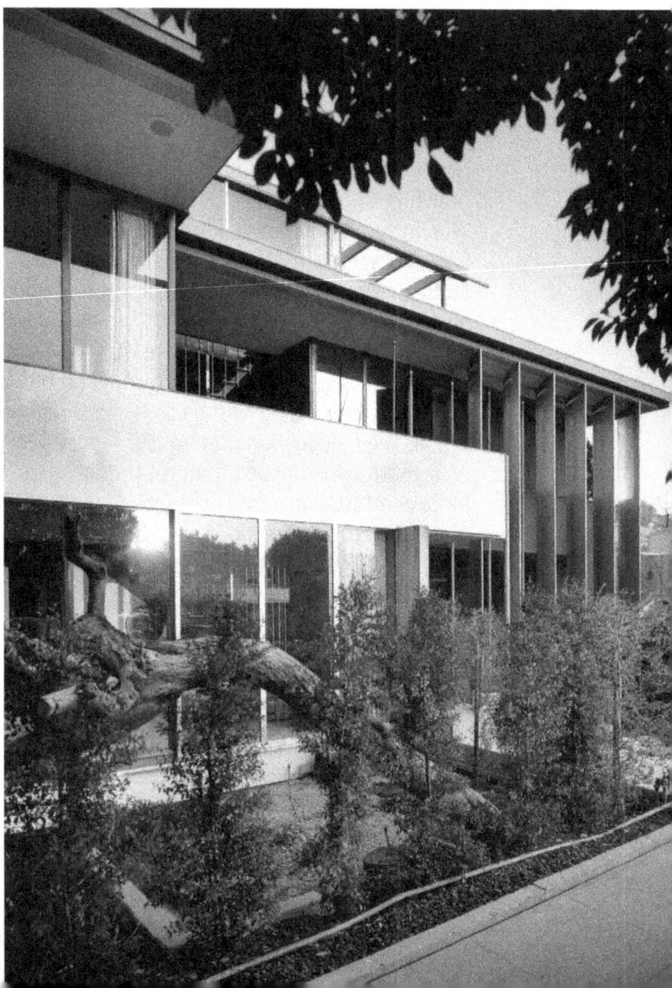

*The technical solutions take on a perhaps excessive
formal prominence, something that had not happened
before, and their presence instills a certain technological
exhibitionism: for instance, in front of Richard Neutra's
bedroom, there's a small terrace, enclosed by a sophisticated triple-layer (a sheet of glass, a mosquito net and
curtains), sliding along a cantilevered steel section that
appears to float. Also now huge revolving aluminum
lâminas, connecting the two floors, regulate the sunlight
on the facade towards the lake: what a large tree, now
scorched, used to do quite effectively, is now realized
by means of a mechanical, mobile and reflective device,
which is, above all, somewhat flashy.*
José Vela Castillo, *Richard Neutra: Un Lugar para el
Orden. Un Estudio sobre la Arquitectura Natural*[25]

Originally built in 1932, on a plot of 378 square meters (18
meters wide x 21 meters deep), VDL House is today surrounded by seven other works signed by the architect and
developed between the 1940s and 1960s: David and Berdine
Treweek House (1948); Sokol House (1948); Reunion House
(1949 1950), now Dion Neutra House; the office headquarters of Richard Neutra (1950); Wong Yew House (1957);
Inadomi House (1960) and Kambara House (1960).

Despite being internationally recognized for the innovative project for the Lovell House– considered a pioneering
example of what historiography generally calls the International Style –, Neutra lived with chronic financial problems
and only came to build a house for his family when the
Dutch industrialist Cornelis Hendrik Van der Leeuw (1890-
1973) offered him a loan – as a tribute, the house was
named after the initials of its sponsor's surname.

Its wooden structure was designed to follow the same
structural modulation as the Lovell House (metallic) and,
with the collaboration of some local companies – who
donated material in exchange for being able to advertise

their companies –, Neutra was able to use aluminum plate
cladding on the external walls and an aluminium-glass-alu-
minium sandwich in the bathrooms for the thermal insulation of the house.[26] In 1939, shortly after the birth of his
youngest son, Raymond Richard Neutra, the architect built
an annex on the eastern end of the plot, for the garage and
a guest apartment, connected to the main volume of the
house through a walkway. This new H-shaped implantation
transformed the garden, which used to advance up to the
entrance at the back, making up a private patio. In 1963,

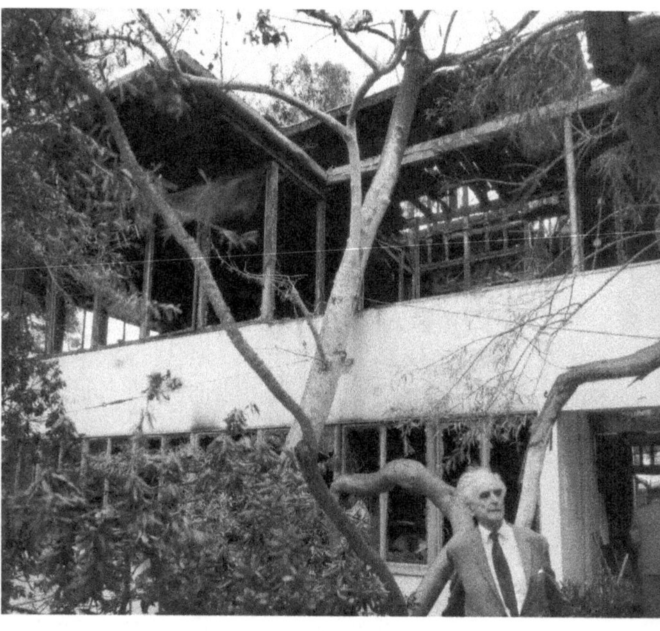

VDL House 2, 1963 fire, Los Angeles.
Richard Neutra, 1965-1966. Photo
Julius Shulman. © J. Paul Getty Trust
Archive. Getty Research Institute, Los
Angeles (2004.R.10)

however, the house suffered a fire that almost completely destroyed it, being rebuilt two years later. It is this second version of the house that is the focus of our commentary.

In the epigraph of this subchapter, the Spanish architect and researcher José Vela Castillo reveals his discomfort regarding the mobile vertical louvers of the VDL 2 House (1965-1966) – according to him a "mechanical, mobile and reflective artifact, which is, above all, somewhat flashy." The strange presence of elements that should not be there, as they do not represent the more austere style of Neutra's early works, attest to how categorical definitions can obscure the understanding of a work. First of all, it is necessary to say that Vela Castilho seems unaware of the severe physical and climatic changes that had taken place on the site. Silverlake, which was once located about 30 meters from the front door of the house, has been remodeled, decreasing in size and now standing at a distance of 180 meters. This increase in distance and the decrease in the area of the lake resulted in higher average temperature in the region, which required a new solution for the façade in question.

However, the main point, which is absent from the Spanish author's analysis, is the understanding that the use of louvers reveals rather an improvement in Neutra's architectural solutions to his concerns about climate issues, which is present in his work ever since the project for the Kaufmann House (1946-1947). Like Thomas Hines in relation to the panel of the Los Angeles Hall of Records building, the movable vertical louvers appear as "uncanny" for Castillo, and their presence is interpreted as a mere technological spectacle. The unfamiliar becomes "excessive," "flashy," "exhibitionist."

The professional relationship with the Swiss landscaper and architect Gustav Ammann in 1919, early on in Richard Neutra's career, the climatic and environmental shock of an Austrian in the Southwest of the United States and the contact with the Californian naturalist wave, with special emphasis on the figure of Philip Lovell, were important factors that explain the architect's interest in the relationship between architecture and the local landscape and climate. This interest triggered an architectural production that always sought to explore this relationship. And this continuous search, both in residential and school projects, took the architect to Puerto Rico – where he developed social projects (hospitals, schools and health centers) as a consultant to the Committee on Design of Public Works (1943-1945) – and then to the countries of South America (1945). Both experiences were vital for Neutra, who assimilated exceptional forms of sun and heat control found in Latin American works.

In the article "Sun Control Devices," published in the *Progressive Architecture* magazine in 1946, Neutra presents the detailed study he developed of the works and the various solutions he found in the countries he visited: canopies,

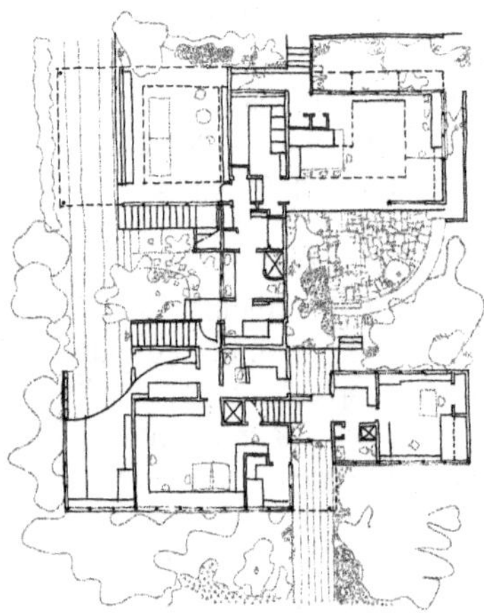

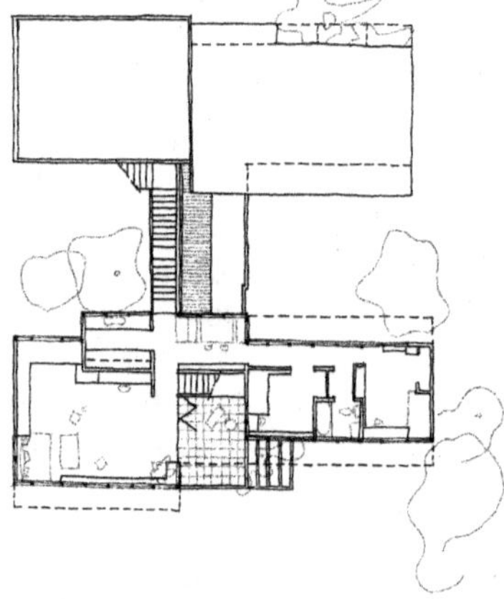

VDL House 1, ground floor and first floor plans, Los Angeles. Richard Neutra, 1932. Croquis Fernanda Critelli

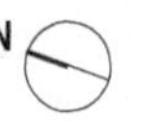
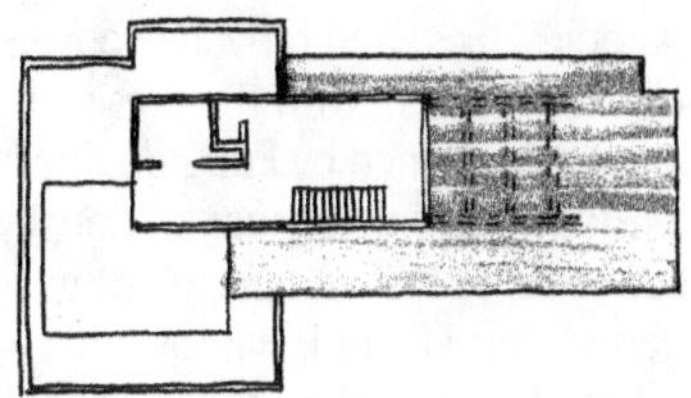

VDL House 2, ground floor, first floor
and cover plans, Los Angeles. Richard
Neutra, 1965-1966. Croquis Fernanda
Critelli

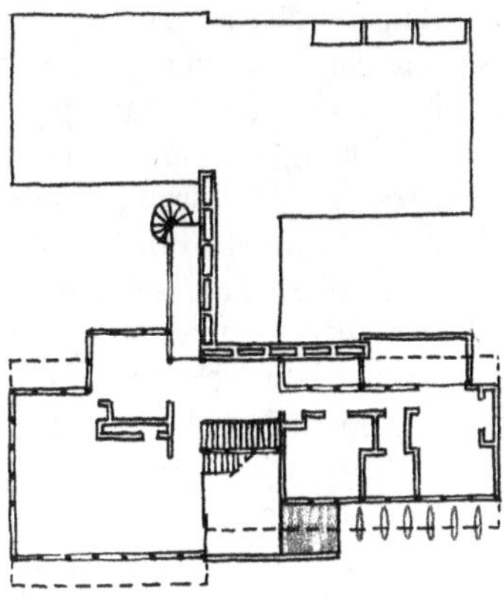

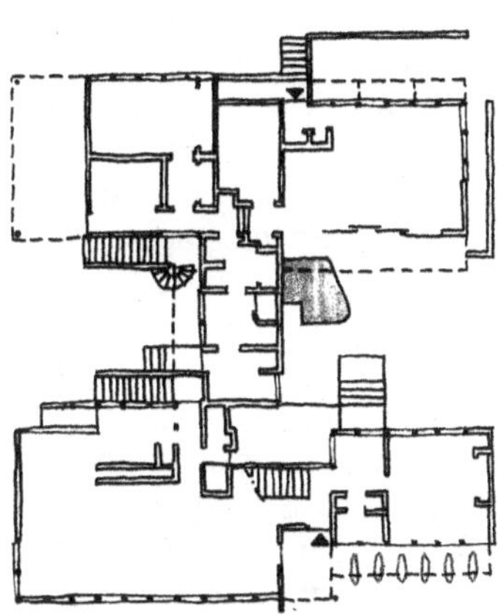

balconies, pierced canopies, fixed and movable louvers. These, in particular, are well documented, with the presence of the Leonidas Moreira Building, designed by Eduardo Kneese de Melo (São Paulo, 1942); the boat passenger station, by Atílio Correa Lima (Rio de Janeiro, 1937); an apartment building designed by the Argentine firm Ferrari, Hardoy and Kurchan (Buenos Aires), where the louver system patented by Julio Villalobos was used; and also the MES, in this case an example of the use of horizontal movable louvers.[27]

Thus, his travels, his research and, of course, the publication of the article evidence his interest in this particular technical solution precisely during the process of rebuilding his own residence. The presence of the six movable vertical louvers on the Southeast façade of VDL House 2 cannot be reduced to mere technological exhibitionism, as José Castillo suggests; rather, it reflects a deep understanding of local specificities, as well as his interest in solutions developed in Latin America and re-elaborated by him throughout his career, in a process of reading and interpretation.

It is also worth pointing out the prominence given to the louvers in the exhibition and in the homonymous catalog *Brazil Builds*, by MoMA of New York. According to the press release divulged at the time, the museum presented to the public, in the central section of the exhibition, "Brazil's great contribution to modern architecture: the control of heat and light externally through sun breaks rather than internally through expensive artificial air cooling or inadequate Venetian blinds."[28] In addition to the photographs taken by Kidder Smith and design drawings, there were models of movable and fixed brises-soleil, as well as vertical and horizontal.[29]

Regarding VDL House 2, Thomas Hines omits the presence of movable vertical louvers, despite the fact that they are quite remarkable no partido and in the final outcome. This symptomatic silence is occupied by the personal accounts made by Dione, the architect's wife, and by their son Dion (also an architect), eight years after Neutra's death.

As in the Neutra & Alexander partnership, Hines reports quarrels and disputes between father and son, both on personal and professional levels. According to him, Dion's plans to leave his father's office and start his own "however, [his plans] were again curtailed by another emergency, which pulled him back closer to the neutral architectural orbit."[30]

According to the historian, father and son decided to plan the reconstruction of the house together:

> When it came to designing and planning 'VDL 2' on the site of the house they had shared so long, it seemed somehow natural to both father and son that they should share in conceptualizing its new form. Perhaps both hoped that this joint enterprise might heal old wounds and prepare the way for a steadier relationship. They agreed the new house would rise on the old slab, and would employ the old modules, but decided to take appropriate cognizance of the changes in Neutra's style and ideas since he built the first house thirty years before. Larger panels of glass, more mirrors and reflecting pools, and softer, more varied textures and materials would give new meaning to VDL 2.[31]

As in the analysis regarding the period of partnership with Robert Alexander, Hines privileges here, as an explanatory factor, the relationship between father and son, which is certainly important, but not decisive for the final configuration of the reform. Richard Neutra, who always maintained a visceral control over his works, vehemently defended his architectural ideals and convictions from the original conception of the project up until the actual construction. As Thomas Hines' narrative itself shows, even though it is a work signed in partnership, Neutra is responsible for the most crucial decisions of the project in terms of structure and also in terms of construction techniques, technological innovations,

choice of materials and the final aesthetics – which makes
the muting of the louvers in Hines' analysis even stranger.

Thomas Hines' deadly silence and José Castillo's assessment of the louvers as technical and formal exaggeration
result from the same problem: both refuse to observe an
important change – or rather, transformation – undergone
by Neutra's work since the mid-1940s. After the experience
in Puerto Rico and the first trip to South America, Richard
Neutra carried out a decantation of the solutions adopted
by Latin American colleagues for issues that also troubled
him. The use of movable vertical louvers as a solution for
sun-damaged façades in the first project that he developed
after the reconn trip – the Kaufmann House – is strange only
to those who ignore this decantation.

VDL House 2, Los Angeles. Richard
Neutra, 1965-1966. Photos Julius
Shulman. © J. Paul Getty Trust
Archive. Getty Research Institute, Los
Angeles (2004.R.10)

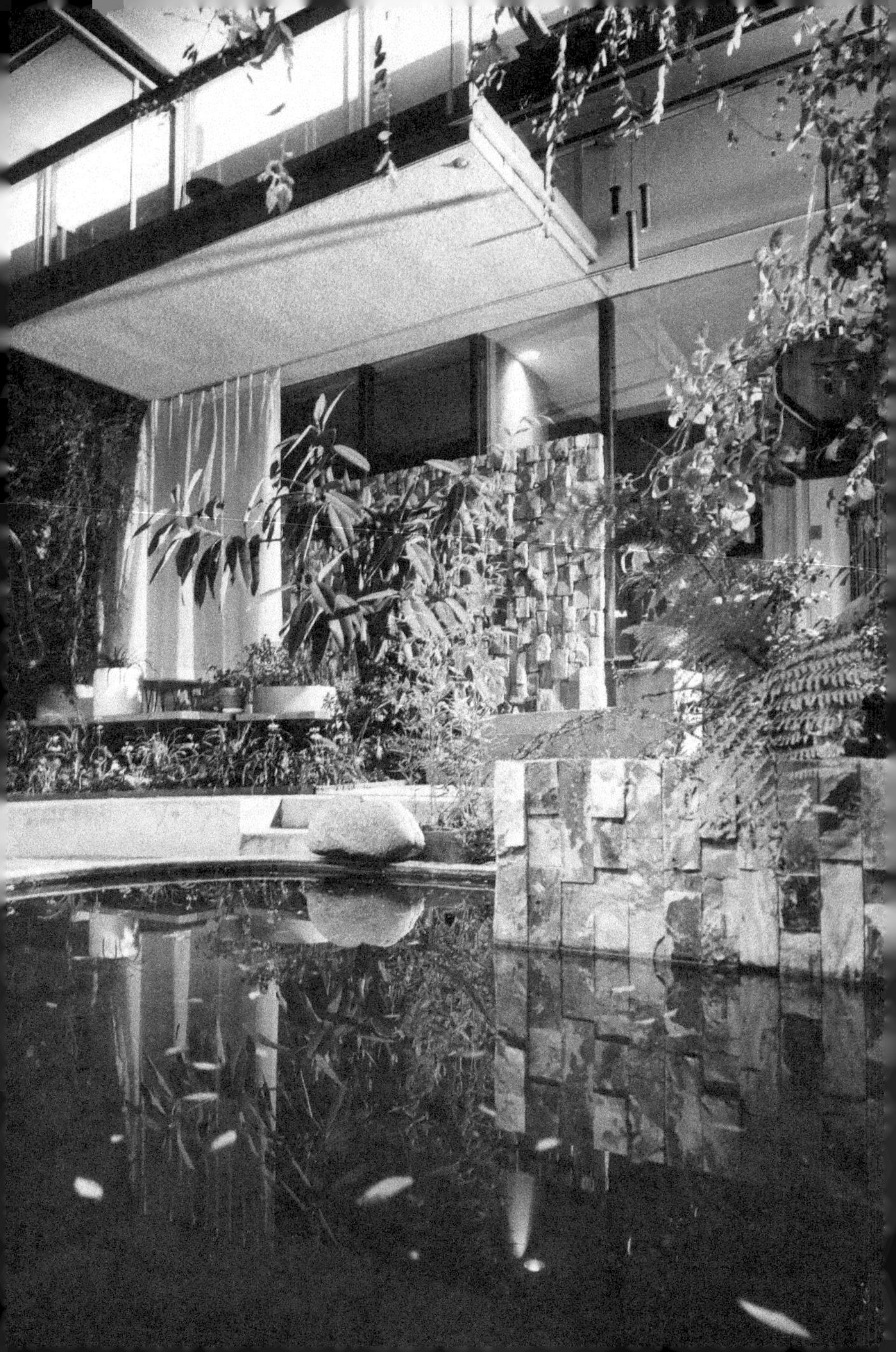

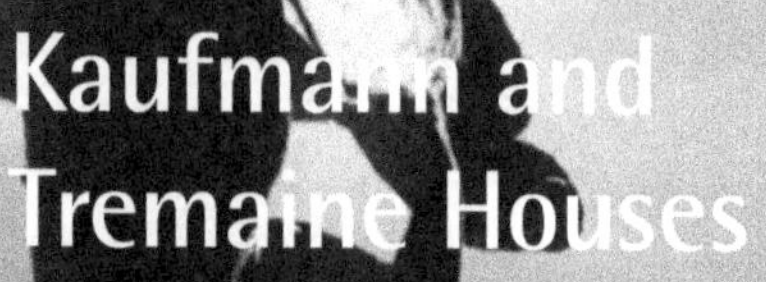

Kaufmann and Tremaine Houses

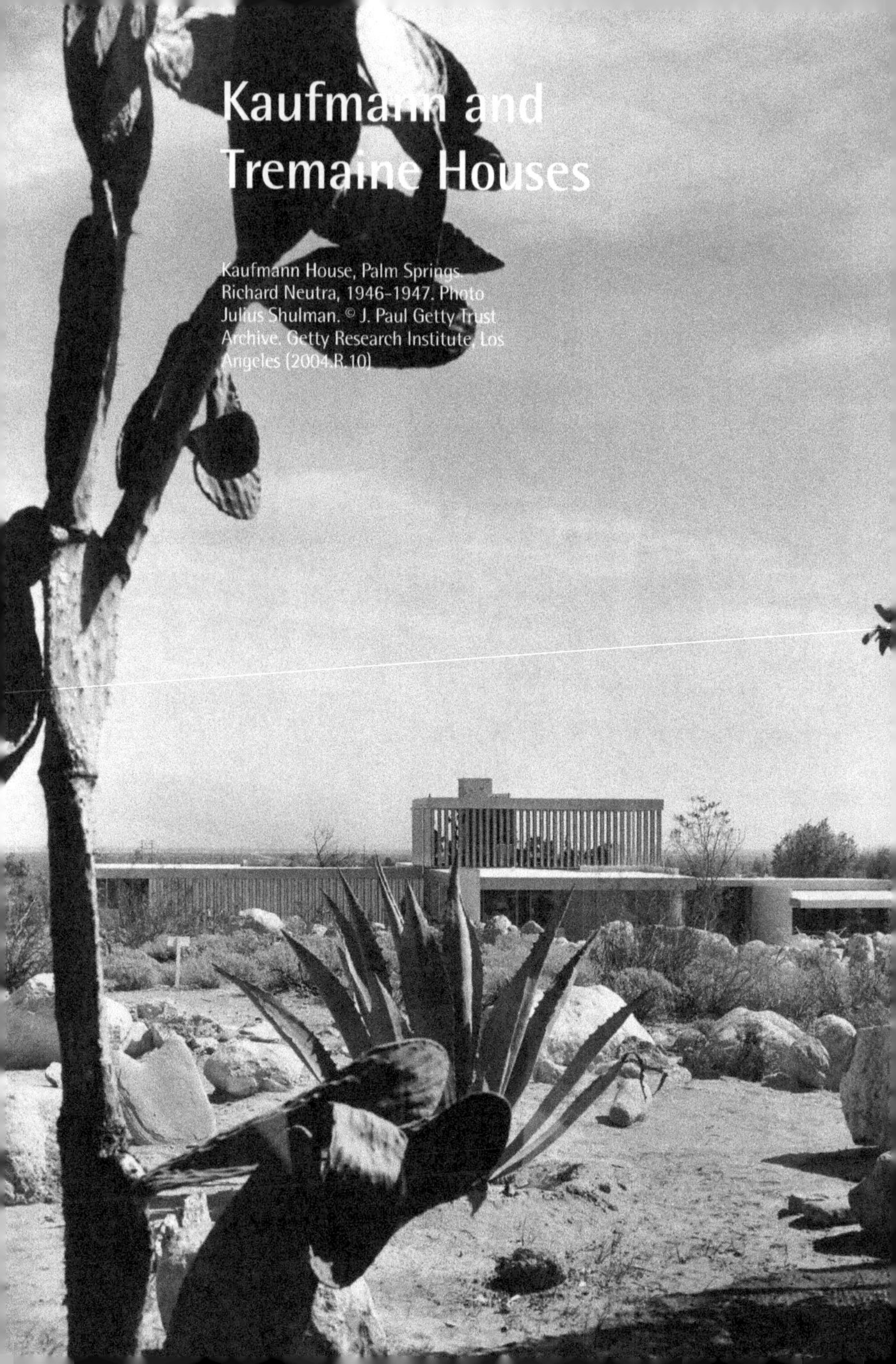

Kaufmann House, Palm Springs.
Richard Neutra, 1946–1947. Photo
Julius Shulman. © J. Paul Getty Trust
Archive. Getty Research Institute, Los
Angeles (2004.R.10)

*Two years before the book on the Puerto Rico projects
and the Tremaine House construction, more or less at
the time he was beginning the Tremaine design (which
was in fact initially sited in Arizona, not California),
he published an article that presented a number of
instruments for modulating solar effects and breezes, as
built in South America by Neutra himself and by other
architects such as Lúcio Costa and Oscar Niemeyer. [...]
All of these devices, and the aims they represent, must
be kept in mind when considering the elaboration of
ceiling or roof space in Tremaine House.*
David Leatherbarrow, *Uncommon Ground: Architecture,
Technology, and Topography*[32]

Unlike the previously mentioned comments by Thomas Hines
and José Castillo, David Leatherbarrow discerned in Richard Neutra's work some elements that may point to a Latin
America influence. Faced with the strangeness of something
he cannot explain, the researcher and professor at the
University of Pennsylvania speculates on a possible connection with South American architects Lúcio Costa and Oscar
Niemeyer. However, demonstrating the pull of established
patterns of thoughst, Leatherbarrow does not put his own
intuition into his analysis, going on to attribute the environmental architectural elements to the architect's previous
trajectory.

Even though the works in Latin America and the study
carried out in the article "Sun Control Devices" had an effect
on the Tremaine House project (1948) – as they certainly
did –, Leatherbarrow nevertheless links "the elaboration of
ceilings or roofs" to projects in Puerto Rico, when Neutra
had not even had contact with Latin American architects
or known their works personally yet. In other words, almost
like in a Freudian slip, Leatherbarrow sheds light on a new
and important interpretation regarding Richard Neutra's
architecture, but ends up reaffirming the conventional

explanation: the endogenous development of his work. Thus, hegemonic historiography refuses to carefully examine the estrangement caused by Neutra's mature work in the Anglo-Saxon context. Digging for the origin and circumstances of this discomfort would inevitably put him in front of what he had originally envisioned – the presence of Latin American architecture –, precisely what this book intends to do by identifying these silenced elements.

At the Tremaine House, there's an aspect overlooked by critics and very little explored in most of the available iconography about it: the presence of wooden-coated movable vertical louvers. Placed on the west façade, under the conjunction of a slab and beam of reinforced concrete, and landing on the terrace, the louvers provide shade to the core of the house. The fact that they are movable allows residents to adjust them according to the intensity of sunlight, which moves along this façade during the afternoon. Clearly, besides an aesthetic issue, they address a thermal comfort issue.

Taking up David Leatherbarrow's comment, a second point comes to mind.

Before Tremaine House, Richard Neutra designed the Kaufmann House (1946-1947), in the period that followed his work in Puerto Rico and his trip through South America. Considered one of the architect's masterpieces, the residence was designed at the time when the article "Sun Control Devices" was written. In other words, while organizing his considerations – and also his photographs of Latin American works – in an article, Neutra designed his first work using brise-soleil.[33]

Thomas Hines, on the other hand, sees in Casa Kaufmann a sophisticated effort in terms of responding to climate issues, without, however, pointing to any relationship with Latin American architecture, not even with the experiences in Puerto Rico. "With its overhangs, adjustable louvers, and radiant floor heating and cooling systems, the house was a model for its time of sophisticated climate control."[34] Very different, however, from his opinion about Tremaine House: "a project that foresaw the "more informal aesthetics of the 1950s."[35]

For Hines, unlike Casa Kaufmann, where all the facades are sculptural, the most interesting views of Casa Tremaine are the North and East facades, where the overhang – formed by the cantilevered reinforced concrete slabs and beams – floats over the large panels of glass.[36] Interestingly, the photo used to illustrate the aspect he appreciates was taken at a stage prior to the installation of the louvers. In fact, there is no mention of these elements in Hines' analysis of the house. It is not known for sure when the work was completed, but it is certain that they were part of the project since the initial drawings, and it is possible to identify them in the photographs that illustrate the publication by Willy Boesiger about the works by Richard Neutra made between 1927 and 1950.[37] Barbara Lamprecht also comments on the installation of the brises on the western façade, which is sunnier, protecting the core of the living room: "On the west side of the 'social quarters', Neutra placed detailed, revolving redwood shade louvers at the edge of the overhang."[38]

The first experiments with louvers, present at Kaufmann and Tremaine houses, will appear again in projects already discussed here for the Los Angeles Hall of Records (1962) and for the reconstruction of the VDL House 2 (1965-1966), but their use was not limited to these projects. In the total set of the architect's works, twelve projects were identified featuring movable vertical louvers,[39] four with fixed vertical louvers,[40] another two where both modalities are applied,[41] and two featuring fixed horizontal louvers.[42] Its use, therefore, becomes quite recurrent after Neutra's first contact with South American architecture and the subsequent publication of the article "Sun Control Devices." With such data in hand, José Castillo's statement about the louvers of the VDL House 2 being a mere "technological exhibitionism,"

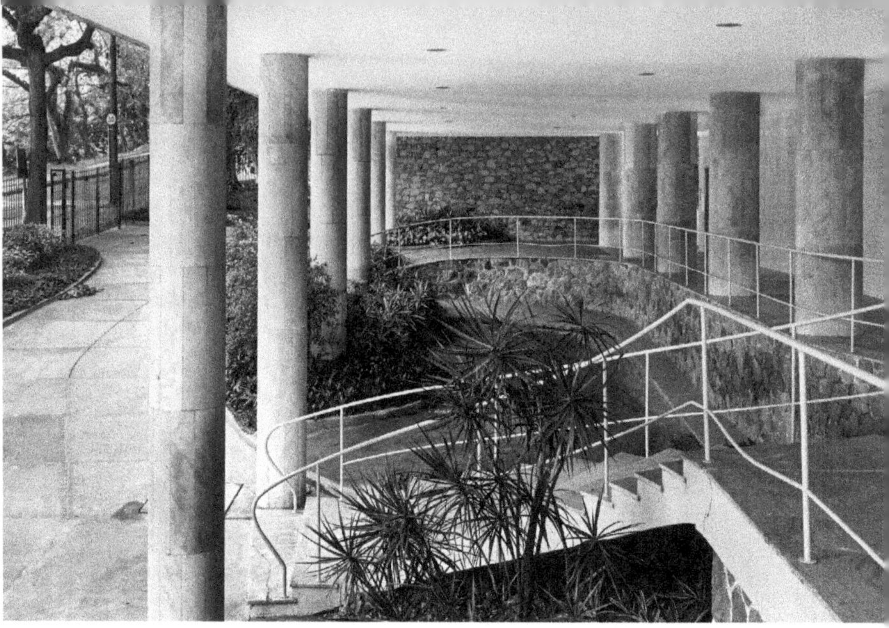

Guinle Park, Rio de Janeiro, Brazil.
Lúcio Costa, 1954. Photo Nelson Kon

without precedent in the architect's previous work, proves to be unfounded. At the same token, Thomas Hines and David Leatherbarrow's choice to exclude the presence of the movable louvers from their analysis of Tremaine House also becomes unreasonable.

In this project, Neutra pays the same attention to climate issues as in the Kaufmann House – louvers on the most sun-damaged section of the façade, elongated overhangs shading the interior of the residence, permanent ventilation through the gaps between beam and slab and a heating system for the terrace floor. However, in Hines' analysis, the Tremaine House does not represent the same model of "sophisticated climate control" as the house in Palm Springs. Instead, the historian dwells on the more imposing presence of the stone walls on the south façade of the house (the entrance façade).

The entrance front of the Tremaine house, on the other hand, with its open garages and relatively dull expanses of flagstones diaper walls, constitutes the building's least impressive façade. [...] The large natural boulders that cover the sites of both houses seem to meld more successfully with the occasional and crisply trimmed flagstone walls of the Kaufmann house than with Neutra's more insistently texture use of the same material at the Tremaine house.[43]

That the use of stone walls was greater in terms of area at Tremaine House than at Kaufmann House, there is no dispute. However, the logic of their presence in both projects is the same: while functioning as visual barriers protecting the privacy of intimate life, they also contribute to the entrance of the house, establishing an interplay with the surrounding nature. The manufactured, almost vernacular tectonics contrast with the purist and industrialized aesthetics that

Kaufmann House, ground floor and first floor plan, Palm Springs. Richard Neutra, 1946-1947. Croquis Fernanda Critelli

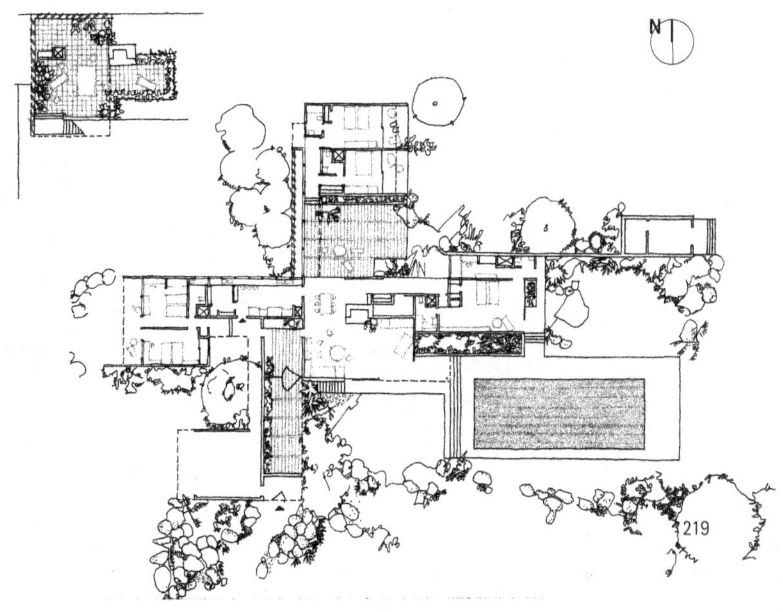

marked Neutra's works up until that moment – metallic or wooden structures, large glass sections, large white planes and the occasional exposed brick walls, usually associated with a fireplace. Closer examination of the architect's works reveals that the use of stone walls was recurrent after 1945: in total, we have identified 36 projects that resort to this particular aesthetic and materiality.[44]

At first, the use of the stone could be attributed simply to the relationship with Frank Lloyd Wright, a mentor that Neutra has always admired. However, it is not possible to discard the prominence that these stone walls, featured almost like a mosaic, had in Brazilian modern architecture – for instance, the residential buildings designed by Lúcio Costa for the Guinle Park (1943-1954) and the Antônio Ceppas Building (1946), designed by Jorge Machado Moreira – with landscaping, tiles and ceramic panel by Roberto Burle Marx –, both visited by Richard Neutra during his November 1945 trip. As in these Brazilian works, this raw element emerges in the facades that Neutra designed, making the relationship between architecture and landscape even more intense.

Understanding the presence of this materiality – the stone walls – as a direct response to the arid surroundings of the Kaufmann House is a simple operation, which does not require the critic to assume any other relationship that could explain such use. However, the same thinking cannot be applied to Tremaine House. The particularity of the surroundings seems to make Thomas Hines uncomfortable when trying to understand the recurrence of the material. The discomfort with the new element points to the existence of a relationship that the American historian does not seem willing to admit: the exchange of ideas flowing from South America to North America, and vice-versa; the real interest and identification that Richard Neutra showed in relation to Latin American architecture – with special emphasis on Brazilian architecture –; and the way he incorporated it to his projects from the second half of the 1940s onwards.

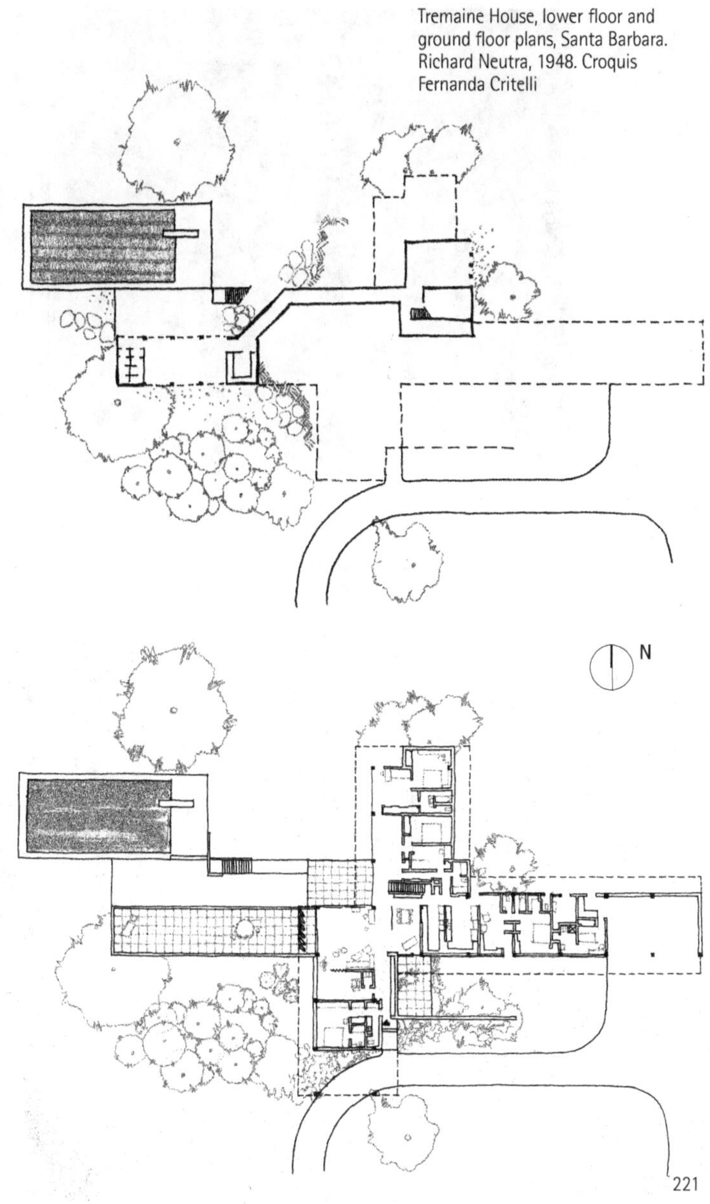

Tremaine House, lower floor and ground floor plans, Santa Barbara. Richard Neutra, 1948. Croquis Fernanda Critelli

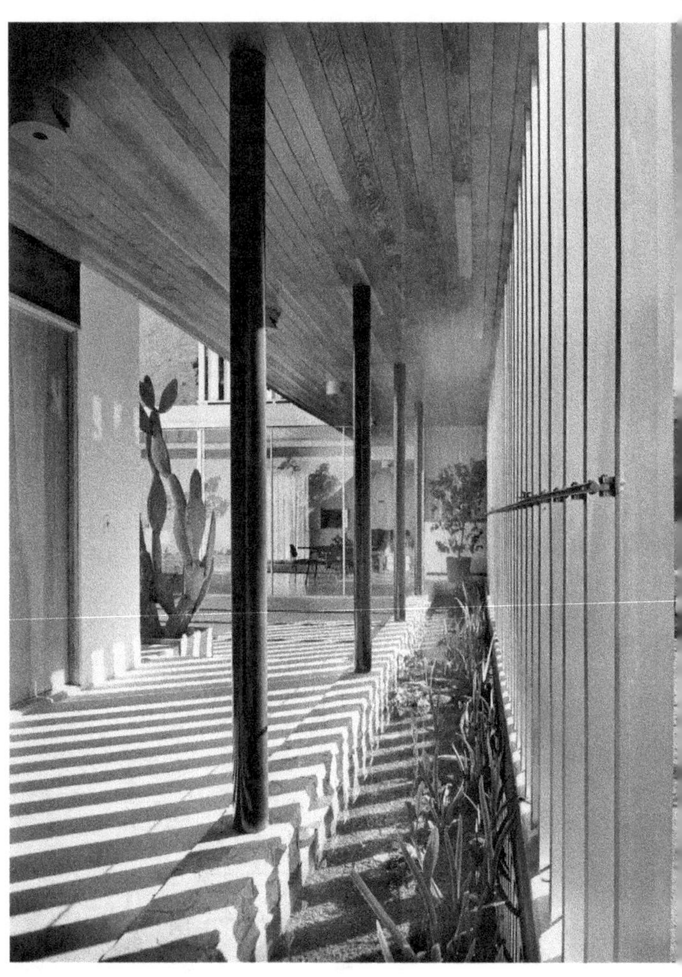

Kaufmann House, Palm Springs.
Richard Neutra, 1946-1947. Photo
Julius Shulman. © J. Paul Getty Trust
Archive. Getty Research Institute, Los
Angeles (2004.R.10)

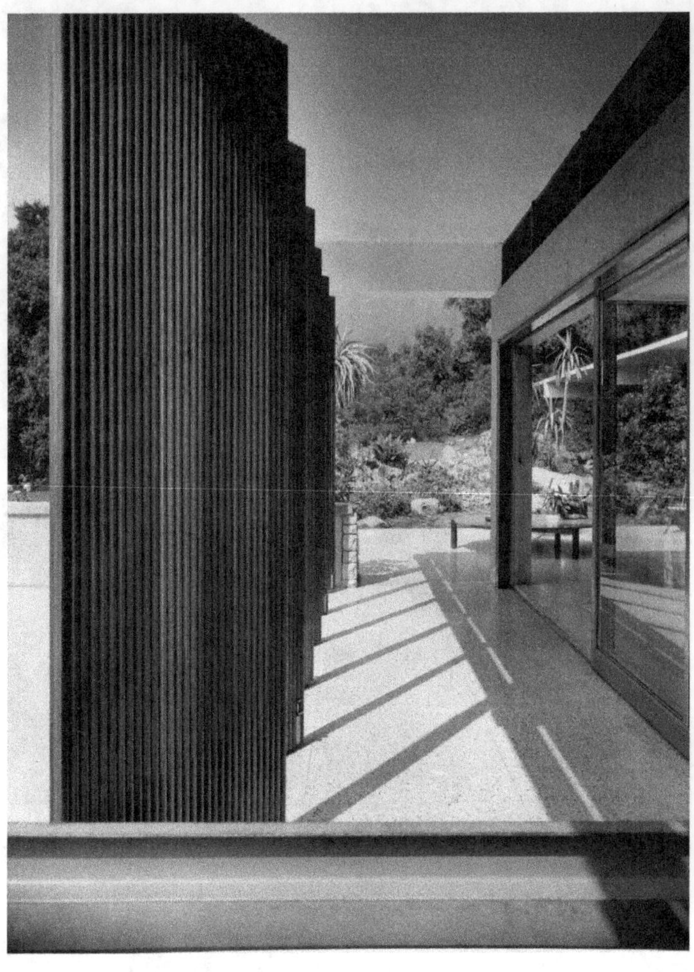

Tremaine House, Santa Barbara.
Richard Neutra, 1948. Photo Julius
Shulman. © J. Paul Getty Trust Archive.
Getty Research Institute, Los Angeles
(2004.R.10)

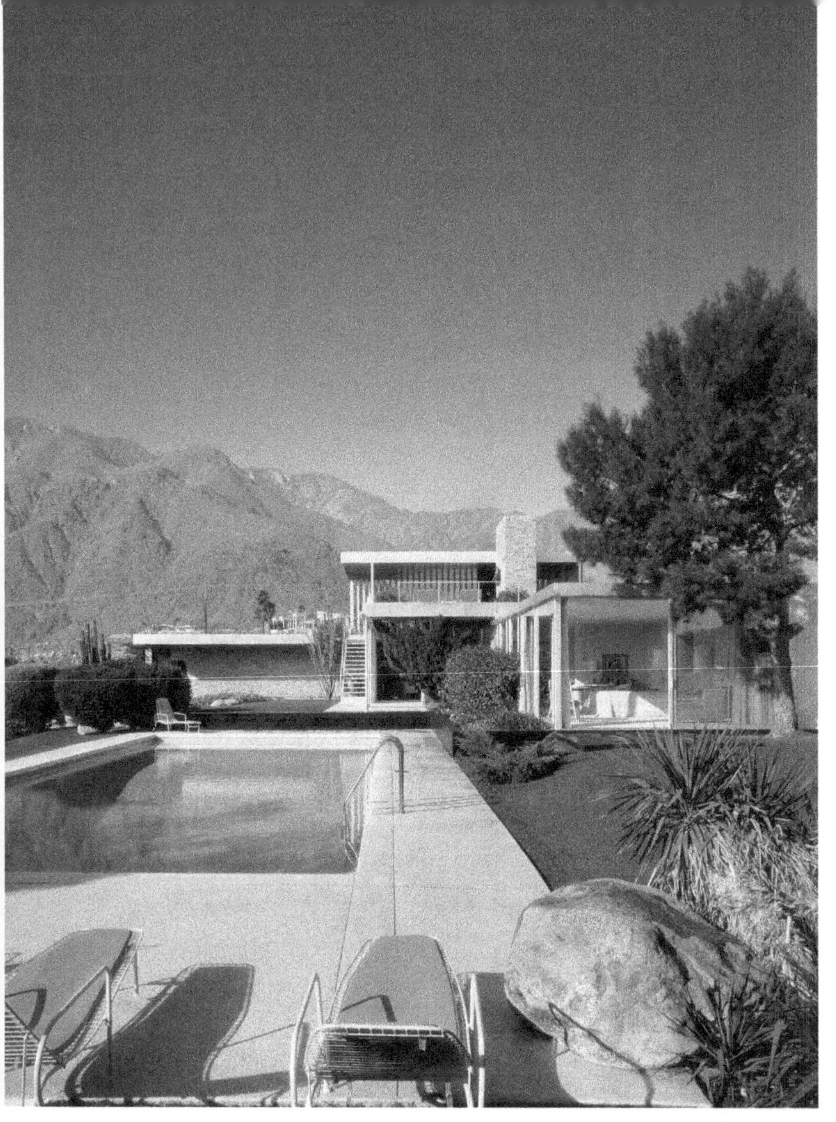

Kaufmann House, Palm Springs.
Richard Neutra, 1946-1947. Photos
Julius Shulman. © J. Paul Getty Trust
Archive. Getty Research Institute, Los
Angeles (2004.R.10)

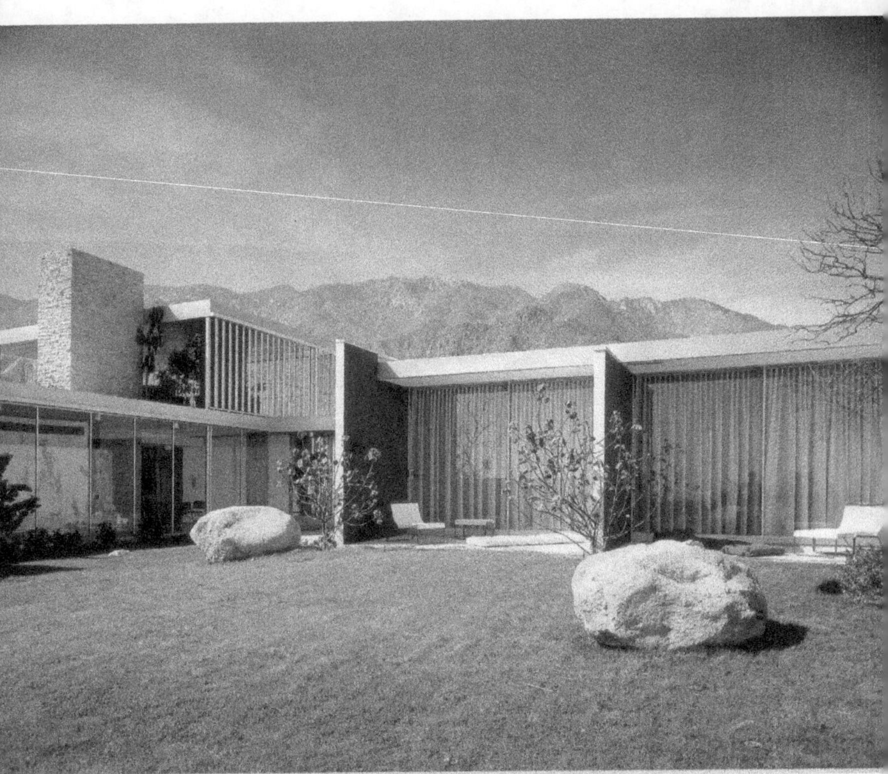

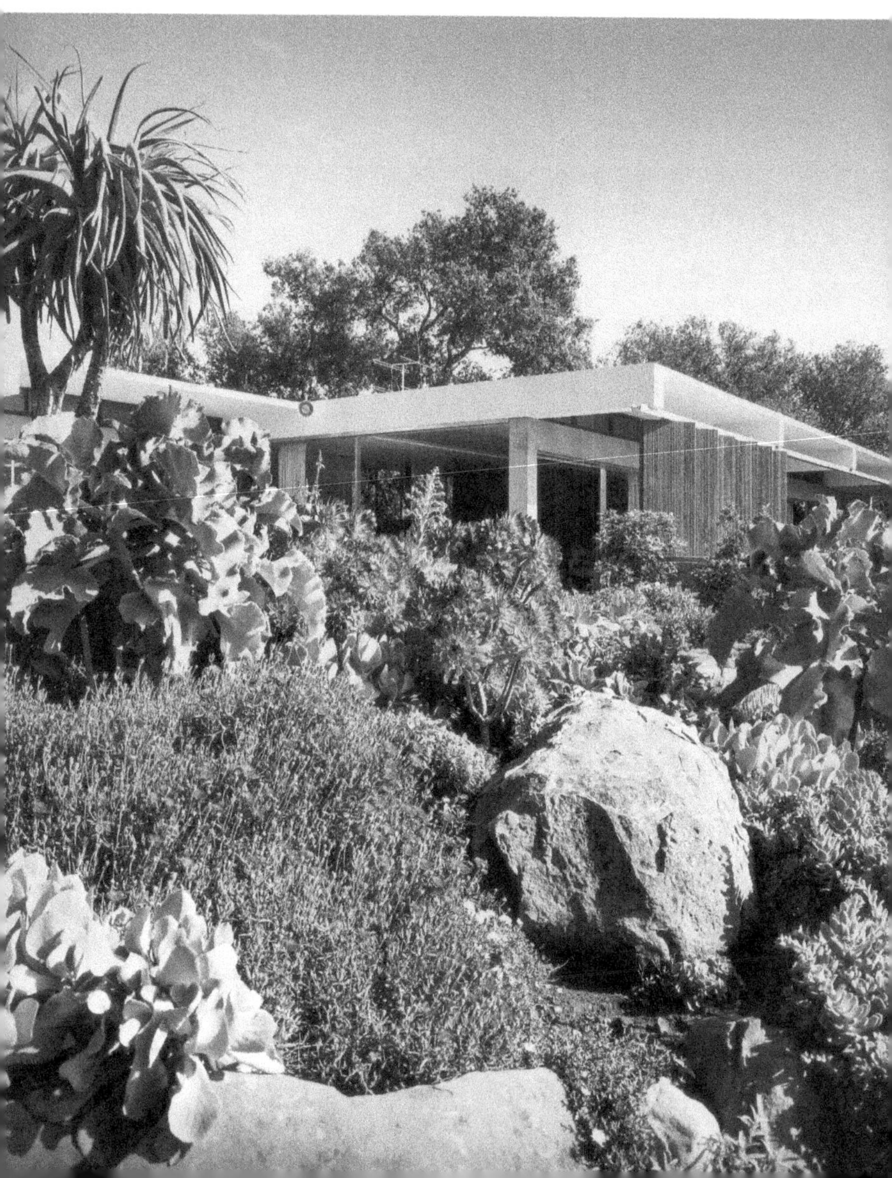

Tremaine House, Santa Barbara. Richard
Neutra, 1948. Photos Julius Shulman. © J.
Paul Getty Trust Archive. Getty Research
Institute, Los Angeles (2004.R.10)

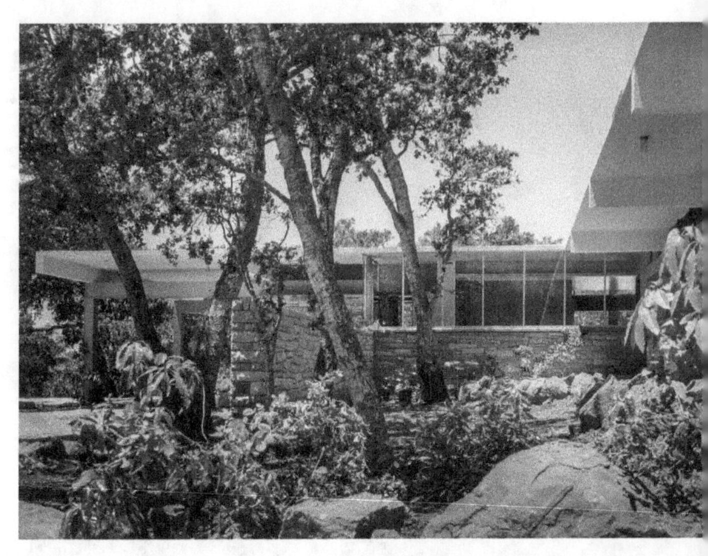

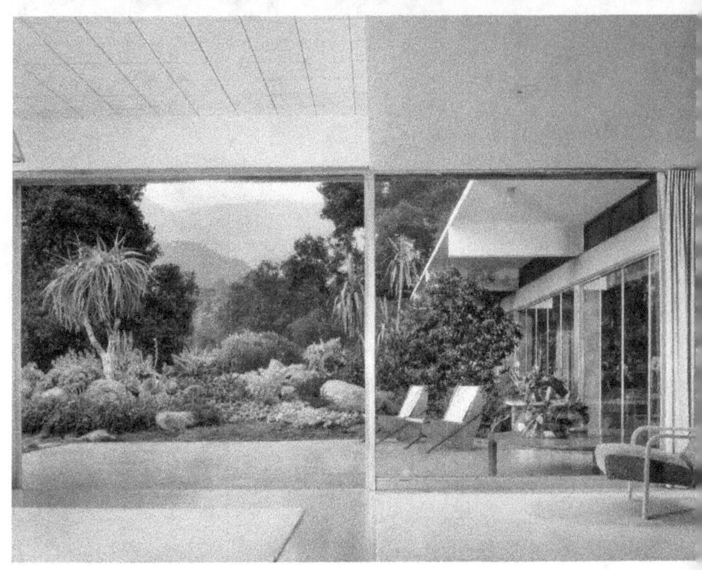

United States Embassy in Karachi

United States Embassy,
Karachi, Pakistan. Richard Neutra,
1955-1958. Photo Julius Shulman.
© J. Paul Getty Trust Archive. Getty
Research Institute, Los Angeles
(2004.R.10)

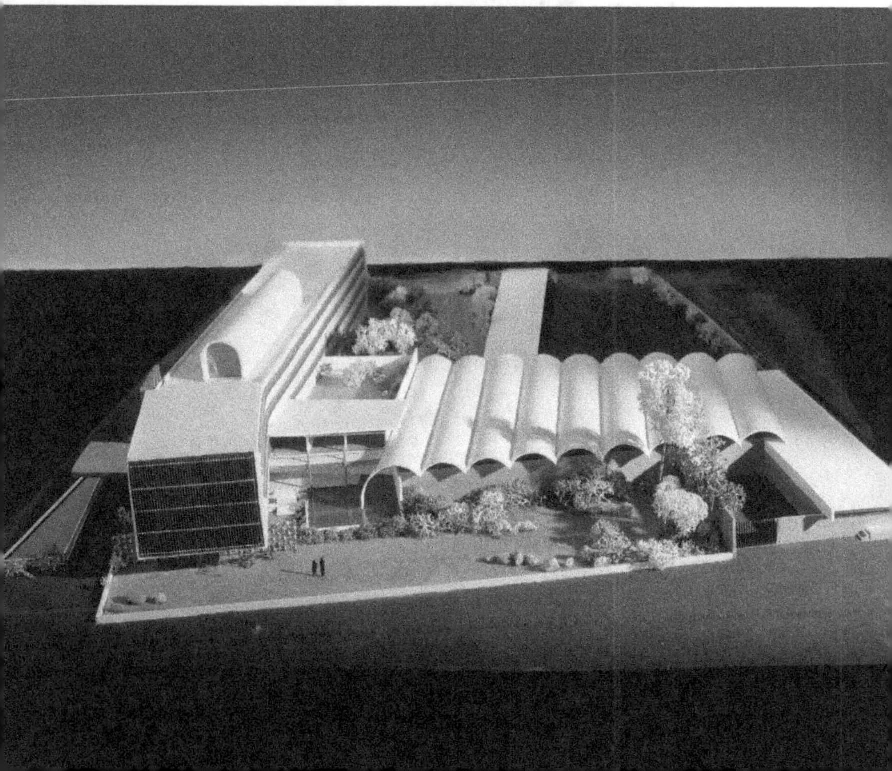

There are many aspects to be addressed in Thomas Hines'
commentary; the first one concerns the program to build
embassies abroad. Taking up the discussions in the first
chapter, this program was part of a larger effort by the
United States to project itself as a world power. For this, the
new embassies should draw "hailed as evidence of American
goodwill and commitment, and their modern architecture,
introduced in the late 1940s, has come to symbolize the
openness of public diplomacy."[46] That is, these new buildings
should represent the country's prosperity, technology and
innovation, as well as – in a period prior to the attack on
the Embassy in Saigon, Vietnam (1965) – the generosity and

goodwill of the Americans, in this case, through ample and accessible spaces.

The monumentality, criticized by Thomas Hines both in the Karachi project and in other embassies of the same period, was not a product of the architects' whim, but a requirement of the Foreign Building Operations – FBO.[47] The agency had a committee responsible for evaluating the projects, which were only approved if they met all the stipulated demands. The case of the Neutra & Alexander embassy was no different:

> The AAC [Architectural Advisory Committee][48] severely criticized Neutra & Alexander's first Karachi presentation, saying that it 'gave the impression of being a commercial enterprise similar to a mail order business.' They demanded a new 'part', but did not discuss replacing the architect.[49]

In his analysis of the project, Hines once again relies on the testimony of Robert Alexander – collected eight years after the death of Richard Neutra – to justify aesthetic decisions that were foreign to him and which, in his opinion, did not correspond to Neutra's architecture. However, the idea that Alexander stumbled across the cylindrical molds for casting concrete vault forms seems to be a weak argument when confronted with the demands of the AAC. Even more so if you consider the Maturity of Neutra, who could very well turn mere chance into a working premise. The expressive use of vaults, conferring monumental character, was present, by instance, in the Igreja da Pampulha (Belo Horizonte, 1940), by Oscar Niemeyer; at the Conjunto Pedregulho School (Rio de Janeiro, 1946), by Affonso Eduardo Reidy; at the Rodoviária de Londrina (Londrina, 1948), by Vilanova Artigas; and at the Auto Posto Clube dos 500 (Guaratinguetá, 1951-1953), by Oscar Niemeyer. As in the case of louvers, Richard Neutra was able to assimilate in his own way the formal and constructive issues of reinforced concrete that caught his attention in Brazilian architecture.

If it was in fact Alexander who found the suitable molds for the vaults of the warehouse building, it was up to Neutra, responsible for the final architectural decisions,[50] to seize the opportunity to develop an aesthetic possibility that was little explored in his work. In this context, his contact with Brazil is crucial in this search for plastic and formal freedom, especially at a "time when there was a need for a national identity that, while based on cultural heritage, also developed the parameters that defined the construction of the country's modernity -- present and future."[51] It was a time when Brazilian architects designed works that announced technical and aesthetic possibilities. In the case of vaults, their use makes it possible to overcome large empty spaces with fewer points of support[52] – the ideal case for a warehouse the size of the one designed for the Karachi Embassy (1955-1958).

As in Brazil, Pakista's industrialization and construction possibilities did not allow for the steel and wood projects characteristic of Richard Neutra's work. The answer, therefore, is the adoption of a reinforced concrete structure, as the architect had already done in the projects for Puerto Rico and the Tremaine and Alfred De Schulthess houses. However, opting for a warehouse that is roofed with an array of vaults goes beyond a simple answer to the materials available. It makes it possible to overcome large empty spaces with few support points – which is ideal when it comes to a storage area –, endowing the project with a particular character. In other words, it represents much more than "a meaningless and uninteresting series of vaults used to decorate the façade," as Thomas Hines put it. Perhaps because this character refers to Brazilian experiences, the historian sees it as an interference in Neutra's work, consequently attributing the idea to Robert Alexander. But the truth is that vaulted roofs, like louvers and artistic panels, show the dexterity of a mature architect who has studied with genuine attention the

Pedregulho Housing, Rio de Janeiro,
Brazil. Affonso Eduardo Reidy, 1946.
Photo Andres Otero

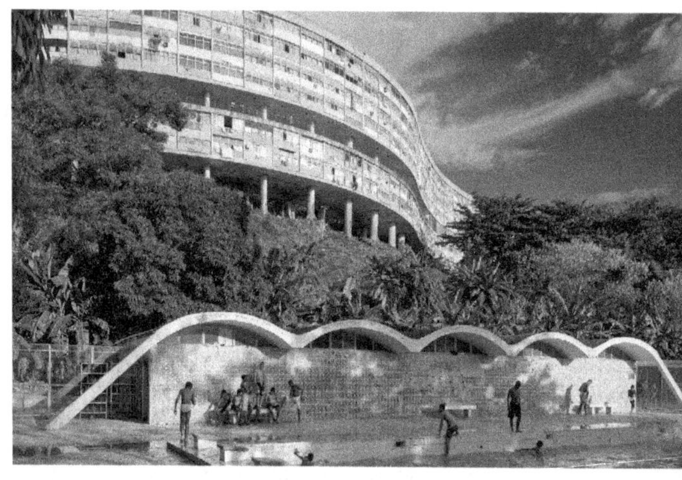

Pampulha Church, Belo Horizonte,
Brazil. Oscar Niemeyer, 1940. Photo
Victor Hugo Mori

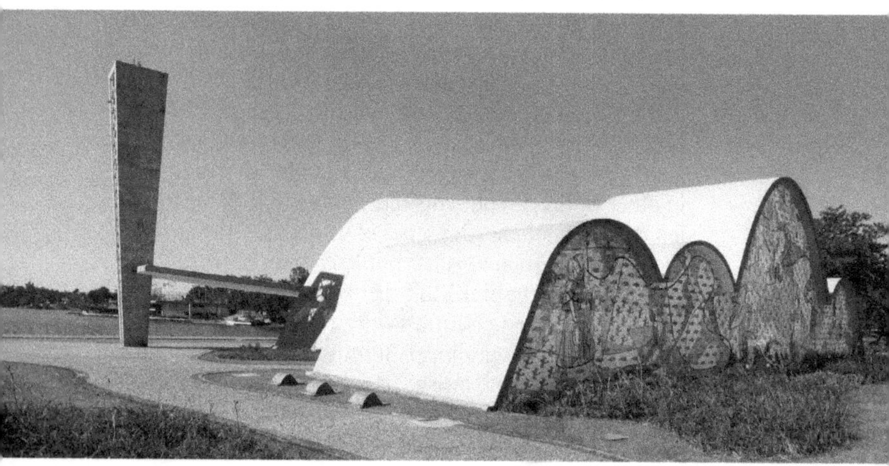

output of his colleagues, recognizing the issues that interested him and developing them in his own projects. Neutra
is, therefore, the agent of action who deliberately chooses
to align himself with a given architectural response and
interpret it in his later work, according to local needs and
conditions.

Another point that calls into question Thomas Hines'
hypothesis that the embassy project highlights the conflicts
of the Neutra & Alexander office is the publication of the
last two volumes of Willy Boesiger's collection, featuring
technical drawings (plan, sections and elevations), perspectives, photos of the scale model and the finished work. In
both books, the presence of the warehouse volume with the
vaulted roof is striking, especially in the photos and views of
the model. In addition, the analysis of the building's location makes important design decisions clear. First, the plot
location, delimited by three streets – a structural one to the
east and two more local in nature to the south and north –
suggests that the longer, three-floored administration building was designed to relate with the larger structural route
that it faces, while the lower volume of the warehouse was
designed for the smaller street. However, it is in the layout of
the driveway at the main entrance that Neutra defines the
most important look of his work.

Due to the angle of the curves and inclination of the
entrance, cars arriving on Collector Street (local route) would
stop under the marquee for the passenger to get out, then
exiting on Victoria Street (structural route). In other words,
when approaching the embassy, the visitor's eye is drawn to
the generous garden, visible from the street, rounded off by
this extensive low volume crowned by nine vaults of reinforced concrete. At the point closest to the administration
building, the last vault finds support in the ground curving
over a generous reflecting pool that, by reflection, creates
an illusion of continuity of the curve. As for the volume of
the administration, however, only the smaller façade is seen,

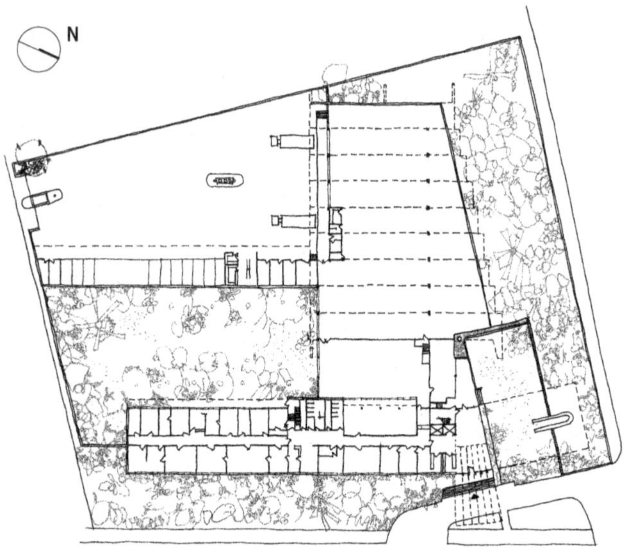

United States Embassy, ground floor
plan, Karachi, Pakistan. Richard

Neutra, 1955-1958. Croqui Fernanda
Critelli

marked by movable vertical louvers. This break from orthog-
onality, exerted precisely on the axis of the marquee, makes
this larger building entirely understandable only from a distance, that is, from the point of view of those moving away
along Victoria Street. It is difficult to imagine that such visual
poetics is the result of an impasse between two architects,
rather than the result of the aesthetic and design mastery of
a mature architect. It is even more difficult to ignore Richard
Neutra's trajectory and, more specifically, his enthusiasm for
modern Latin American architecture.

The material published by Boesiger shows that, between
the final project and the finished work, there were some
modifications – such as, for example, the rectangular volume
at the west end of the warehouse identified on the model –
an idea that was eventually abandoned. But it is clear that

the idea of a vaulted roof, representing the predominant visual impact on the way to the building, was already part of the project from the very beginning. The availability of the molds, as well as the local conditions, was the excuse for Neutra to try out a new aesthetic from the decantation and assimilation of Brazilian works that he had examined with great care and interest. In addition, the US Embassy in Karachi was not the only work on which Richard Neutra worked with reinforced concrete cascas. In 1963, he again proposed the use of vaults in the design for the laboratories of the University of Mymensingh, Bangladesh (not built).

United States Embassy, Karachi, Pakistan.
Richard Neutra, 1955-1958. Photo Julius
Shulman. © J. Paul Getty Trust Archive.
Getty Research Institute, Los Angeles
(2004.R.10)

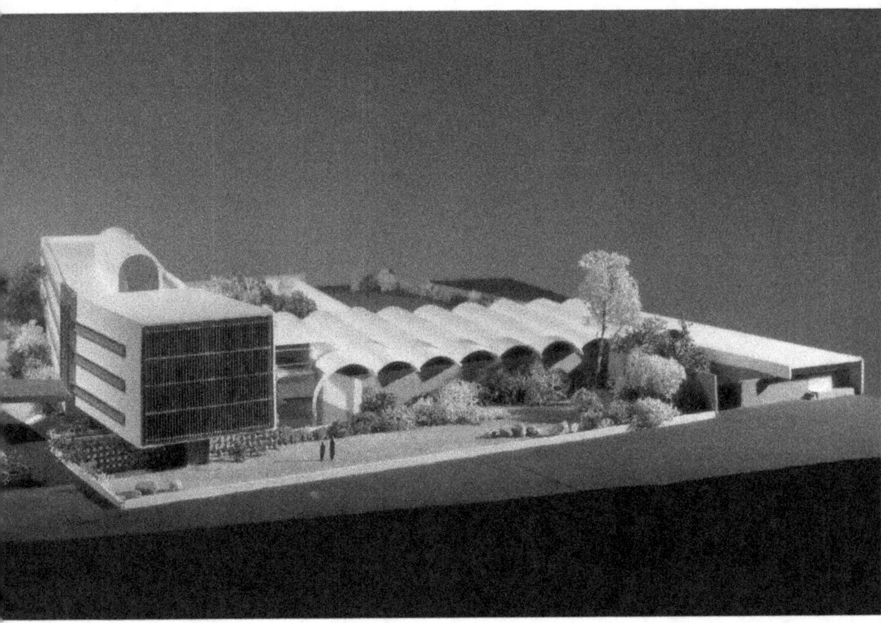

Once again, Thomas Hines expresses his estrangement regarding the project, blaming the delicate health condition in which the architect found himself at the time. According to the historian, organizational problems in Richard Neutra's practice led to a decline in the quality of large works in the 1960s.

> Despite such exceptions as the residentially scaled Mariner's Medical Center, a general sense of fatigue characterized Neutra's later, larger buildings – as indeed it did the work of so many of his modernist peers. Political and budgetary constraints could not alone account for the bland lifelessness of such late modernist monuments as the Roberson Arts Center, Binghamton, New York (1965); the University of Pennsylvania dormitories, Philadelphia (1969); the La Veta Medical Tower, Orange, California (1966); and the university laboratories for Mymensingh, Bangladesh [sic] (1963). As he had with numerous buildings in the Alexander years, Neutra reflected the anxious vulnerability of his modernist generation by attempting to 'warm' such structures with superfluous and disingenuous gimmicks.[53]

The persistence of the expression "warming Neutra's stark modernity" in Hines' commentary shows his discomfort regarding certain "uncanny" aspects of Richard Neutra's work. Formal and constructive solutions that blur the idea he holds about what is special in the output of the architect are seen as resulting from external factors, be it partnerships – Robert Alexander and Dion Neutra – or even the architect's health in the last years of his life. Hines approaches these projects by dismissing the influence of Richard Neutra's own professional career. Apart from the residences and a few small-sized commercial projects, where the austere modernism of the first works is evident – metallic or wooden structures, large glass sections and white walls, featuring a hegemony of industrial aesthetics –, the other projects are frowned upon. This is the case, for instance, of Alfred De Schulthess House (1956), in Havana. Built with a concrete structure and landscaping signed by Roberto Burle Marx, Thomas Hines sees it as a disaster, resulting from the architect's incompetence in dealing with large-scale projects.[54] The "uncanny" in Richard Neutra's work, which bothers

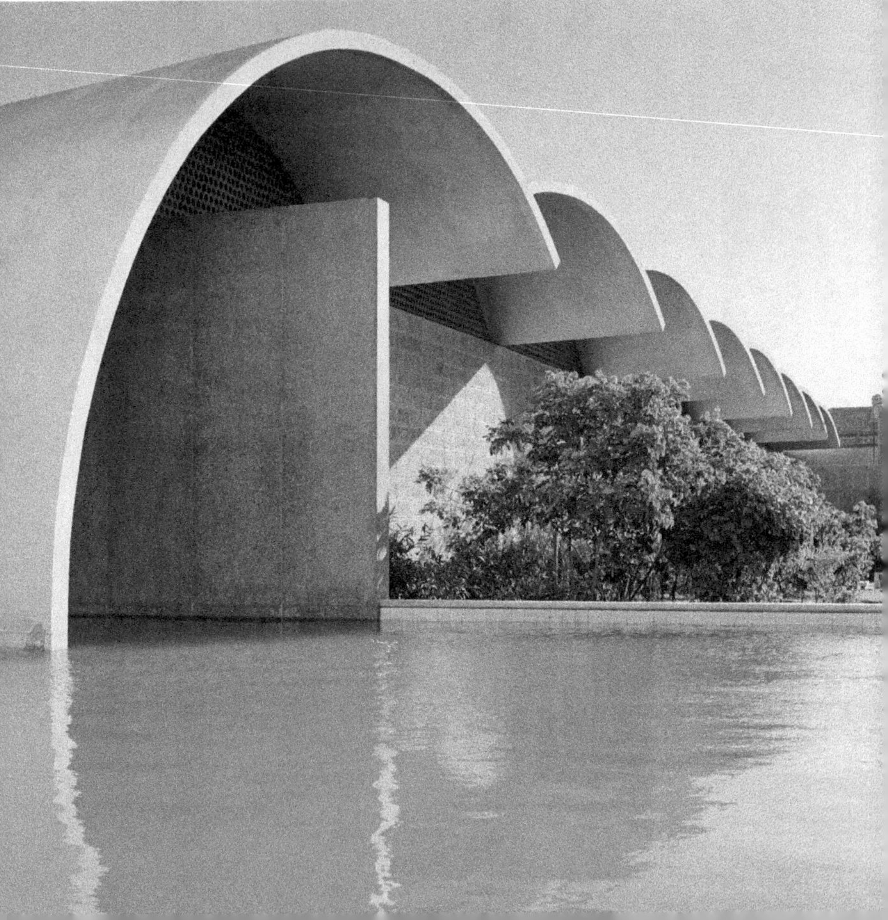

United States Embassy, Karachi,
Pakistan. Richard Neutra, 1955-1958.
Photo Rondal Partridge. Rondal
Partridge Archive

Hines and other historians, is the weird feeling that springs from something hidden that haunts them. The influence of modern Latin American architecture, especially Brazilian modernism, seems to take on that role – it's always there, but it does not fit into what is expected of the work of one of the most renowned architects of the 20th century. In any case, it is an influence that was assimilated and interpreted by an established architect with his own mind. An elaborate "misreading", developed when local conditions – climate, landscape and technology – demanded or allowed it.

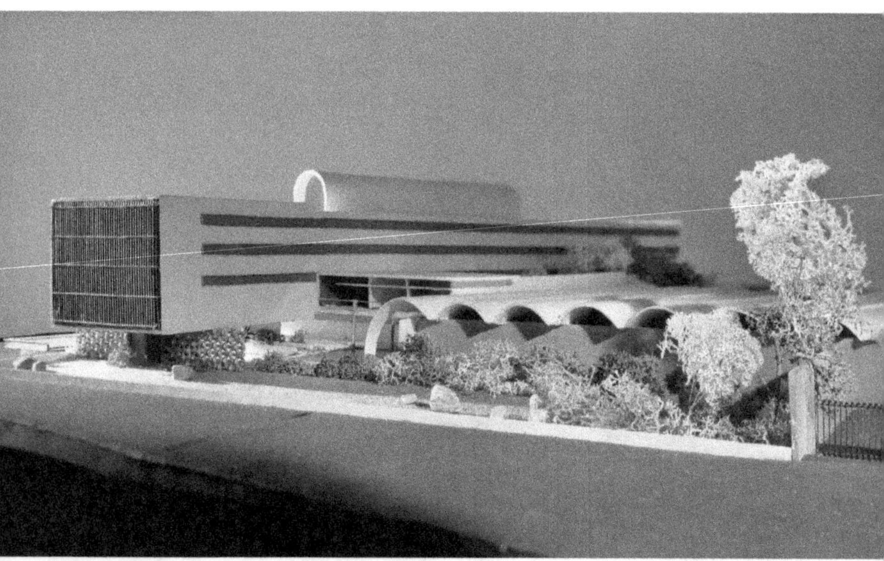

United States Embassy, Karachi,
Pakistan. Richard Neutra, 1955-1958.
Photo Julius Shulman. © J. Paul Getty
Trust Archive. Getty Research Institute,
Los Angeles (2004.R.10)

Thus, instead of repeating Thomas Hines' familiar readings – and estrangements –, what is proposed here is to contemplate these works with a new understanding. The architect's professional trajectory and his desire to stay connected with his colleagues around the world, whether through publications or correspondence, become an integral part of the narrative for analyzing the works. These aspects, therefore, are no longer seen with the pejorative connotation of a "Great Man act"[55] and become clues to the understanding of new aesthetics and new constructive materials that pop up in the course of his works. Moreover, as this is a research developed in Latin America, we try to escape from imported concepts and impositions and to relocate the episodes of historiography through a reverse perspective, as Marina Waisman puts it.[56]

Schulthess House

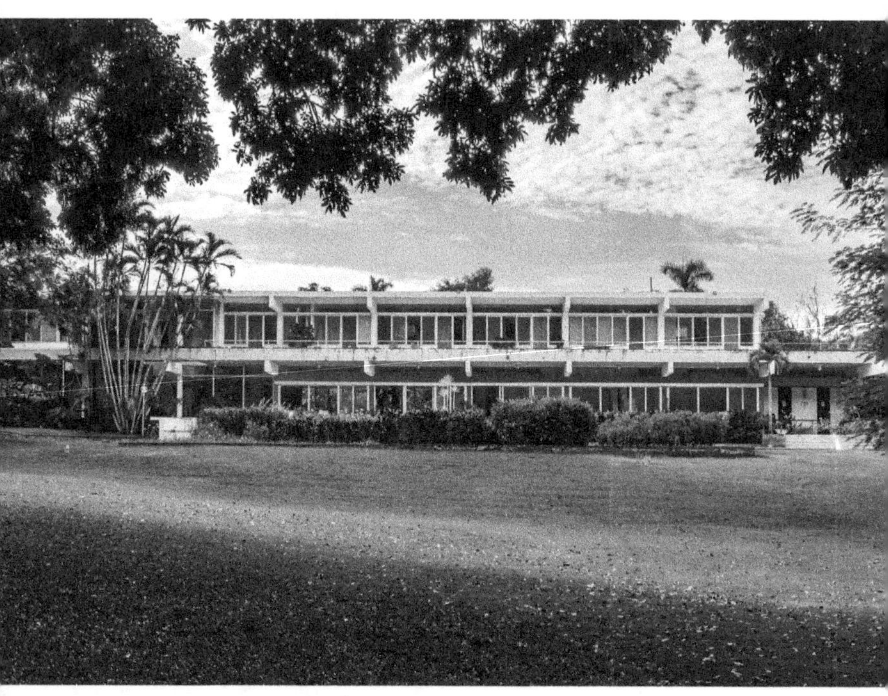

Alfred De Schulthess House, Havana,
Cuba. Richard Neutra, 1956. Photo
André Marques

*Besides the three volumes edited by Willy Boesiger on
Neutra, there are really two significant publications
about his work, both featuring inaccuracies. Thomas
S. Hines' Richard Neutra and the Search for Modern
Architecture is undoubtedly the most valuable analysis
of Neutra's output; it is an extensive and passionate
account of his life and works; however, despite contain-
ing 360 illustrations – many of them of smaller projects
–, it doesn't include a single photo of the Schulthess
House, which is only mentioned in a three line commentary. This approach contrasts with that of Boesiger and
Neutra himself, who, in the second volume published by
Editorial Girsberger, from Zurich, in 1959, dedicated ten
pages and eighteen illustrations to this particular house.
The opportunity to present and discuss one of the few
works produced by Neutra in the tropics – a circumstance that in itself adds interest – was lost. Also, in
the same book by Hines, page 243, there is a photo of a
mural designed by Burle Marx in another work by Neutra, in Los Angeles, and the person working on the mural
is erroneously identified as Burle Marx himself. This error
reappeared in the edition of Neutra's complete works in
1999 by Taschen, a publishing house in Cologne, whose
main author is Barbara Mac Lamprecht – an essential
book, for sure, but it also contains a few other inaccuracies regarding Schulthess House. It states that the
structure is made of steel, when, in reality, it is made
of reinforced concrete; the south façade is described
as glass, when it is, for the most part, enclosed and
hermetic; finally, the best photograph of the house in
the book is identified on page 415 as if it were of the
González-Gorrondona house, built by Neutra in Caracas
in 1962.*
Eduardo Luis Rodríguez, *Modernidad Tropical. Neutra,
Burle Marx y Cuba: La Casa De Schulthess*[57]

This accurate review, written by Cuban architect and historian Eduardo Luis Rodríguez, in the opening pages of his book-catalogue dedicated to the Schulthess House, points to important fissures in the hegemonic historiographical discourse regarding the work of Richard Neutra. The near omissions and confusions about the works in Latin America featured in these two famous publications to this day are replicated in narratives concerning the architect, even in those written by Latin American researchers. For instance, despite the cover of the book *Richard Neutra en América Latina – Una Mirada Desde el Sur* being illustrated by a photo of the north façade of the Cuban house, Catherine Ettinger devotes no more than a single paragraph to the actual work, and even then she says that Neutra designed it in a "steel frame that was coated with concrete"[58] and that the general layout as well as the playful element on the roof reflect Neutra's experience in Puerto Rico.[59] Besides the clear misunderstanding as to the structural system used in the house – due to hurricanes, which are farily common in the region, Neutra chose a reinforced concrete structure – and apparently not aware of the catalog *Modernidad Tropical – Neutra, Burle Marx y Cuba: La Casa de Schulthess*, produced by Eduardo Rodríguez, Ettinger ends up reinforcing the assertions made by Hines and Lamprecht, which carry their ideological position.

In the case of the North American and German publications, one could speculate that the Cuban political situation after 1959 created an obstacle in terms of accessing the house and learning about its history. Eduardo Rodríguez indeed reports the difficulty encountered by both foreign and local architects to visit the work.[60] But even this is not enough to justify the absence of a deeper analysis in such narratives; after all, a large part of the collection of drawings and photos is featured in the second volume edited by Boesiger[61] and archived in the UCLA *Neutra Collection* (the architectural project) and the Burle Marx & Cia. Ltda. office (the landscaping project). That is, at the time of the development of Thomas Hines' research on Richard Neutra's biography, material on the Schulthess House was largely available and, even so, was not incorporated into the account.

Moreover, there is the historian's assessment in the small excerpt of the book where he comments on the house[62] and in a testimony to the researcher:[63] for him, this project represented the architect's ineptitude in face of large-scale works. It is not the purpose here to devalue Hines' critical stance on the residency. It indeed distinguishes itself from the vast majority of his residential projects – economical houses with more modest measurements, designed with a metallic or

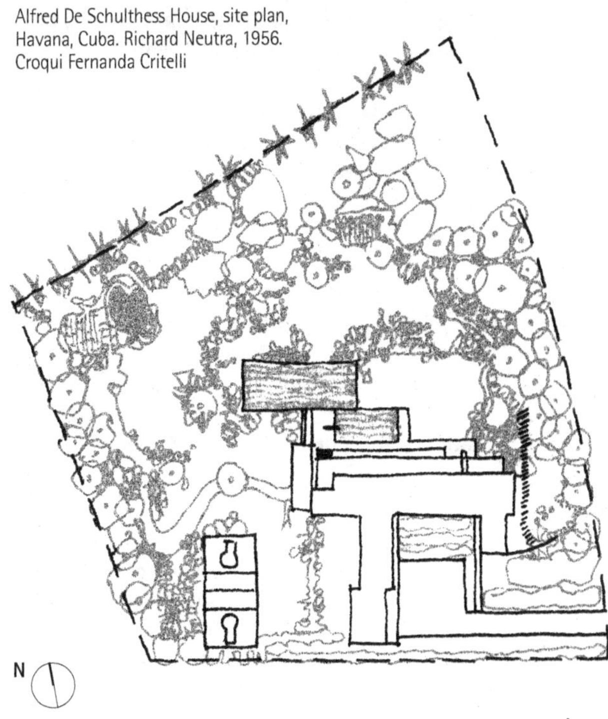

Alfred De Schulthess House, site plan,
Havana, Cuba. Richard Neutra, 1956.
Croqui Fernanda Critelli

wooden structure. However, if Hines' opinion were due solely
to a question of scale, the later González-Gorrondona House
– which the historian compares to Lovell House – would not
be reduced to an instance of "happy memories" from another
time. If we return to the Freudian notion of "*unheimlich*,"
Thomas Hines' position obscures the historian's inability to
face his own discomfort. Not because the use of concrete
and the generosity of the areas are new, but because of what
this project represents: the materialization of Neutra's relationship with Latin American architecture and landscaping.

To claim that Schulthess House is the first materialization of this relationship so important to Neutra does not
mean to ignore the previous publication of *Architecture
of Social Concern*, a book generally seen by historiography
as an imposition of a so-called central architecture on a
supposedly peripheral region. According to this discourse,
the architect's later works, including the Latin American
ones – which push forward the issues between climate and
landscape – would be reflections of the experience in Puerto
Rico. Despite being repeated several times,[64] this statement
omits or reduces the importance of the recognition trip to
South America in 1945 and the professional and personal
ties that were formed at that time and which lasted until
Neutra's death. The experience of Puerto Rico brought new
elements to Neutra's concerns regarding the relationship
between architecture and the local environment. Concerned
with these issues, the architect found possible solutions in
Latin America; he photographed and studied them, resulting
in the article "Sun Control Devices," published by *Progressive
Architecture* magazine in 1946.

In addition to the article, the relationship with Roberto
Burle Marx is also very significant. As studied in our master's
degree, Richard Neutra not only admired the Brazilian landscape artist but also urged his clients to hire him to develop
landscape as well as mural projects.[65] One of these clients
was Alfred De Schulthess, a Swiss resident in New York who,

in 1952, had been transferred to Havana to assume the
vice-presidency of Banco Garrigó.[66] Implemented on a ten
thousand square meter plot in the Country Club, a luxurious
residential neighborhood designed during the government
of Fulgêncio Batista (1952-1959),[67] the house has clearly
sectored environments, distributed over two floors: the
service areas (kitchen , laundry and employee quarters) and
social areas (dining and living rooms, office, toilet and guest
bedroom) are located on the ground floor, while the intimate
area (private bedrooms and bathrooms and intimate living
room) appears on the upper floor.

From an axis at the entrance, marked by a portico at
a higher level than the rest of the ground floor, Richard
Neutra organizes the circulation in the interior of the house.
From this niche, a variety of functions follow: on the left –
down about three steps –, the dining and living rooms and
the service rooms; on the right, an office, guest bedroom
and bathroom; finally, the stairs – embedded in the office
wall and braced in the structure of the upper floor, with a
structural logic quite similar to that adopted by Rino Levi
at the Olivo Gomes residence (1949-1951), in São José dos
Campos – leading to the bedrooms and family room. On
this floor, Neutra chooses to occupy the center of the plant,
leaving a passage on one side and a balcony on the other
for contemplating the landscape. On the front façade, which
corresponds to the upper floor, the fechamento with wooden
panels transforms into cabinets facing the corridor. In the
living room, the presence of a fireplace marks the division
with the entrance niche, thus structuring the social area. This
element, which points to an influence of Frank Lloyd Wright's
works on Richard Neutra's repertoire, is entirely covered with
stone, thus standing out from the rest of the house's internal
areas.

Neutra arranges the structure of the house in eight
modules, dislocating the volume on the ground floor in
relation to the upper floor in order to create a balcony on the

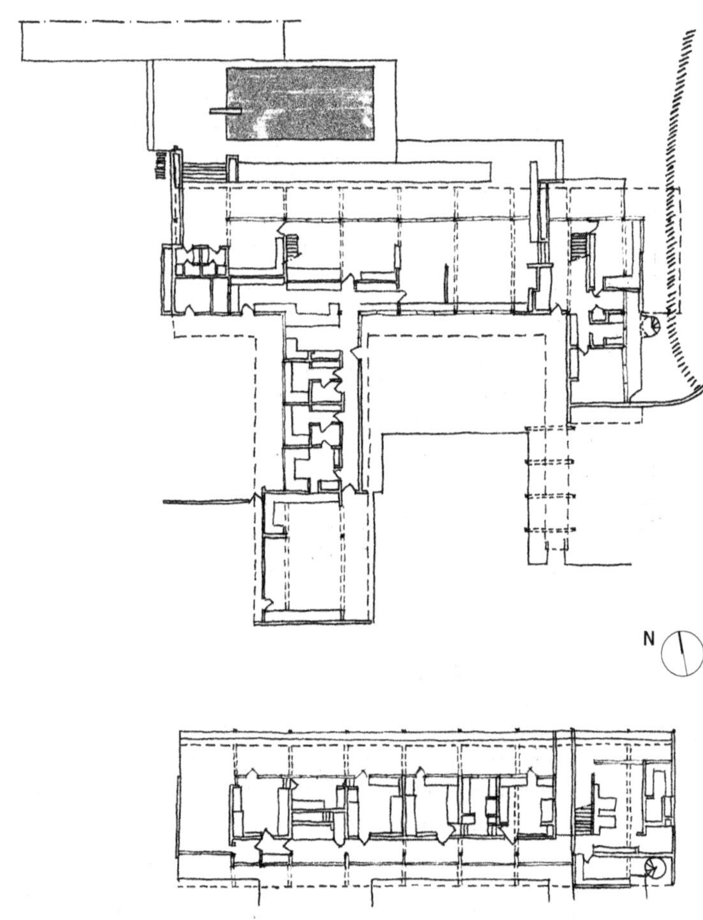

Alfred De Schulthess House, ground
floor and first floor plans Havana,
Cuba. Richard Neutra, 1956. Croquis
Fernanda Critelli

upper part and, on the lower part, a garden that penetrates
the house. In the transversal direction, the architect takes up
the studies carried out for the article "Sun Control Devices"
and solves the architecture using a cantilever/gap/cantilever
scheme, protecting the North façade with an overhang of
approximately 2,45 meters. On the south façade, the upper
floor advances over the cantilever, forming a narrower overhang as protection for spaces on both floors: on the ground
floor, the windows of the rooms; at the top, the windows of
the corridor that leads to the rooms. Regarding the treatment of the facades, despite Barbara Lamprecht's mistake –
pointed out by Eduardo Luis Rodríguez in the epigraph at the
beginning of this analysis –, Richard Neutra worked on them
in order to guarantee the privacy of the interior life while
providing the view of the landscape designed by Roberto
Burle Marx. In other words: to the south (view from the
entrance), the windows are high, allowing for natural lighting and ventilation, the external walls working as support
for the cabinets on the inside; to the east and west (views,
respectively, towards the street and the edge of the land),
great blind walls enclose the limits of the house like stone
curtains loose from the ground; finally, the north façade is
entirely composed of large sliding glass floor-to-ceiling doors
that open onto the landscape, integrating the internal and
external areas.

The landscaping proposed by Burle Marx uses plants
with different heights, colors and textures that harmonize
with the architecture in three different moments. In the
farthest contour, large trees create a dense mass, almost like
a virgin forest where the physical limits of the plot cannot
be seen. Around the house, the matrix of right angles of the
architecture is reflected towards the garden design, proposed
in a concrete grid that houses smaller plants of various colors
and textures, as a counterpoint to the green mass at the
edge of the land. Here the water mirror and the pool meet,
giving way to the living room that extends to the outside.

The relationship between this geometric landscaping and the almost in natura vegetation develops through a looser design of the walk in curved lines, with a movement of the topography that, in addition to providing distinct and surprising views of the house, creates a new limit for the terrain. The feeling is that Schulthess House is located in a clearing of a virgin and unexplored forest. These transitions and the creation of visual boundaries in landscaping are very similar to what was proposed for the Museum of Modern Art in Rio de Janeiro a few years earlier, in 1953. According to Roberto Burle Marx, the distinct textures, colors and sizes of the vegetation make it possible a harmonious composition with the architecture.[68]

The mastery with which the conditions of climate and local technology, the client's demands and the relationship

Alfred De Schulthess House, Havana,
Cuba. Richard Neutra, 1956. Photos
André Marques

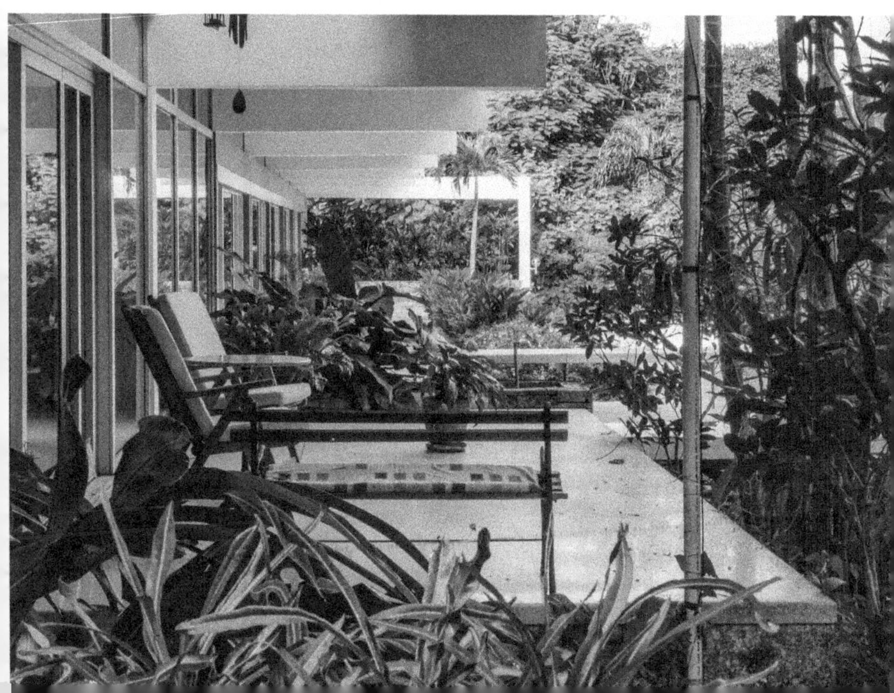

between architecture and landscape are resolved in the Schulthess House project attests to the architect's maturity at that time. Richard Neutra had his own convictions and knew how to rework his references, which he saw and studied with enthusiasm in Latin America. We are not talking about a rookie architect who came to Latin American territory as an experiment. On the contrary, this work – as well as the González-Gorrondona House, which will be discussed below – represents the architect at his peak, constantly looking for innovations, having established with his Latin American colleagues (with whom he identified culturally, as well as on those questions relating to climate and landscape) dialogues through which it was possible to get to the answers he was looking for. Still, this house has been dismissed as peripheral by hegemonic historiographical discourse, and this clearly reveals the discomfort in the face of what seems uncanny.

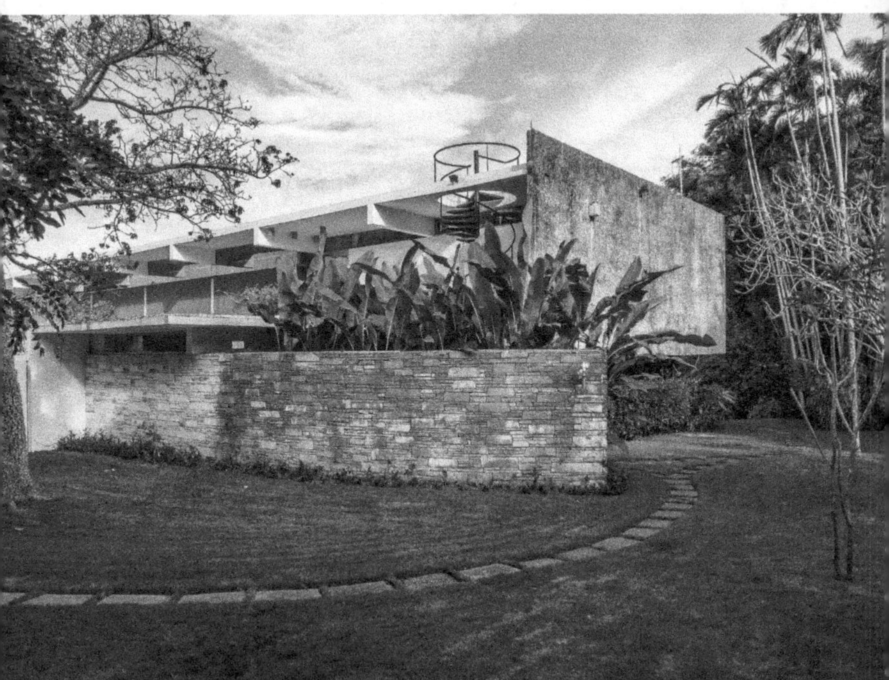

González-Gorrondona House

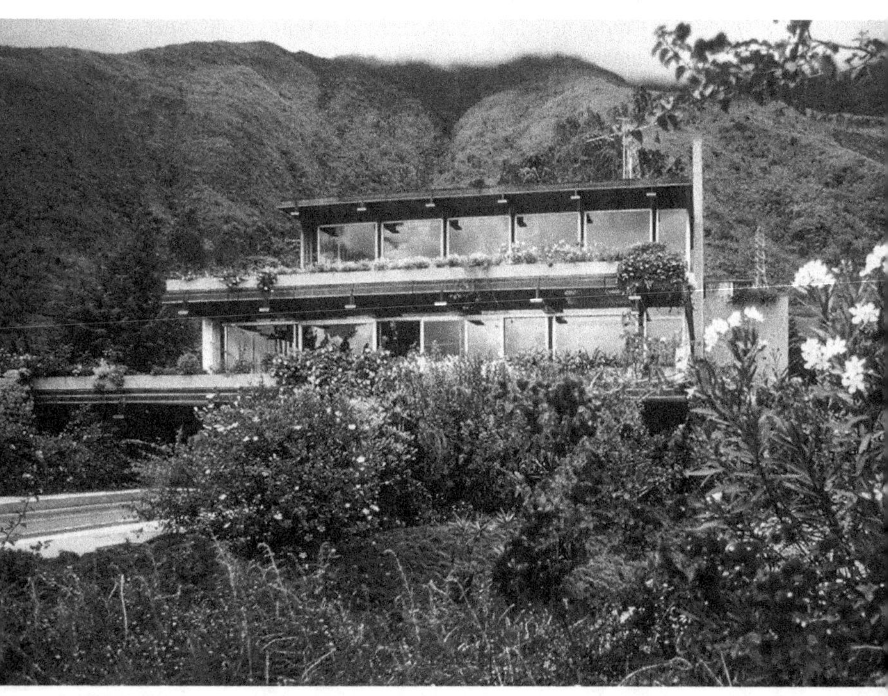

González-Gorrondona House, Caracas,
Venezuela. Richard Neutra, 1958-
1965. Photo Raymond Richard Neutra

Neutra's late houses outside the United States ranged from merely competent to excellent. Of the first category, the De Schulthess house, Havana, Cuba (1956), exemplified Neutra's problems in the too-large, too-rich category, while the González-Gorrondona house, Caracas, Venezuela (1962), recalled, in its stepped hillside layering, happier memories of his larger thirties' houses.
Thomas S. Hines, *Richard Neutra and the Search for Modern Architecture*[69]

Designed for the lawyer, economist and banker José Joaquim González-Gorrondona (1910-1988), in the middle of El Ávila National Park, Caracas, the story of this house is quite curious, starting with the place where it was built. A man of great influence in Venezuela, González-Gorrondona was president of the National Economy Council, an advisory body to the state between 1949 and 1959; governor at the International Monetary Fund – IMF; representative of Venezuela at the World Bank; founder, in 1957, of the National Discount Bank; and Minister of Transport and Communications between 1964 and 1966.[70] During the dictatorship of General Pérez Jiménez, he hired Italian architect Gio Ponti to fulfill his dream of building a mansion outside the urban perimeter and in front of Los Palos Grandes, La Castellana, Santa Eduvigis, La Carlota and the US Embassy. Ponti sketched an initial project for the house, but never actually finished it.[71]

So, in January 1958, after the end of the dictatorship and the election of the new democratic government, González-Gorrondona hired Richard Neutra to design his house.[72] In the third volume published on the architect's works, Willy Boesiger states that this house took eight years to build: "From a library of thousands of volumes and art treasures, which the owner, a ministry of his country's government, has collected, down to the spacious pool, the multistoried steel structure has been studied in all its rooms and functions by Neutra through eight years of creative attention to a singular site and program."[73]

Although Thomas Hines and, consequently, Barbara Lamprecht date this project to 1962, its construction was finished only in 1965.[74] During this long period between design and construction, the work suffered a few setbacks. Due to the fact that the plot was located in the thousandth quota of the slope on which the construction of the El Ávila National Park was being considered, the new Venezuelan government prevented the project from going forward until, in December 1958, it was decreed that the area of the park

González-Gorrondona House, lower
floor and ground floor plans, Caracas,
Venezuela. Richard Neutra, 1958-
1965. Croquis Fernanda Critelli

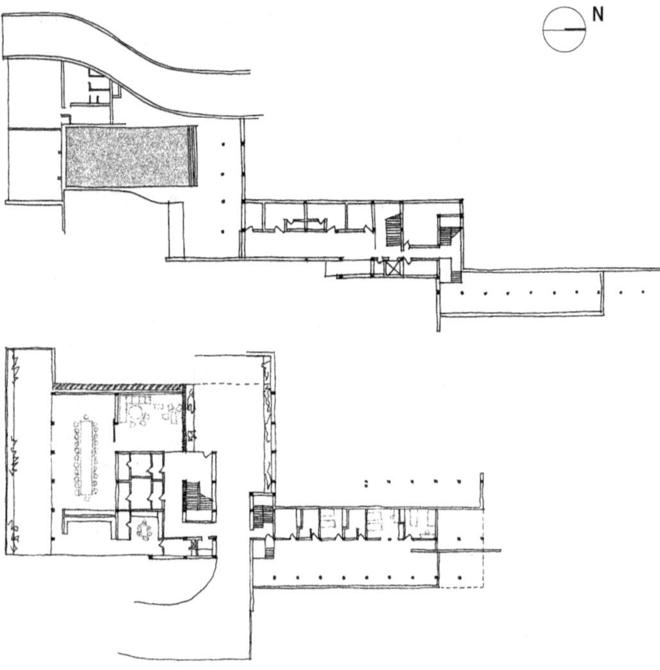

would start from that point. Thus, the project was approved. However, permission for its actual construction and ultimate use by its owners was given only in 1963, when the National Parks Institute of Venezuela granted González-Gorrondona the title of forest ranger.[75]

Even though it was extensively published in Boesiger's third volume, González-Gorrondona House enjoys little prominence in hegemonic historiography. Thomas Hines, in the epigraph of this text, mentions it only to compare it with the residential works of the 1930s: according to the historian, its quality is an exception when it comes to works

González-Gorrondona House, first floor,
second floor and cover plans, Caracas,
Venezuela. Richard Neutra, 1958-1965.
Croquis Fernanda Critelli

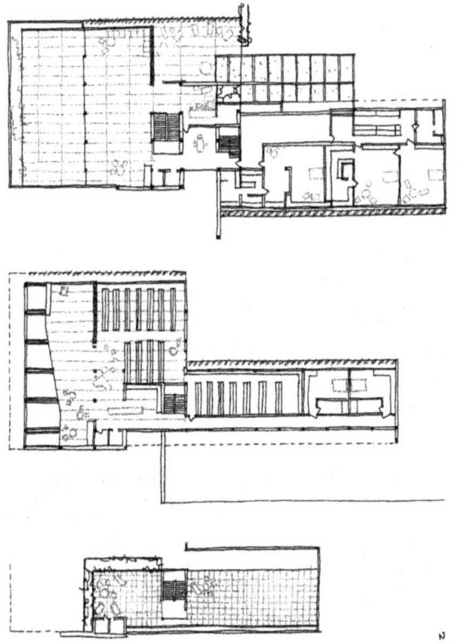

built outside North American soil. Along the same lines, Barbara Lamprecht compares the Venezuelan house with the well-known Casa Lovell, on account of both projects being designed for sloping terrain. What is not mentioned, however, is that, unlike Lovell House, which is situated on sloping terrain, Gorrondona House is situated on an acclivitous terrain on the mountainside.

Because it has a smaller area when compared to the South American project, Richard Neutra solves the entire private area of Lovell House on the access floor: the rooms are placed in the southwestern portion of the house, thus ensuring good lighting and a view of Griffith Park and the city of Los Angeles. The two lower floors are reserved for the guest rooms, kitchen, living rooms, library, as well as the leisure and gym areas. In the Venezuelan house, the political office its owner occupied demanded areas for conferences and receptions that differ from the normal social areas of a house. In this case, the separation and connection of different environments makes this project even more complex.

To solve these particularities in terms of use and plot, Neutra divided the house into two volumes: one half-buried on the hillside where, on one floor, we have the employees' facilities and, on the other, those of the family; and a back volume for leisure, social and private areas, all overlooking the valley where the city of Caracas is located. The second floor above the pool gives access to cars and pedestrians. On this floor, we have the reception: a small living room that opens onto a dining room for 26 people, taking up almost the entire south façade, with an unobstructed view of the city. Also on this floor are the service areas, kitchen and employee dormitories. On the third floor, the social areas – living room, terrace and gallery – and the private area – bedrooms – for the family; while the fourth floor is practically entirely reserved for the owner's library and art collection, with space only for the two guest rooms in the northern portion of the slimmer volume. Crowning this generous house is a covered terrace with a privileged view of the city and the entire Parque El Ávila.

Given the Ecuadorian climate conditions where the house is located, Richard Neutra extensively elaborated the sun control mechanisms that he had studied on his first visit to South America: the balconies, the wider overhangs and, above all, the vertical movable louvers. In the architect's previous works, movable vertical louvers appeared in a discreet manner; now, they gain prominence in the Venezuelan house. This treatment is applied to the East and West façades, featuring, in some situations, double-height ceilings – as illustrated by the perspective sketched by the architect of the Northwest façade.

Despite the similarity of being set on a sloping terrain with majestic views of the city and park, González-Gorrondona House is totally different from the Lovell House in terms of the relationship with the sun. In California, where the sun, albeit present, is not as intense as in the Ecuadorian climate, facades and openings constantly invite light and heat, following the wishes of the naturopathic physician who commissioned the house and who advocated healing through the sun. On the other hand, in the Venezuelan house, which is more challenged by the intensity of the sun, the facades were designed sometimes to avoid excess light and heat and sometimes to open itself up to it. The technologies and materials used are totally different: from the white prismatic volume cut by horizontal strips of glass almost forty years earlier, Neutra reached his peak through a composition of horizontal and vertical planes of different materials, which on one side rest on the slope of the mountain and, on the other, project from it towards the valley, opening up to the view. As at Schulthess House – and perhaps with even greater maturity –, Richard Neutra masterfully worked the solutions studied in the article "Sun Control Devices," manipulating them in his own way in this project for Gorrondona House. And despite being mentioned as an example of the quality of Neutra's work, Thomas Hines and Barbara Lamprecht did so with a strange discomfort, associating the project with what they were familiar with from an architecture prior to Neutra's relationship with Latin America.

Also, in the same way as in the Cuban house, Richard Neutra gives great prominence to the landscaping at the Casa González-Gorrondona – developed here by the Venezuelan Eduardo Robles Piquer – by integrating it into internal environments through visuals and small gardens. The construction possibilities and local conditions in Venezuela made it possible for the house to be built entirely with a metallic structure. However, despite all its complexity and quality, the commentary on this house repeats to this day the same few assertions made by Lamprecht and Hines. Catherine Ettinger, for example, singles out one paragraph to present the house in her book *Richard Neutra en América Latina: Una Mirada desde el Sur*, saying that the project employs strategies used in Lovell House.[76] However, she goes on to say that the environments are distributed over two floors with a roof terrace,[77] when in fact the house has five staggered floors.

The fact that Richard Neutra's only two projects in South America are mostly dismissed in hegemonic historiographical discourse does not seem to be a matter of mere neglect or ignorance. After all, both projects were published and extensively illustrated in the collection edited by Willy Boesiger. Moreover, Neutra's attention during the production of these books highlights the importance of such projects for the

González-Gorrondona House, Caracas, Venezuela. Richard Neutra, 1958-1965. Photo Raymond Richard Neutra

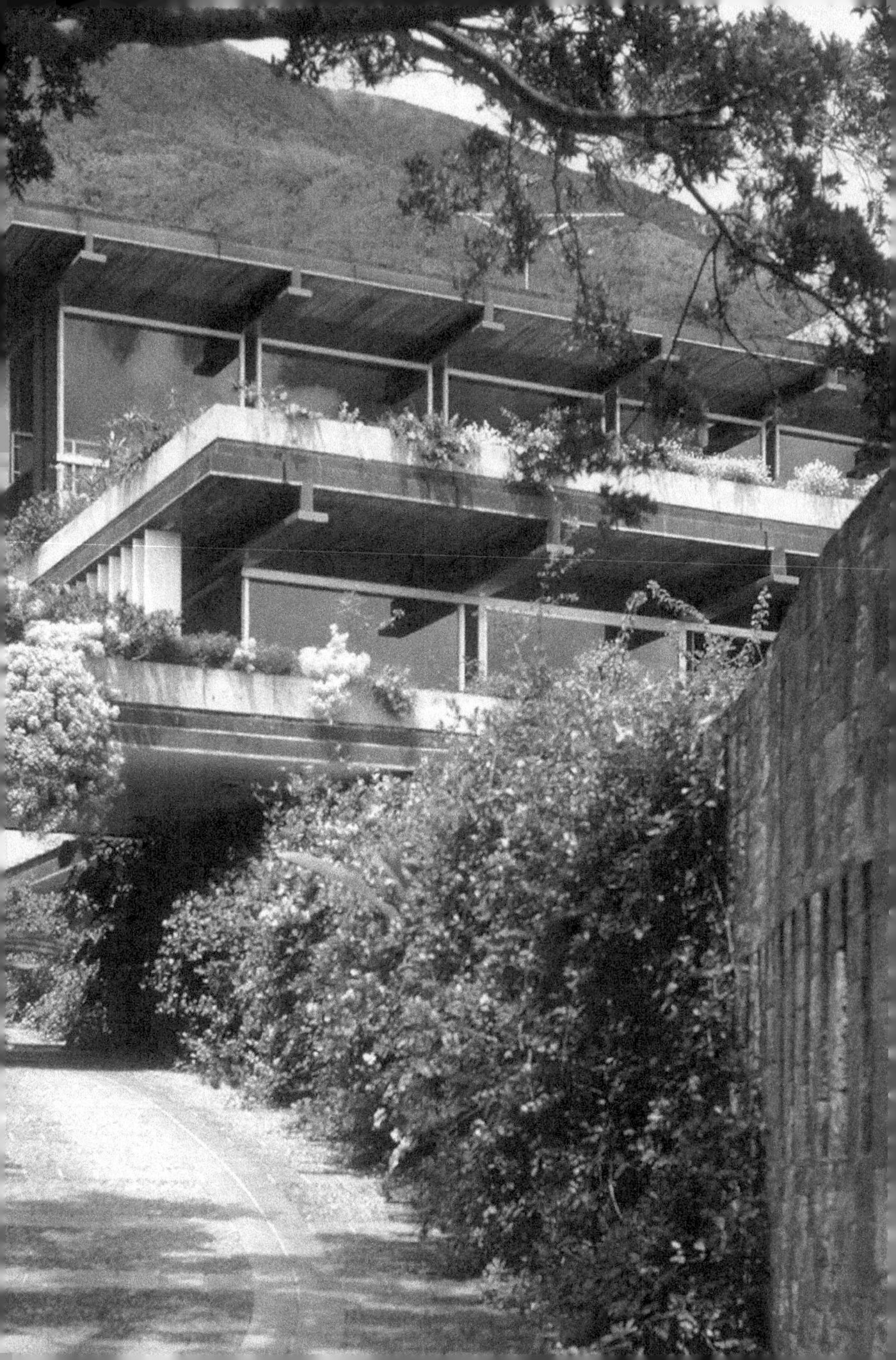

architect: "It seems to me, dear Mr. Boesiger, that to a certain extent I'm writing you my testament."[78] Besides, the drawings and correspondence relating to both projects are featured in the UCLA's *Neutra Collection* – a collection that Thomas Hines and Barbara Lamprecht themselves helped to organize. So why are the Alfred de Schulthess and González-Gorrondona houses virtually dismissed in the analysis of these historians? Is it because both point to a manifestation that they would prefer to keep hidden?

The ideological stance of both historians is evident, even in the statement that the Venezuelan house represents a good example of Neutra's output, given that the issues they raised were limited to a comparison with one of Neutra's first works in the United States, avoiding any further analysis. Not even the extensive use of movable vertical louvers, fairly unprecedented in Neutra's output – at least with regard to the composition of the façade – was apparently not worthy of analysis. The truth is that both Gorrondona House and Schulthess House point to the consolidation of Richard Neutra's personal and professional contact with Latin America. Pushing the argument even further, they evidence the architect's gradual transformation after this contact, attesting to the fact that modern architecture was not developed in Europe and the United States and then imposed or adapted in Latin America. In fact, these new experiments evolved through a network of influences, some of them happening simultaneously, others becoming references even for the most established architects. And, as a network that connects points in multiple directions, answers elaborated by Latin American architecture became indeed a reference for architects in the Northern hemisphere.

If it is true that architects are in constant search for renewal and transformation – whether through appropriation, assimilation, adaptation, opposition or interpretation, as Michael Baxandall puts it –, then it is not reasonable to say that Richard Neutra came to Latin America only to spread the word about his own architecture – the modern American architecture of the so-called International Style – among us. It would be advisable to assume that, instead of a one-way transit, from the center to the periphery, the exchanges between architects did happen in multiple directions, according to the interests of agents who single out an influence, among many others, either to follow it – or oppose it.

Notes

1. Robert E. Alexander, "Unpublished Memoirs." Alexander Papers, Cornell University, quoted in Thomas S. Hines, *Richard Neutra and the Search for Modern Architecture*, 268.

2. Previous books published about the architect only presented compendiums of his works. See: Willy Boesiger, *Buildings and Projects: Richard Neutra, 1927-1950* (Zurich: Girsberger, 1951); Willy Boesiger, *Buildings and Projects: Richard Neutra, 1950-1960* (Zurich: Girsberger, 1959); Willy Boesiger, *Buildings and Projects: Richard Neutra, 1961-1966* (Zurich: Girsberger, 1969); Esther McCoy, *Richard Neutra* (New York: George Braziller, 1960); Manfred Sack, *Richard Neutra* (Barcelona: Gustavo Gili, 1994); Bruno Zevi, *Richard Neutra* (Italy: Il Balcone, 1954).

3. Both in the memoirs in the Cornell University Archive (Robert E. Alexander, "Unpublished Memoirs." Alexander Papers, Cornell University) and in an interview conducted by Hines with the architect in December 1978.

4. Hines, *Richard Neutra and the Search*, 255 and 268.

5. Ibid., 255.

6. Entry "Robert Evans Alexander (Architect)." In Pacific Coast Architecture Database – PCAD. Available in <https://bit.ly/41xJDOM>.

7. Hines, *Richard Neutra and the Search*, 247.

8. Ibid.

9. Ibid., 245.

10. The Neutra & Alexander office, headquartered in the Glendale Boulevard building, developed urban planning and public and commercial architecture projects; on the other hand, in the studio on Silverlake Boulevard (on the ground floor of Casa VDL), Neutra was developing the residential projects. Ibid., 246.

11. Ibid.

12. Ibid., 268.

13. Ibid., 267.

14. Although not referenced, it is likely to be the architect's unpublished memoirs (present in the Cornell University Archive) or the interview conducted in December 1978.

15. Hines, *Richard Neutra and the Search*, 267-268.

16. Boesiger, *Buildings and Projects: Richard Neutra, 1950-1960*, 189-191.

17. Boesiger, *Buildings and Projects: Richard Neutra, 1961-1966*, 200-211.

18. Fernanda Critelli, "Richard Neutra e o Brasil."

19. Both at the Museum of Modern Art – MoMA in New York: Portinari of Brazil, October 9th to November 17th, 1940; Twenty Centuries of Mexican Art, May 15 to September 30, 1940.

20. Cf. Diego Rivera Mural Projects. Available in <https://bit.ly/3s1TRpO>.

21. Roberto Segre, "Oscar Niemeyer: tipologias e liberdade plástica," 168. Free translation.

22. Critelli, "Richard Neutra e o Brasil," 271-223.

23. Ibid., 225.

24. Boesiger, *Buildings and Projects: Richard Neutra, 1950-1960*, 189-191.

25. José Vela Castillo, *Richard Neutra: Un Lugar para el orden. Un estudio sobre la arquitectura natural*, 95. Free translation.

26. Barbara Mac Lamprecht, *Richard Neutra: Complete Works* (Koln: Taschen, 2010), 30.

27. Richard Joseph Neutra, "Sun Control Devices," 88-91; Critelli, "Richard Neutra e o Brasil," 105-110.

28. *Brazilian government leads Western Hemisphere in encouraging modern architecture. Exhibition of Brazilian architecture opens at Museum of Modern Art*, 2.

29. Ibid.

30. Hines, *Richard Neutra and the Search*, 321. The emergency was the fire that struck the architect's residence on the morning of March 27, 1963.

31. Ibid., 321-322.

32. David Leatherbarrow, *Uncommon Ground: Architecture, Technology, and Topography*, 57.

33. In addition to these two initial projects, movable vertical louvers were used in several other works, as will be seen later.

34. Hines, *Richard Neutra and the Search*, 228.

35. Ibid.

36. Ibid., 229.

37. Boesiger, *Buildings and Projects: Richard Neutra, 1950-1960*, 80-89.

38. Lamprecht, *Richard Neutra: Complete Works*, 201. Here, there are also photos prior to the installation of the louvers.

39. Here's: Kaufmann House (1946-1947), Tremaine House (1948), Northwestern Fire Association headquarters building (1950), Amalgamated Clothing Workers of America Union headquarters building (1956, Neutra & Alexander), US Embassy in Karachi (1955-1958, Pakistan, Neutra & Alexander), Gettysburg Cyclorama Center (1958-1961, Neutra & Alexander), headquarters of the Santa Ana Police Facilities (1961), Gonzáles-Gorrondona House (1962-1965, Venezuela), Adelphi Library University (1963), Mariners Medical Center (1963) and VDL House 2 (1965-1966).

40. Here's: California State University School of Fine Arts building (1959), Bewobau House (1960, Germany), Martin Rang House (1961, Germany) and the headquarters building of Sung Flour Mill (1968, Malaysia).

41. Here's: Los Angeles Hall of Records Building (1962, Neutra & Alexander) and Orange County Courthouse Building (1968).

42. Here's: Medical Buildings La Veta (1966) and the School of Fine Arts at California State University (1959).

43. Hines, *Richard Neutra and the Search*, 229.

44. Here's: Kaufmann House (1946-1947), William Atwell House (1948), Sokol House (1948), Tremaine House (1948), David Treweek House (1948), Charles Chase House (1949), Benedict Freedman House (1949), Wilkins House (1949), Dion Neutra House (1949-1950), O'Brien House (1950), Frederick Fischer House (1951), Milton Goldman House, (1951), James Moore House (1950-52), Frederick Auerbacher House (1953), Elliot House (1953), Loren Price House (1951-1953), Roberts House (1955), Philip Livingstone House (1956), Frank Miller House (1956), Alfred De Schulthess House (1956, Cuba), John Clark House (1957), Louis Nash House (1955-1957), Claremont Methodist Church (1959), Dailey House (1959), Larsen House (1959), Henry Singleton House (1959), David Coveney House (1960), Inadomi House (1960), Kambara House (1960), Gettysburg Cyclorama Center (1958-1961, Neutra & Alexander), Martin Rang House (1961), Casa Gonzáles-Gorrondona (1962, Venezuela), Eugen Erman House (1962), Harold Goldman House (1962), Feodor Pitcairn House (1962) and Guenter Pescher House (1968, Germany).

45. Hines, *Richard Neutra and the Search*, 266-267.

46. Jane C. Loeffler, *The Architecture of Diplomacy: Building America's Embassies*, 3.

47. It is worth remembering that, at that time, it was believed that monuments symbolized man's ideals, goals and actions, and that monumental architecture should be more than merely functional, it could achieve a new level of freedom and develop new creative possibilities. Cf. Josep Lluis Sert, Ferdnand Léger and Sigfried Giedion (1943), "Nine Points on Monumentality," 48-51.

48. The Architectural Consulting Committee, created within the Federal Building Operations – FBO, was formed by architects and operated by reviewing and approving the projects of the embassies between 1954 and 1956.

49. AAC Minutes, 16 August 1955, 2, quoted in Loeffler, *The Architecture of Diplomacy*, 208.

50. Hines, *Richard Neutra and the Search*, 255.

51. Segre, "Oscar Niemeyer," 171. Free translation.

52. Ibid., 169.

53. Hines, *Richard Neutra and the Search*, 305-311.

54. Hines, *Richard Neutra and the Search*, 303. A similar statement was made by the historian to the researcher during an interview carried out in December 2014.

55. Hines, *Richard Neutra and the Search*, 268.

56. Marina Waisman, *O interior da história: historiografia arquitetônica para uso de latino-americanos*, 97.

57. Eduardo Luis Rodríguez, *Modernidad Tropical. Neutra, Burle Marx y Cuba: La Casa De Schulthess*, 8. Free translation.

58. Catherine Ettinger, *Richard Neutra en América Latina: Una Mirada desde el Sur*, 86. Free translation.

59. Cf. Ibid.

60. Rodríguez, *Modernidad Tropical*, 8.

61. Boesiger, *Buildings and Projects: Richard Neutra, 1950-1960*, 52-61.

62. Hines, *Richard Neutra and the Search*, 303.

63. Thomas S. Hines, Interviewed by Fernanda Critelli at his home. Los Angeles, December 20, 2014.

64. To mention just two examples: Leatherbarrow, *Uncommon Ground*, 57; Ettinger, *Richard Neutra en América Latina*, 86.

65. Critelli, "Richard Neutra e o Brasil," 215-229.

66. Rodríguez, *Modernidad Tropical*, 10. Catherine Ettinger claims that Alfred De Schulthess was Nestle's representative in Cuba. Ettinger, *Richard Neutra en América Latina*, 86.

67. Roberto Segre, *Arquitetura e urbanismo da revolução cubana*.

68. Roberto Burle Marx, quoted in Nabil Bonduki, ed., *Affonso Eduardo Reidy*, 180.

69. Hines, *Richard Neutra and the Search*, 303.

70. "Casa González-Gorrondona, un Privilegio in El Ávila," *Institutional Assets and Monuments of Venezuela – IAM Venezuela*, Caracas, November 2, 2017. Available in https://bit.ly/3uVDXNI; Narciso Guaramato Parra, "J.J. Gonzalez Gorrondona. Protagonists in the Venezolan Economy," *Protagonistas en la Economia Venezolana*, Caracas, June 6, 2009. Available in <https://bit.ly/2TLT4fy>.

71. Cf. "Casa González-Gorrondona."

72. Ibid.

73. Boesiger, *Buildings and Projects: Richard Neutra, 1961-1966*, 14.

74. "Casa González-Gorrondona;" Rosa Remón Royo, "Casa González Gorrondona o Alto Claro, Caracas Venezuela Obra del Arquitecto Richard J. Neutra: Posiblemente la Residencia Unifamiliar más Grande Proyectada por Richard J. Neutra," *Arquitectura y Empresa*, Godella, November 9, 2017. Available in <https://bit.ly/3gekt1i>.

75. Ibid.

76. Ettinger, *Richard Neutra en América Latina*, 86.

77. Ibid., 87.

78. Letter from Richard Neutra to Willy Boesiger, July 7, 1964, quoted in Boesiger, *Buildings and Projects: Richard Neutra, 1961-1966*, 10.

Afterword
Neutra and Brazil
Raymond Richard Neutra

April 24, 2021

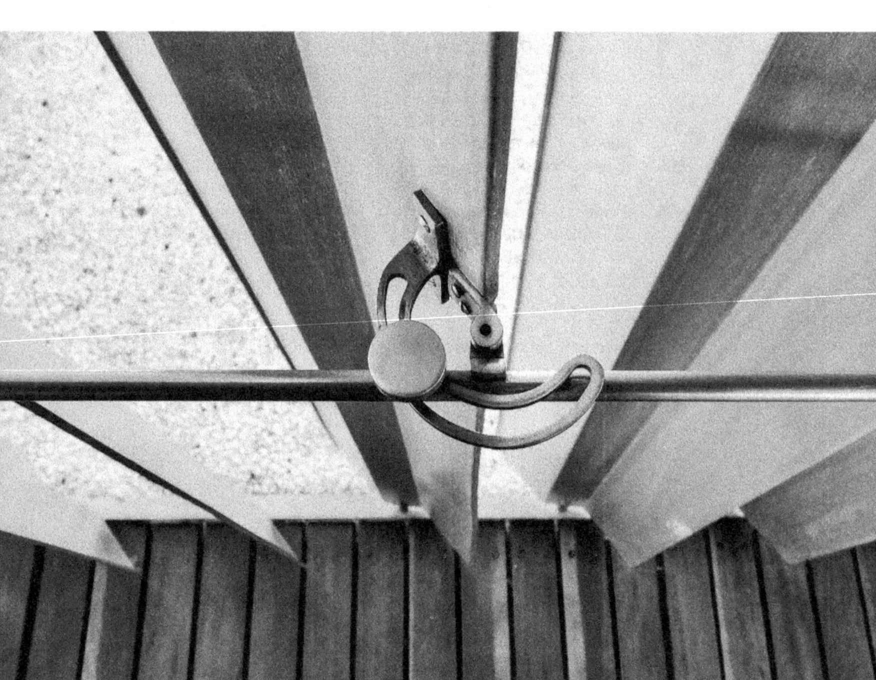

Kaufmann House, detail of the
opening mechanism of the brise-soleil,
Palm Springs. Richard Neutra, 1946-
1947. Photo Raymond Richard Neutra

Dr. Fernanda Critelli makes a good case that my father's various trips to Mexico and South America influenced the way he subsequently thought and worked. She makes the case that some of these changes struck some architectural historians as unpleasantly uncharacteristic of his other works, "strange." How behavior and attitudes change has been a topic of importance in my career in public health. For example how can we change attitudes and behavior to the use of cigarettes? It was something my father thought about too, what elements of argument will influence the Los Angeles Board of Supervisors to accept the extra expense of 150-foot-high sun louvers on its new Hall of Records? Like all causal processes many factors work simultaneously sometimes interacting with each other to influence forms of thought and behavior. Some are present from past experiences.

My father grew up as an outsider, a second-generation Hungarian Jewish immigrant to Vienna in the multi-cultural Habsburg Empire. Unlike me, who was educated to think of South America as a Spanish and Portuguese invention, he remembered that the consolidation of European dominance and management of much of South America and Mexico was conducted under the aegis of the Habsburg Empire that for a time also included Austria and the near countries. So when he talked of the lands to the south and their many indigenous and European immigrant cultures, he seemed to have a sense that "we were once all part of one complex interesting mosaic." His long journey on horseback with his artillery pieces through Croatia, Serbia, Bosnia and Albania during World War I honed his tendency to be curious about current cultural differences and the historical lines of descent, which contributed to them.

As part of the Good Neighbor Policy, my father visited South America in the fall of 1945. Although free riding on the complex foreign policy agenda of elite stakeholders in the American polity, he saw it as an opportunity for his own agenda, to broaden his perspective on developing countries and to proselytize for his vision of an architecture that used natural elements and industrial and local technologies to satisfy human needs. I would guess he was hoping that there would be opportunities for joint architectural projects on that continent. His strategy, as Critelli points out, was to ask for intense reconnaissance visits with local politicians and planners to detect local issues and then orient his lectures to relate to them. In Argentina this even involved a visit to Juan Peron who gave him a photographic portrait with his signature. In Peru he met architect and later Peruvian president Fernando Belaunde Terry. He seems to have arrived in Brazil, just around the time that Getúlio Vargas was removed from office in October of 1945.

One of the intellectual challenges that engaged my father in Puerto Rico and then on this South American tour was how the form and means of current architecture should respond to climate, culture and history. Just as in his adopted home in California, he was unsympathetic with the idea that a regional architecture should be constrained to display historical stylistic elements. For example he avoided the California Mission tile roofs unless they were forced upon him by local regulation. When so forced, the result, would not be mistaken for a mission.

My father would probably facetiously ask why the white Anglo-Saxon protestant students of Palos Verdes High School should feel a warm sense of belonging when seeing the ceramic roof coverings similar to those that Franciscan friars needed to keep the sun and rain off them as they worked to convert the aboriginal hunter-gatherers into God fearing Roman Catholics and loyal Spanish peons. An explanation may be that we were propagandized to feel that way. As a Californian school child it seems to have been mandated seventy years ago, that we all built cardboard Mission models and were taught what a great thing it was that Padre Serra[1] built the tile covered missions and *civilized* the Indians.

Although some of us now know the dark side of Padre Serra as a person and the dark side of his project, red ceramic roof tiles are back in vogue with commercial and institutional California architecture. Mid-century California modern, which really does reflect a regional subculture and a regional climate is now a fringe regionalism for sophisticates.

But back then my father was always thinking of economic broad application, so he focused on locally available inexpensive industrial material and local crafts when they were economically appropriate. He also advocated for paying careful attention to local sociological needs and climactic conditions. For him *that* would serve as regionalism. In this position he was not so different from the modernist architects that he encountered on his trip. As these local modernist architects eschewed stylistic features of structures by indigenous peoples or those of architects serving the church,

Palos Verdes School, use of ceramic tiles as local request, Palos Verdes. Neutra and Alexander, 1961. Photo

Raymond Richard Neutra

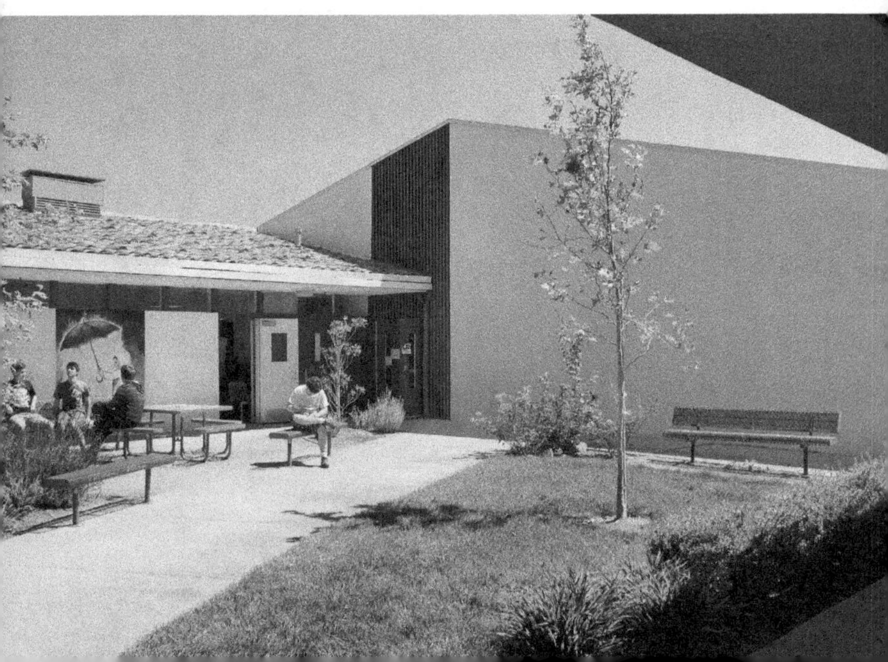

the colonial government or earlier elites, the architects of countries like Brazil and Mexico who served current governments and elites, started to have a unique national *modernist* character which became a source of regionalist pride. So it seems that my father was wrong to think that locally available technology, programmatic needs and climate should be the main drivers of a region's architecture. Complex political, psychological and economical processes produce powerful fashionable considerations like those that yielded our Californian red tile roofs.

My father was struck by the many ingenious ways that his South American colleagues controlled the southern sun. His visit to the Buenos Aires Los Eucalypos apartment house

Los Eucalyptos Apartment, detail of
wood brise-soleil, Buenos Aires, Argentina. Kurchan and Ferrari Hardoy, 1941.
Photo Raymond Richard Neutra

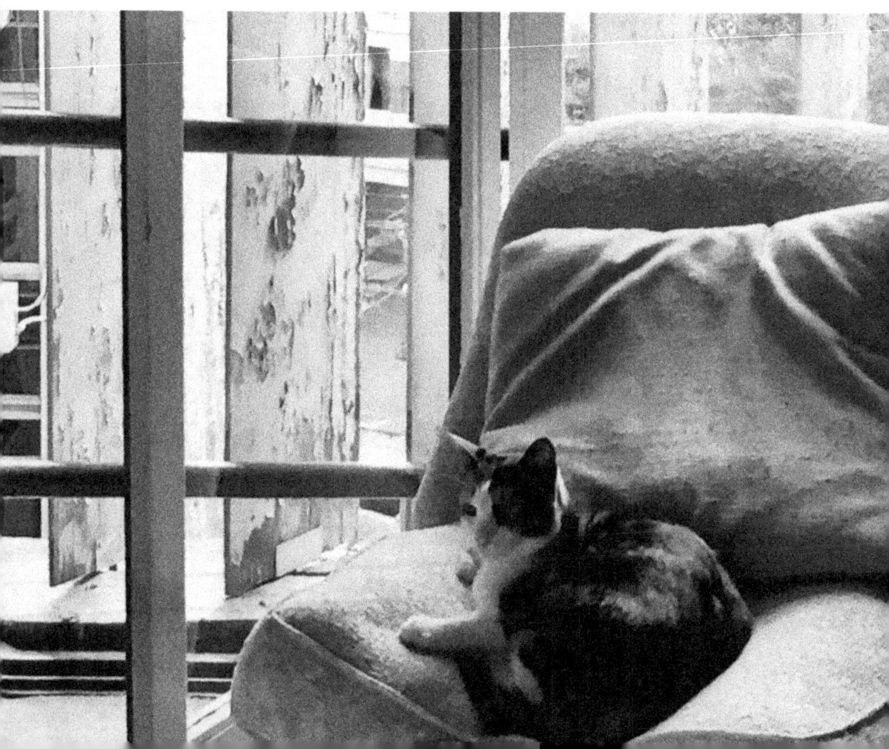

designed by Jorge Ferrari Hardoy and Kurchan in 1941, introduced him to the idea of vertical rotating sun louvers previously designed by architect Villalobos.

They could be rotated or could be cranked on a cable to fold together at the side of the window. As Critelli says, my father wrote an article in *Progressive Architecture* in 1946 approvingly describing these and other sun devices. He then redesigned Hardoy's vertical louvers so that they could lock closed against the strong wind descending on the 1946 Kaufmann Desert house each evening from the mountains. This protected those sitting on the roof deck enjoying the cool desert evening.

Devices like these were used so often in Southern California through the 1960's that the Lemlar company, unrelated to my father, found it profitable to supply them. So this is an example of straight-forward borrowing and adapting from a South American model. Critelli shows the use of these louvers in enormous size at the 1962 Los Angeles Hall of Records, which according to my brother, did indeed require my father to argue for them before the Board of Supervisors in a public meeting.

She quotes a Spanish architectural historian as thinking that their use in a similar width at the VDL II as "technological exhibitionism." That side of the VDL II compound definitely needs shade from the western sun, so some kind of sun control is needed. However, these louvers were donated. The 1966 VDL II project like the 1932 VDL I benefited from donations of materials and appliances from manufacturers who looked forward to using them in advertisements. It is my recollection that my brother Dion received these particular sized louvers from the Lemlar company. For my taste narrower louvers shading the same area would please me more, but apparently those sizes were not available for donation. Whether narrower louvers would placate our Spanish colleague remains to be seen.

Architectural historians are given to clothing their *evaluations* of architectural compositions and features as statements of objective facts, almost equivalent to statements about the performance, say, of an automobile. One can objectively say that a 1967 Ford can go faster than a 1927 Ford. But not everyone would agree that a 1927 Neutra building is "better resolved" than a 1967 Neutra Building. It is in this way that some architectural historians characterize the composition of the variety of materials at the Los Angeles Hall of Records as inferior to compositions and components of other works. As Critelli points out the subjective preferences presented as enduring objective truths tend to be repeated by other architectural critics until someone sees the same objective features and is delighted by them, thus making the very same features soar suddenly into vogue. The same thing happens in other domains of art. For example Johan Sebastian Bach was considered a minor dry musical mathematician for much of the 18th century until Mendelsohn's aunt and music teacher introduced the young Mendelsohn to Bach and gave him the hand copied manuscript of the Saint Matthew's Passion which he performed in 1829. After that, the appreciation for Bach spread exponentially and has grown ever greater.[2] It turns out that the appearance of so many materials in the Los Angeles Hall of Records was partially caused by a local regulation. This is explained on page 98 of my brother's self-published book *The Neutras Then and Later*:

> To satisfy a policy requiring a percentage of the overall budget to be spent on "art", we employed the services of Malcolm Leland, sculptor. Rather than have him create a statue to place in the plaza, he was encouraged to design a custom drinking fountain in cast bronze, which later became a standard of the Haws fountain company. Dozens of these were first produced for use in our building. Malcolm was also responsible for the design

of several screens that were integrated into the exterior design of the building.

We also employed Joseph Young, muralist, who designed and carried out a mosaic mural on the North wall of the auditorium fronting Temple Street. This depicted the development of water resources in the region by featuring water running down a map of the county ending up in a reflecting pool at the street and courtyard.[3]

So, here, a local regulation specified *some* art, but my father and brother declined to use the art budget for a sculpture standing independently of the building while retaining the kind of spare materiality that the architecture critic would have found to his taste and framed as objectively "better."

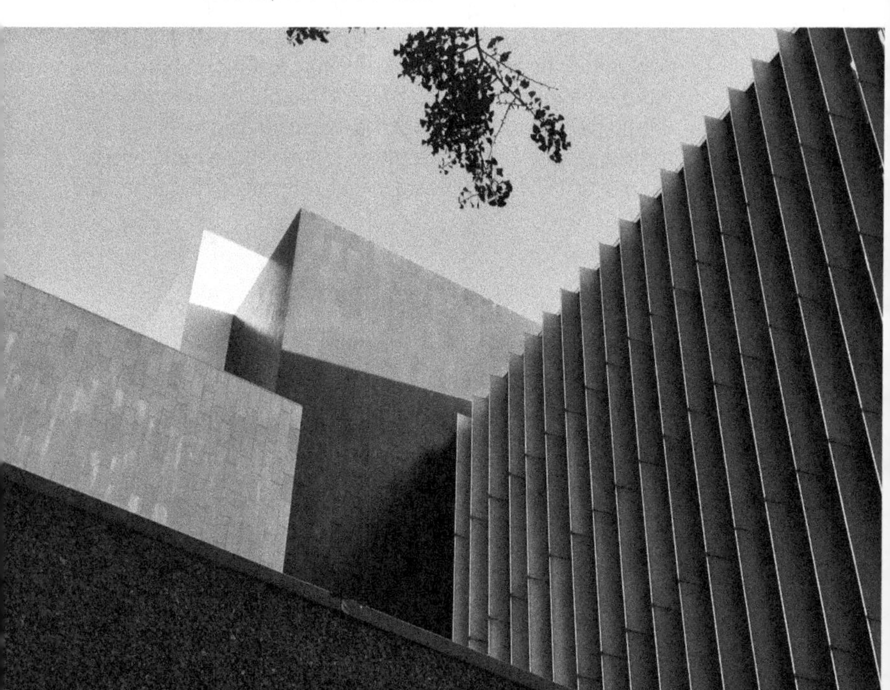

Los Angeles Hall of Records, Los Angeles. Neutra and Alexander, 1962. Photo Raymond Richard Neutra

Instead Neutra and Alexander went with a policy of integrating the art as part of the building. They chose to artfully follow the seventh point of Wright's 1930 Kahn lecture on Modern Architecture[4] about integrating mechanical systems into the design.[5] The building's ventilation system required grates and the building needed drinking-fountains. Let the ceramic artist Malcolm Leland design the fountains and a patterned portion of the wall which would cast different shadows on itself as the sun moved. The ventilation openings required some kind of grate, but these would be hidden behind this large surface integrated into the larger design.

Both the drinking fountains and the grate served dual functional and an esthetic purposes. Other than my father's Spider Leg, which similarly serves two purposes: support and expansion of space as seen from the inside, this was the closest my father ever came to ornamentation. Would Adolf Loos have approved? The fact that my father chose to integrate the mandated art into the overall design instead of pursuing the easier option of providing a plinth next to the building to place some costly sculpture, as well as the *way* my father integrated the art to the building, may, as Critelli argues, have been influenced by strategies that my father saw on his many trips to South America. His modernist architect colleagues there, shared some of his same earlier influences. So practice and thought are indeed influenced through many pathways.

Los Angeles Hall of Records, Joseph
Young artistic mural, Los Angeles EUA.
Neutra and Alexander, 1962. Photo
Raymond Richard Neutra

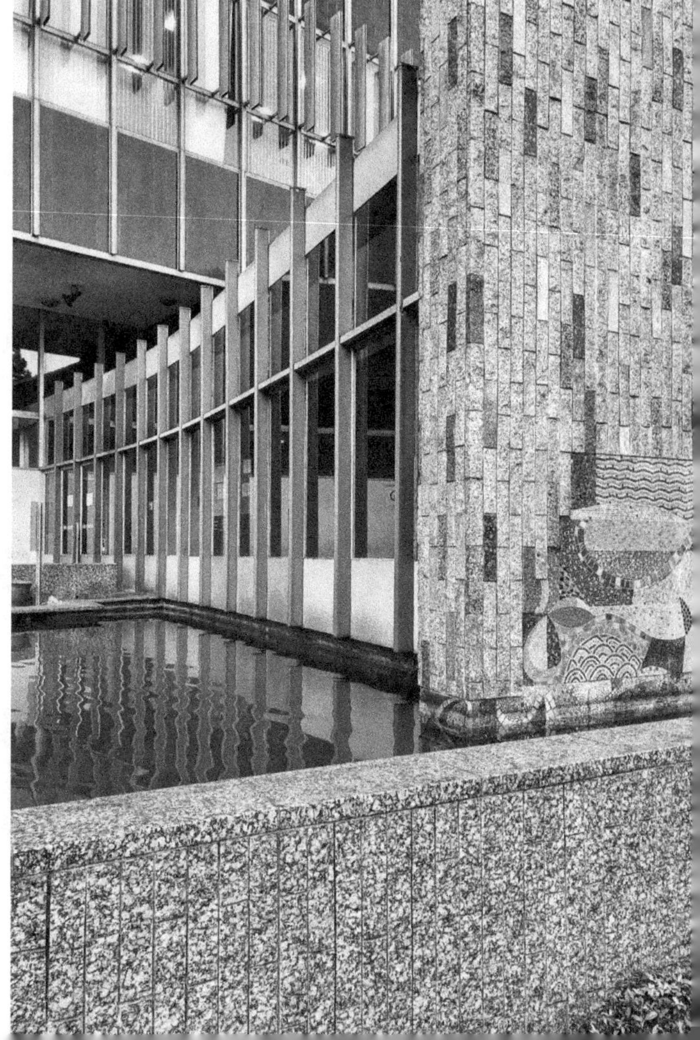

Los Angeles Hall of Records, detail of
Malcolm Leland ceramic mural, Los
Angeles. Neutra and Alexander, 1962.
Photo Raymond Richard Neutra

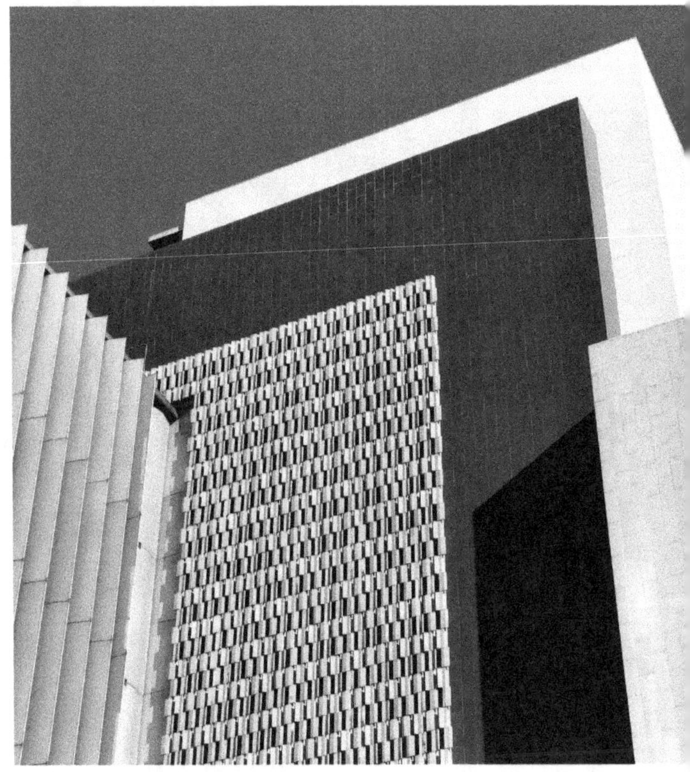

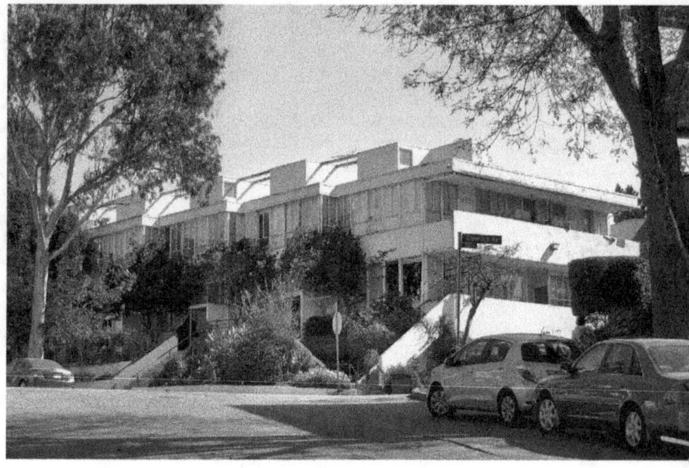

Notes

1. Junípero Serra y Ferrer (1713-1784) was a Roman Catholic Spanish priest and friar of the Franciscan Order. Founder of the Missions, he was appointed to the charge of the one to be established in California, where he spent all the reminder of his life.
2. "Felix Mendelssohn: Reviving the Works of J.S. Bach."
3. Dion Neutra, *The Neutras Then & Later*, 98.
4. Held by the Department of Art and Archaeology of Princeton University, the Kahn Lectures were a series of lectures sponsored by New York banker Otto Hermann Kahn that took place from 1929 to 1931. The series of Frank Lloyd Wright's lectures on Modern Architecture consisted of six lectures and one exhibition of his most recent works, all of them during 1930. Originally published in 1931 in the Princeton monograph series for art and archaeology, a new edition was released in 2008, also by Princeton University: Frank Lloyd Wright, *Modern Architecture: Being the Kahn Lectures of 1930*.
5. Edgar Kaufmann and Ben Raeburn Wright, eds., *Frank Lloyd Wright: Writings and Buildings*, 47-49.

Bibliography

"Casa González-Gorrondona, un Privilegio en El Ávila." *Institutional Assets and Monuments of Venezuela – IAM Venezuela*, Caracas, November 2, 2017 <https://bit.ly/3uVDXNI>.

"Felix Mendelssohn: Reviving the Works of J.S. Bach." Library of Congress <https://bit.ly/3vXbkR9>.

"Summary of AG-018 United Nations Relief and Rehabilitation Administration (UNRRA) (1943-1946)." United Nations Archives <https://bit.ly/3cgk4u3>.

Acayaba, Marcos, Guilherme Wisnik, Hugo Segawa and Júlio Roberto Katinsky. *Marcos Acayaba*. São Paulo: Cosac Naify, 2010.

Acayaba, Marlene Milan. *Branco e Preto: uma história do design brasileiro nos anos 50*. São Paulo: Instituto Lina Bo Bardi, 1994.

Acayaba, Marlene Milan. *Residências em São Paulo 1947-1975*. São Paulo: Romano Guerra, 2011.

Almeida, Maisa Fonseca de. "Revista Acrópole publica residências modernas: análise da revista Acrópole e sua publicação de residências unifamiliares modernas entre os anos 1952 a 1971." Master thesis, EESC USP, 2008.

Alvarez Prozorovich, Fernando, and Abilio Guerra. "Construindo a casa paulista. O rigor e a clareza de Marcio Cotrim na análise da obra de Vilanova Artigas." *Resenhas Online* 19, no. 220.02, Vitruvius 2020 <https://bit.ly/3kOLg3C>.

Atique, Fernando. *Arquitetando a "Boa Vizinhança": Arquitetura, cidade e cultura nas relações Brasil-Estados Unidos 1876-1945*. São Paulo: Pontes, 2010.

Ayerbe, Luis Fernando. *A revolução cubana*. São Paulo: Unesp, 2004.

Bandeira, Luiz Alberto Moniz. *Presença dos Estados Unidos no Brasil*. Rio de Janeiro: Civilização Brasileira, 1973.

Banham, Reyner. *The Architecture of the Well-Tempered Environment*. Chicago: The University of Chicago Press, 1984.

Barbosa, Marcelo. "Franz Heep. Um arquiteto moderno." PhD diss., FAU Mackenzie, 2012.

Barbosa, Marcelo. *Adolf Franz Heep. Um arquiteto moderno*. São Paulo: Monolito, 2018.

Bardi, Pietro Maria. *Neutra: residências/residences*. São Paulo: Museu de Arte de São Paulo, 1950.

Bastos, Maria Alice Junqueira and Ruth Verde Zein. *Brasil. Arquiteturas após 1950*. São Paulo: Perspectiva, 2011.

Baxandall, Michael. *Patterns of Intention. On the Historical Explanation of Pictures*. New Haven/London: Yale University Press, 1985.

Behling, Stefan and Sophia Behling. *Sol Power: La Evolución de la Arquitectura Sostenible*. Barcelona: Gustavo Gili, 2002.

Belgaumi, Arif. "Legacy of the Cold War: Richard Neutra Neutra in Pakistan." *Int|AR – Interventions Adaptative Reuse 3*, October 2010, 83-88.

Bergdoll, Barry and Delfim Sardo. *Modern Architects*. New York: Museum of Modern Art, 2011.

Berman, Marshall. *Tudo que é sólido desmancha no ar. A aventura da modernidade*. São Paulo: Companhia das Letras, 2001.

Beting, Gianfranco. "Pan Am: a pioneira mundial no Brasil." *Flap*, April 2012 <https://bit.ly/3UKDk7Y>.

Bloom, Harold. *The Anxiety of Influence: A Theory of Poetry*. New York/Oxford: Oxford University Press, 1997.

Blumenthal, Michael D. "The Economic Good Neighbor Aspects of United States Economic Policy Toward Latin America in the Early 1940s as Revealed by the Activities of the Office of Inter-American Affairs." PhD diss., University of Wisconsin, 1968.

Boesiger, Willy. *Buildings and Projects: Richard Neutra, 1927-1950*. Zurich: Girsberger, 1951.

Boesiger, Willy. *Buildings and Projects: Richard Neutra, 1950-1960*. Zurich: Girsberger, 1959.

Boesiger, Willy. *Buildings and Projects: Richard Neutra, 1961-1966*. Zurich: Girsberger, 1969.

Bonduki, Nabil, ed., *Affonso Eduardo Reidy*. Lisbon: Blau, 2000.

Bourdieu, Pierre. *O poder simbólico*. Rio de Janeiro: Bertrand, 1989.

Bourdieu, Pierre. "Os modos de produção e modos de percepção artísticos." In *A economia das trocas simbólicas*. Coleção Estudos no. 20, 3rd edition. São Paulo: Perspectiva, 1992, 269-294.

Brasil, Luciana Tombi. *David Libeskind*. São Paulo: Romano Guerra/Edusp, 2007.

Brazilian government leads Western Hemisphere in encouraging modern architecture. Exhibition of Brazilian architecture opens at Museum of Modern Art. New York: The Museum of Modern Art, 1943 <https://mo.ma/3gjtMgh>.

Brinkley, Alan. *Franklin Delano Roosevelt: o presidente que tirou os Estados Unidos do buraco*. Barueri: Amarilys, 2014.

Bruand, Yves. *Arquitetura contemporânea no Brasil*. São Paulo: Perspectiva, 2010.

Bullrich, Francisco. *New Directions in Latin American Architecture*. London: Studio Vista, 1969.

Camargo, Mônica Junqueira de. "Princípios de arquitetura moderna na obra de Oswaldo Arthur Bratke." Phd diss., FAU USP, 2000.

Capello, Maria Beatriz Camargo. "Congresso Internacional de Críticos de Arte 1959. Difusão nas revistas internacionais e nacionais especializadas." In *Annals of VIII Seminário Docomomo Brasil*. Rio de Janeiro, September 2009 <https://bit.ly/3z4gNYy>.

Capello, Maria Beatriz Camargo. "Recepção e difusão da arquitetura moderna brasileira nos números especiais das revistas especializadas europeias (1940-1960)." In *Annals of XIX Seminário Docomomo Brasil*. Brasília, June 2010 <https://bit.ly/3x0wv53>.

Cardinal, Silvia Arango. *Ciudad y Arquitectura: Seis Generaciones que Construyeran la America Latina Moderna*. Mexico: Fondo de Cultura Económica, 2012.

Castillo, José Vela. *Richard Neutra: Un Lugar para el Orden. Un Estudio sobre la Arquitectura Natural.* Sevilla: Editora Universidad de Sevilla/Consejería de Obras Públicas y Transportes, 2003.

Cavalcanti, Lauro and Farès El-Dahdah. *Roberto Burle Marx 100 anos: a permanência do instável.* Rio de Janeiro: Rocco, 2009.

Cavalcanti, Lauro. *Arquitetura moderna carioca 1937-1969.* Rio de Janeiro: Fadel, 2013.

Cavalcanti, Lauro. *Moderno e brasileiro: a história de uma nova linguagem na arquitetura (1930-60).* Rio de Janeiro: Jorge Zahar, 2006.

Cavalcanti, Lauro. *Quando o Brasil era moderno: guia de arquitetura 1928-1960.* Rio de Janeiro: Aeroplano, 2001.

Cheviakoff, Sofia. *Josep Lluís Sert.* Gloucester: Rockport Publishers, 2003.

Ciampaglia, Fernanda. "Galiano Ciampaglia. Razões de uma arquitetura." Master thesis, FAU USP, 2012.

Cobbers, Arnt. *Mendelsohn.* Koln: Taschen, 2010.

Cody, Jeffrey W. *Exporting American Architecture, 1870-2000.* London: Routledge, 2005.

Congresso Internacional Extraordinário de Críticos de Arte. Cidade nova: síntese das artes. Rio de Janeiro: FAU UFRJ, 2009.

Costa, Alcilia Afonso de Albuquerque. "As contribuições arquitetônicas habitacionais propostas na Cidade dos Motores (1945-46). Town Plannings Associates. Xerém, RJ." *Arquitextos* 11, no. 124.01, Vitruvius, September 2010 <https://bit.ly/3wRzBs6>.

Cotrim, Marcio. "Construir a casa paulista: o discurso e a obra de Vilanova Artigas entre 1967 e 1985." PhD diss., ETSAB/UPC, 2008.

Cotrim, Marcio. "Mies e Artigas: a delimitação do espaço através de uma única cobertura." *Arquitextos* 09, no. 108,01, Vitruvius, May 2009 <https://bit.ly/3ik1Awp>.

Cotrim, Marcio. *Vilanova Artigas. Casas paulistas 1967-1981.* São Paulo: Romano Guerra, 2017.

Cramer, Gisela and Ursula Prutsch. ¡Américas Unidas! Nelson A. Rockefeller's Office of Inter-American Affairs (1940-46). Madrid/Frankfurt: Iberoamericana/Vervuert, 2012.

Cramer, Gisela and Ursula Prutsch. "Nelson A. Rockefeller's Office of Inter-American Affairs and the Quest for Pan-American Union: An Introductory Essay." In ¡Américas Unidas! Nelson A. Rockefeller's Office of Inter-American Affairs (1940-46), edited by Gisela Cramer and Ursula Prutsch. Madrid/Frankfurt: Iberoamericana/Vervuert, 2012, 15-52.

Critelli, Fernanda. A questão social da arquitetura. O livro de Neutra: "Arquitetura social em países de clima quente". *Resenhas Online,* n. 106.03, Vitruvius, October 2010 <https://bit.ly/3wW7c4b>.

Critelli, Fernanda. "Richard Neutra e o Brasil." Master thesis, FAU Mackenzie, 2015.

Critelli, Fernanda. "Richard Neutra no Brasil." Scientific initiation research, FAU Mackenzie, 2012.

Critelli, Fernanda. "Richard Neutra: conexões latino-americanas." PhD diss., FAU Mackenzie, 2020.

Crosse, John. The Taliesin Class of 1924: A Case Study in Publicity and Fame. *Southern California Architectural History*, June 25, 2019 <https://bit.ly/3pqJz0Q>.

Curtis, William J. R. *Arquitetura moderna desde 1900*. Porto Alegre: Bookman, 2008.

Czajkowski, Jorge. *Jorge Machado Moreira*. Rio de Janeiro: Centro de Arquitetura e Urbanismo, 1999.

De Wit, Wim and James Alexander. *Overdrive: L.A. Constructs the Future 1940-1990*. Los Angeles: The Getty Research Institute, 2013.

Dedecca, Paula Gorenstein. "Aproximações, diferenciações e embates entre a produção do Rio de Janeiro e de São Paulo nas revistas de arquitetura (1945-1960)." In *Annals of VIII Seminário Docomomo Brasil*. Rio de Janeiro, September 2009 <https://bit.ly/3igU45z>.

De Lucca, Guss. "Those responsible for the attacks on the event in 2008 will take part in the next edition to debate the *'pixo'*. *IG*, June 15, 2010 <https://bityli.com/L3wuhW>.

Del Real, Patrício. "Building a Continent: The Idea of Latin American Architecture in the Early Postwar." PhD diss., Columbia University, 2012.

Dent, David W. *Historical Dictionary of U.S.-Latin American Relations*. Westport/London: Greenwood Press, 2005.

Dourado, Guilherme Mazza. *Modernidade verde: jardins de Burle Marx*. São Paulo: Senac, 2009.

Durand, José Carlos. "Le Corbusier no Brasil: negociação política e renovação arquitetônica. Contribuição à história social da arquitetura brasileira." *RBCS*, no.16, July 1991 <https://bit.ly/3ggJRnb>.

Ettinger, Catherine R. *Richard Neutra en América Latina: Una Mirada desde el Sur*. Guadalaraja: Arquitetônica, 2018.

Faggin, Carlos Augusto Mattei. "Carlos Millán. Itinerário profissional de um arquiteto paulista." PhD diss., FAU USP, 1992.

Fernández-Galiano, Luis. "El Constructor en el Espejo." *AV Monografias*, no. 132, Madrid, July/August 2008, 3.

Ferroni, Eduardo Rocha. "Aproximações sobre a obra de Salvador Candia." Master thesis, FAU USP, 2008.

Figueroa, Carmen A. Rivera de. *Architecture for the Tropics*. San Juan: Editorial Universitaria/Universidad de Puerto Rico, 1980.

Fonseca, Maurício A. "Le Corbusier e a conquista da América." *Resenhas Online*, no. 001.08, Vitruvius, January 2002 <https://bit.ly/34Y5Nhj>.

Foresti, Débora Fabbri. "Aspectos da arquitetura orgânica de Frank Lloyd Wright na arquitetura paulista: a obra de José Leite de Carvalho e Silva." Master thesis, IAU USP, 2008.

Forte, Miguel. *Diário de um jovem arquiteto: minha viagem aos Estados Unidos em 1947*. São Paulo: Editora Mackenzie, 2001.

Fragelli, Marcelo. *Quarenta anos de prancheta*. São Paulo: Romano Guerra, 2010.

Frampton, Kenneth. *História crítica da arquitetura moderna*. São Paulo: Martins Fontes, 2008.

Franco, Tiago Seneme. "A trajetória de Jacques Pilon no Centro de São Paulo. Análise das obras de 1940 a 1947." Master thesis, FAU Mackenzie, 2009.

Fraser, Valerie. *Building the New World: Studies in the Modern Architecture of Latin America, 1930-1960*. London/New York: Verso, 2000.

Freud, Sigmund (1919). "The Uncanny." https://bit.ly/3laUonK

Fujioka, Paulo Yassuhide. "Princípios da arquitetura organicista de Frank Lloyd Wright e suas influências na arquitetura moderna paulistana." PhD diss., FAU USP, 2003.

Galeazzi, Ítalo. "Mies van der Rohe no Brasil. Projeto para o Consulado dos Estados Unidos em São Paulo, 1957-1962." *Arquitextos* 05, no. 056.03, Vitruvius, January 2005 <https://bit.ly/3gfYbfk>.

Gay, Peter. *Freud para historiadores*. São Paulo: Paz e Terra, 1989.

Gimenez, Luis Espallargas. *Pedro Paulo de Melo Saraiva, arquiteto*. São Paulo: Romano Guerra/Instituto Lina Bo e P.M. Bardi, 2016.

Ginzburg, Carlo. "Controlando a evidência: o juiz e o historiador." In *Nova história em perspectiva. Propostas e desdobramentos*, edited by Fernando A. Novais and Rogerio F. da Silva. São Paulo: Cosac Naify, 2011, 341-358.

Ginzburg, Carlo. "Microhistory: Two or Three Things that I Know About It." *Critical Inquiry*, no. 20, March/June 1993, 10-35.

Ginzburg, Carlo. *Mitos, emblemas, sinais: morfologia e história*. São Paulo: Companhia das Letras, 2002.

Ginzburg, Carlo. *O queijo e os vermes: o cotidiano e as ideias de um moleiro perseguido pela Inquisição*. São Paulo: Companhia das Letras, 1987.

Ginzburg, Carlo. "Sinais: raízes de um paradigma indiciário." In *Mitos, emblemas, sinais: morfologia e história*, 143-179. São Paulo: Companhia das Letras, 2002.

Glinkin, Anaioly. *Inter-American Relations: From Bolívar to the Present*. Moscou: Pregress Publishers, 1990.

Gnoato, Luis Salvador. "O Brasil novamente no MoMA de Nova York. Latin American in Construction: Architecture 1955-1980." *Drops*, no. 092.03, May 2015 <https://bit.ly/3zfSA1A>.

Goldberger, Paul. "Wallace Harrison Dead at 86; Rockefeller Center Architect." *The New York Times*, December 3, 1981 <https://nyti.ms/3il9pSl>.

Gomes, Angela de Castro, ed. *História do Brasil nação: 1808-2010*. Volume 4: Olhando para dentro 1930-1964. Rio de Janeiro: Objetiva, 2013.

Gonzáles, Robert. *Designing Pan-America: U.S. Architectural Visions for the Western Hemisphere*. Austin: University of Texas Press, 2011.

Goodwin, Philip L. *Brazil Builds: Architecture New and Old 1652-1942*. New York: The Museum of Modern Art, 1943.

Gravagnuolo, Benedetto. *Adolf Loos: Theory and Works*. New York: Rizzoli, 1982.

Guerra, Abilio and Fernanda Critelli. "Richard Neutra e o Brasil." *Arquitextos* 14, no.159.00, Vitruvius, August 2013 <https://bit.ly/3w8oESM>.

Guerra, Abilio. "Como se escreve uma dissertação." *Resenhas Online* 19, no. 227.03, Vitruvius, November 2010 <https://bit.ly/3k31iu0>.

Guerra, Abilio, ed. *Textos fundamentais sobre história da arquitetura moderna brasileira – parte 1.* São Paulo: Romano Guerra, 2010.

Guerra, Abilio, ed. *Textos fundamentais sobre história da arquitetura moderna brasileira – parte 2.* São Paulo: Romano Guerra, 2010.

Guerra, Abilio. "Lúcio Costa – modernidade e tradição. Montagem discursiva da arquitetura moderna brasileira." PhD diss., IFCH Unicamp, 2002.

Guerra, Abilio. "Lúcio Costa, Gregori Warchavchik e Roberto Burle Marx: síntese entre arquitetura e natureza tropical." *Revista USP*, no. 53, March/May 2002, 18-31.

Guerra, Abilio. "Monografia sobre Salvador Candia e a necessidade de um diálogo acadêmico." *Resenhas Online*, no. 078.03, Vitruvius, June 2008 <https://bit.ly/2Rw9FDq>.

Guerra, Abilio. O brutalismo paulista no contexto paranaense. A arquitetura do escritório Forte Gandolfi. *Resenhas Online*, no. 106.02, Vitruvius, October 2010 <https://bit.ly/2Sgj1Dr>.

Guimarães, Marília Dorador. "Roberto Burle Marx: a contribuição do artista e paisagista no Estado de São Paulo". Master thesis, Minter Mackenzie/Unifor, 2015.

Hart, Justin. *Empire of Ideas. The Origins of Public Diplomacy and the Transformation of U.S. Foreign Policy.* New York: Oxford University Press, 2013. Kindle edition.

Hines, Thomas S. and Arthur Drexler. *The Architecture of Richard Neutra: From International Style to California Modern.* New York: The Museum of Modern Art, 1982.

Hines, Thomas S. *Richard Neutra and the Search for Modern Architecture.* New York: Rizzoli, 2005.

Hormain, Débora da Rosa Rodrigues Lima. "O relacionamento Brasil-EUA e a arquitetura moderna: experiências compartilhadas, 1939-1959." PhD diss., FAU USP, 2012.

Irigoyen Touceda, Adriana Marta. "Da Califórnia a São Paulo." PhD diss., FAU USP, 2005.

Irigoyen Touceda, Adriana Marta. "Frank Lloyd Wright e o Brasil." Master thesis, EESC USP, 2000.

Irigoyen Touceda, Adriana Marta. *Wright e Artigas: duas viagens.* São Paulo: Ateliê Editorial, 2002.

Josep Lluís Sert: A Nomadic Dream, film by Pablo Bujosa Rodríguez, 2013, 73 min.

Kaplan, Wendy. *California Design 1930-1965: Living in a Modern Way.* Los Angeles/Cambridge: Los Angeles County Museum of Art/MIT Press, 2011.

Kaufmann, Edgar and Ben Raeburn Wright, editors. *Frank Lloyd Wright: Writings and Buildings.* New York, Horizon Press, 1960.

Khan, Hasan-Uddin. *Estilo Internacional: arquitetura modernista de 1925-1965.* Koln: Taschen, 2009.

Kilston, Lyra. *Sun Seekers. The Cure of California*. Los Angeles/London: Atelier Éditions, 2019.

Lamprecht, Barbara Mac. *Richard Neutra 1892-1970: formas criadoras para uma vida melhor*. Koln: Taschen, 2010.

Lamprecht, Barbara Mac. *Richard Neutra: Complete Works*. Koln: Taschen, 2010.

Lamprecht, Barbara Mac. "The Obsolescence of Optimism? Neutra and Alexander's U.S. Embassy, Karachi, Pakistan." *Modern Resources*, June 23, 2012 <https://bit.ly/3psKtdA>.

Lapuerta, José María. "Casa VDL, Los Ángeles (Estados Unidos) / VDL House, Los Angeles (United States)." *AV Monografias*, no. 132, July/August 2008, 30-41.

Lapuerta, José María. "Casas de maestros / House of Masters." *AV Monografias*, no. 132, July/August 2008.

Lassala, Gustavo. "Em nome do pixo. A experiência social e estética do pixador e artista Djan Ivson." PhD diss., FAU Mackenzie, 2014.

Lassala, Gustavo and Abilio Guerra. "Cripta Djan Ivson, profissão pixador. Pixar é crime num país onde roubar é arte". *Entrevista* 13, no. 049.04, Vitruvius, March 2012 <https://bityli.com/gOR8k9>.

Lassance, Guilherme, ed. *Leituras em teoria da arquitetura – volumes 2 and 3*. Rio de Janeiro: Viana&Mosley, 2010.

Lavin, Sylvia. *Form Follows Libido: Architecture and Richard Neutra in a Psychoanalytic Culture*. Cambridge: MIT Press, 2004.

Leatherbarrow, David. *Uncommon Ground: Architecture, Technology, and Topography*. Cambrigde: MIT Press, 2002.

Leet, Stephen. *Richard Neutra's Miller House*. New York: Princeton Architectural Press, 2004.

Leonard, Thomas M. *United States-Latin American Relations, 1850-1903*. Tuscaloosa/London: The University of Alabama Press, 1999.

Levi, Giovanni. "Sobre a micro-história." In *A escrita da história: novas perspectivas*, edited by Peter Burke. São Paulo: Editora UNESP, 1992, 133-162.

Liernur, Jorge Francisco. "'The South american way'. O milagre brasileiro, os Estados Unidos e a Segunda Guerra Mundial – 1939-1943." In *Textos fundamentais sobre história da arquitetura moderna brasileira – parte 2*, edited by Abilio Guerra. São Paulo: Romano Guerra, 2010.

Liernur, Jorge Francisco. "Latin America: The Places of the "Other"." In *At the End of the Century: One Hundred Years of Architecture*, edited by Richard Koshalek, Elizabeth A. T. Smith and Celik Zeynep. New York: Abrams, 1998.

Lins, Paulo de Tarso Amendola. "Arquitetura nas bienais internacionais de São Paulo (1951-1961)." PhD diss., IAU USP, 2008.

Lira, José. "From Mild Climate's Architecture to 'Third World' Planning: Richard Neutra in Latin America." In *Annals of 14th International Planning History Society Conference*. Istambul, July 2010 <https://bit.ly/3gbbayX>.

Lira, José. "Redes, fronteiras e vetores: três arquitetos estrangeiros em São Paulo." In *Annals of II Enanparq: Teorias e práticas na arquitetura e na cidade contemporâneas.* Natal, September 2012.

Lira, José. *Warchavchik: fraturas da vanguarda.* São Paulo: Cosac Naify, 2011.

Loeffler, Jane C. *The Architecture of Diplomacy: Building America's Embassies.* New York: Princeton Architectural Press, 2011.

Loureiro, Claudia, and Luiz Amorim. "Por uma arquitetura social: a influência de Richard Neutra em prédios escolares no Brasil." *Arquitextos* 2, no. 020.03, Vitruvius, January 2002 <https://bit.ly/3clOnj0>.

Lübken, Uwe. "Playing the Cultural Game: The United States and the Nazi Threat to Latin America." In ¡Américas Unidas! Nelson A. Rockefeller's Office of Inter-American Affairs (1940-46), edited by Gisela Cramer and Ursula Prutsch. Madrid/Frankfurt: Iberoamericana/Vervuert, 2012, 53-76.

Maior, Armando Souto. *História geral.* São Paulo: Companhia Editora Nacional, 1966.

Marlin, Willian. *Nature Near: Late Essays of Richard Neutra.* Santa Barbara: Capra Press, 1989.

Marques, André. "Aldary Toledo – entre arte e arquitetura." PhD diss., FAU Mackenzie, 2018.

Marques, André. "A obra de João Filgueiras Lima, Lelé: projeto, técnica e racionalização." Master thesis, FAU Mackenzie, 2012.

Marques, André. *Lelé: diálogos com Neutra e Prouvé.* São Paulo/Austin: Romano Guerra/Nhamerica, 2020.

Martins, Carlos Alberto F. "Estado, cultura e natureza na origem da arquitetura moderna brasileira: Le Corbusier e Lúcio Costa (1929-1936)." *Caramelo,* no. 6, 1993, 129-136.

Mccann Jr., Frank D. *The Brazilian-American Alliance, 1937-1945.* Princeton: Princeton University Press, 1973.

McCoy, Esther. *Richard Neutra.* New York: George Braziller, 1960.

McCoy, Esther. *Vienna to Los Angeles: Two Journeys. Letters between R. M. Schindler and Richard Neutra. Letters of Louis Sullivan to R. M. Schindler.* Santa Monica: Arts + Architecture Press, 1979.

Mendonça, Fernando de Magalhães. "Pedro Paulo de Melo Saraiva: 50 anos de arquitetura." Master thesis, FAU Mackenzie, 2006.

Minchillo, Carlos Cortez. *Erico Verissimo, escritor do mundo: circulação literária, cosmopolitismo e relações interamericanas.* São Paulo: EDUSP, 2015.

Mindlin, Henrique. *Arquitetura moderna no Brasil.* Rio de Janeiro: Aeroplano, 1999.

Montaner, Josep Maria. *Arquitetura e crítica na América Latina.* São Paulo: Romano Guerra, 2014.

Morais, Fernando. *Chatô: o rei do Brasil.* São Paulo: Companhia das Letras, 1994.

Moreira, Pedro. "Alexandre Altberg e a Arquitetura Nova no Rio de Janeiro." *Arquitextos* 05, no. 058.00, Vitruvius, March 2005 <https://bit.ly/3ilHuSo>.

Moura, Gerson. *Brazilian Foreign Relations 1939-1950: The Changing Nature of Brazil-United States Relations During and After the Second World War*. Brasília: Fundação Alexandre Gusmão, 2013.

Moura, Gerson. *Tio Sam chega ao Brasil: a penetração cultural americana*. São Paulo: Brasiliense, 1984.

Munford, Eric. "The CIAM Discourse on Urbanism, 1928-1959." PhD diss., Princeton University, 1996.

Munford, Eric. *The CIAM Discourse on Urbanism, 1928-1960*. Cambridge: The MIT Press, 2000.

Nahas, Patricia Viceconti. "Brasil Arquitetura: memória e contemporaneidade. Um percurso do Sesc Pompéia ao Museu do Pão (1977-2008)." Master thesis, FAU Mackenzie, 2009.

Nedelykov, Nina and Pedro Moreira. "Caminhos da arquitetura moderna no Brasil: a presença de Frank Lloyd Wright." *Arquitextos* 02, no. 018.03, Vitruvius, November 2001 <https://bit.ly/3ggjXQn>.

Neto, Lira. *Getúlio: da volta pela consagração popular ao suicídio (1945-1954)*. São Paulo: Companhia das Letras, 2014.

Neto, Lira. *Getúlio: do Governo Provisório à ditadura do Estado Novo (1930-1945)*. São Paulo: Companhia das Letras, 2013.

Neutra, Dion. *The Neutras Then & Later*. Barcelona/Vienna: Triton, 2012.

Neutra, Dione. *Richard Neutra: Promise and Fulfillment, 1919-1932*. Illinois: Southern Illinois University, 1986.

Neutra, Dione. *To Tell the Truth: Interviewed by Lawrence Weschler*. Los Angeles: University of California, 1983.

Neutra, Raymond Richard. "Encontros porto-riquenhos." *Arquitextos* 14, no.158.01, Vitruvius, August 2013 <https://bit.ly/3ppiGdL>.

Neutra, Raymond Richard. *Cheap and Thin: Neutra and Frank Lloyd Wright*, 2017. Kindle edition.

Neutra, Richard Joseph. "Arquitetura funcional." *Revista de Engenharia Mackenzie*, no. 67, October 1937, 132-133.

Neutra, Richard Joseph. "Dos aspectos formais não visuais do plano da cidade e seu contexto urbanístico." *Habitat*, no. 57, October/November 1959, 16-17.

Neutra, Richard Joseph. "Observations on Latin America." *Progressive Architecture*, no. 5, May 1946, 67-72.

Neutra, Richard Joseph. "Planejamento: um problema humano, com base no indivíduo." *Módulo*, no. 15, 1959, 14-17.

Neutra, Richard Joseph. "Sun Control Devices." *Progressive Architecture*, no. 10, October 1946, 88-91.

Neutra, Richard Joseph. "Uma casa inédita de Neutra." *Pilotis*, no. 4, February 1950, 4-9.

Neutra, Richard Joseph. *Architecture of Social Concern in Countries of Mild Climate*. São Paulo: Todtmann, 1948.

Neutra, Richard Joseph. *El Mundo y la Vivienda*. Barcelona: Gustavo Gili, 1962.

Neutra, Richard Joseph. *Life and Shape*. New York: Appleton Century Crofts, 1962.

Neutra, Richard Joseph. *Planificar para sobrevivir*. Mexico/Buenos Aires: Fondo de Cultura Económica, 1957.

Neutra, Richard Joseph. *Realismo Biológico. Um Nuevo Renacimiento Humanístico en Arquitectura*. Buenos Aires: Nueva Visión, 1958.

Neutra, Richard Joseph. *Survival Through Design*. New York: Oxford University Press, 1954.

Neutra, Richard Joseph. *Vida y forma*. Buenos Aires: Marymar, 1972.

Newhouse, Victoria. *Wallace K. Harrison, Architect*. New York: Rizzoli, 1989.

Oliveira, Liana Paula Perez de. "A capacidade de dizer não. Lina Bo Bardi e a Fábrica da Pompeia." Master thesis, FAU Mackenzie, 2007.

Ortenblad Filho, Rodolpho. "A arquitetura de Richard Neutra." *Acrópole*, no. 230, December 1957, 56-57.

Our Architects en Caracas: Arquitectura Norteamericana en Caracas, 1925-1975. Exhibition catalogue (Room TAC, Caracas, July 25 to October 1, 2017). Caracas: Fundación Trasnocho Cultural/Docomomo Venezuela, 2017.

Paquette, Catha. "Soft Power: The Art of Diplomacy in US-Mexican Relations, 1940-1946." In ¡Américas Unidas! Nelson A. Rockefeller's Office of Inter-American Affairs (1940-46), edited by Gisela Cramer and Ursula Prutsch. Madrid/Frankfurt: Iberoamericana/Vervuert, 2012, 143-180.

Parra, Narciso Guaramato. "JJ Gonzalez Gorrondona." *Protagonistas en la Economia Venezolana*, Caracas, June 6, 2009 <https://bit.ly/2TLT4fy>.

Pereira, Ana Larla Olimpio and Paulo Yassuhide Fujioka. "A residência do arquiteto: uma análise gráfica das casas de Vilanova Artigas." *Risco*, no. 21, January/June 2015, 36-59.

Pereira, Sabrina Bom. "Rodolpho Ortenblad Filho: estudo sobre as residências." Master thesis, FAU Mackenzie, 2010.

Peter, John. *The Oral History of Modern Architecture*. New York: Harry N. Abrams, 2000.

Puglisi, Mariana de Carvalho. "Habitação e cidade – espaços coletivos na habitação de interesse social. Análise das obras do arquiteto Hector Vigliecca em São Paulo – 1989 a 2016." Master thesis, FAU Mackenzie, 2017.

Quantrill, Malcom. *Latin American Architecture: Six Voices*. College Station: Texas A&M University, 2000.

Queiroz, Rodrigo. "Projeto moderno e território americano: a arquitetura de uma nova paisagem." In *Annals of VIII Seminário Docomomo Brasil*. Rio de Janeiro, September 2009 <https://bit.ly/3cn1KPT>.

Rabell, Leonardo Santana. *Planificación y Política Durante la Administración de Luis Muñoz Marin: Un Análisis Crítico*. Puerto Rico: Analisis, 1984.

Radford, Antony, Selen Morkoç and Amit Srivastava. *The Elements of Modern Architecture: Understanding Contemporary Buildings*. London: Thames and Hudson, 2014.

Ribeiro, Patrícia Pimenta Azevedo. "A participação do arquiteto Richard Neutra no Congresso Internacional Extraordinário de Crítico de Arte em 1959." In *Annals of VIII Seminário Docomomo Brasil*. Rio de Janeiro, September 2009 <https://bit.ly/3xdIUTx>.

Ribeiro, Patrícia Pimenta Azevedo. "Teoria e prática. A obra do arquiteto Richard Neutra." PhD diss., FAU USP, 2007.

Robin, Ron. *Enclaves of America: The Rhetoric of American Political Architecture Abroad, 1900-1965*. New Jersey: Princeton University Press, 1992.

Rocha, Fernanda Cláudia Lacerda. "Os jardins residenciais de Roberto Burle Marx em Fortaleza: entre descontinuidades e conexões." Master thesis, Minter Mackenzie/Unifor, 2015.

Rocha, Ricardo. "Resenhar Brazil Builds." *Resenhas Online*, no. 142.05, Vitruvius, October 2013 <https://bit.ly/3ildu9y>.

Rodrigues, Felipe de Souza Silva. "Aurelio Martinez Flores: a produção do arquiteto mexicano no Brasil (1960-2015)." Master thesis, FAU Mackenzie, 2019.

Rodríguez López, Luz Marie. "¡Vuelo al porvenir! Henry Klumb y Toro-Ferrer: proyecto moderno y arquitectura como vitrina de la democracia – Puerto Rico, 1944-1958." PhD diss., Universitat Politècnica de Catalunya, 2008.

Rodríguez, Eduardo Luis. "Theory and Practice of Modern Regionalism in Cuba." *Docomomo Journal*, no. 33, September 2005 <https://bit.ly/3uW83Ac>.

Rodríguez, Eduardo Luis. *Modernidad Tropical. Neutra, Burle Marx y Cuba: La Casa de Schulthess*. Havana: Embassy of Switzerland in Cuba, 2007.

Rodríguez, Eduardo Luis. *The Havana Guide: Modern Architecture 1925-1965*. New York: Princeton Architectural Press, 2000.

Rossetti, Eduardo Pierrotti. "Brasília, 1959: a cidade em obras e o Congresso Internacional Extraordinário dos Críticos de Arte." In *Annals of VIII Seminário Docomomo Brasil*. Rio de Janeiro, September 2009 <https://bit.ly/3wUKWYc>.

Rovira, Josep M. *José Luis Sert: 1901-1983*. Milan: Electa Architecture, 2003. [English version]

Rowland, Donald W., ed. *History of the Office of the Coordinator of Inter-American Affairs: Historical Reports on War Administration*. Washington: Government Printing Office, 1947 <https://bit.ly/34UfQ78>.

Royo, Rosa Remón. "Casa González Gorrondona o Alto Claro, Caracas Venezuela obra del Arquitecto Richard J. Neutra: posiblemente la residencia unifamiliar más grande proyectada por Richard J. Neutra." *Arquitectura y Empresa*, Godella, November 9, 2017 <https://bit.ly/3gekt1i>.

Ruchti, Valeria. "Jacob Ruchti: a modernidade e a arquitetura paulista (1940-1970)." Master thesis, FAU USP, 2011.

Rydell, Robert W. and Laura Burd Schiavo. *Designing Tomorrow: America's World's Fairs of the 1930s*. London: Yale University Press, 2010.

Sack, Manfred. *Richard Neutra*. Barcelona: Gustavo Gili, 1994.

Safran, Yehuda and Wilfried Wang. *The Architecture of Adolf Loos.* London: The Arts Concil, 1985.

Said, Edward W. *Cultura e imperialismo.* São Paulo: Companhia das Letras, 2011.

Santos, Daniela Ortiz, Mário Luis Carneiro Pinto Magalhães and Priscilla Alves Peixoto. "Cartas sobre cartas – a contribuição silenciosa brasileira na construção dos primeiros Congressos Internacionais de Arquitetura Moderna." In *Annals of VIII Seminário Docomomo Brasil.* Rio de Janeiro, September 2009 <https://bit.ly/2Rr65u5>.

Santos, Maria Cecília Loschiavo dos. *Móvel moderno no Brasil.* São Paulo: Studio Nobel, 1995.

Segawa, Hugo, and Guilherme Mazza Dourado. *Oswaldo Arthur Bratke.* São Paulo: PW Editores, 2012.

Segawa, Hugo. "Arquitetos peregrinos, nômades e migrantes." In *Arquiteturas no Brasil/Anos 80,* edited by Hugo Segawa. São Paulo: Projeto, 1988, 9-13.

Segawa, Hugo. *Arquiteturas no Brasil 1900-1990.* São Paulo: EDUSP, 2010.

Segre, Roberto. "Ideias e invenções de Buckminster Fuller são analisadas por Roberto Segre." *Projeto,* no. 212, November 2011.

Segre, Roberto. "Oscar Niemeyer: tipologias e liberdade plástica." In *Tributo a Niemeyer,* edited by Alberto Petrina. Rio de Janeiro: Viana&Mosley, 2009, 163-175.

Segre, Roberto. *Arquitetura e urbanismo da revolução cubana.* São Paulo: Nobel, 1987.

Segre, Roberto. *La Vivienda en Cuba en el Siglo XX: Republica y Revolucion.* Mexico: Concepto, 1980.

Segre, Roberto. *Ministério da Educação e Saúde: ícone urbano da modernidade brasileira.* São Paulo: Romano Guerra, 2013.

Sennott, Stephen. *Encyclopedia of Twentieth Century Architecture.* New York: Fitzroy Dearborn, 2004.

Sert, José Luis, Ferdnand Léger and Sigfried Giedion (1943). "Nine Points on Monumentality." In Giedion, Sigfried. *Architecture You and Me: The Diary of a Development.* Cambridge: Harvard University Press, 1958, 48-51.

Sheine, Judith. *R. M. Schindler.* London: Phaidon, 2001.

Silva, Helena Ayoub. *Abrahão Sanovicz, arquiteto.* São Paulo: Romano Guerra, 2017.

Silva, Joana Mello de Carvalho. "O arquiteto e a produção da cidade: a experiência de Jacques Pilon em perspectiva (1930-1960)." PhD diss., FAU USP, 2010.

Siqueira, Vera Beatriz. *Burle Marx.* São Paulo: Cosac Naify, 2009.

Smith, Elizabeth A. T. *Case Study Houses.* Koln: Taschen, 2010.

Smith, Kathryn. *Frank Lloyd Wright: America's Master Architect.* New York: Abbeville Press, 1998.

Smith, Richard Cándida. "Érico Veríssimo, a Brazilian Cultural Ambassador in the United States." *Revista Tempo* 17, no. 34, January/June 2013, 147-173 <https://bit.ly/3pnNAU1>.

Sodré, João Clark de Abreu. "Roteiros americanos: as viagens de Mindlin e Artigas pelos Estados Unidos, 1943-1947." PhD diss., FAU USP, 2016.

Sombra, Fausto. "Luís Saia e o restauro do Sítio Santo Antônio: diálogos modernos na conformação arquitetônica paulista." Master thesis, FAU Mackenzie, 2015.

Sombra, Fausto. "Três pavilhões de Sérgio Bernardes: Volta Redonda, Bruxelas e São Cristóvão. Contribuição à vanguarda arquitetônica moderna brasileira em meados do século 20." PhD diss., FAU Mackenzie, 2020.

Sosa, Marisol Rodríguez; Segre, Roberto. "Do coração da cidade – a Otterlo (1951-59). Discussões transgressoras de ruptura, a semente das novas direções pós-CIAM." In *Annals of VIII Seminário Docomomo Brasil*. Rio de Janeiro, September 2009, https://bit.ly/3fR4gQC.

Steele, James. *Los Angeles Architecture: The Contemporary Condition*. London: Phaidon, 1993.

Steele, James. *Schindler*. Koln: Taschen, 2005.

Stevens, Garry. *O círculo privilegiado: fundamentos sociais da distinção arquitetônica*. Brasília: Editora UnB, 2003.

Stuchi, Fabiana Terenzi. "Revista Habitat: um olhar moderno sobre os anos 50 em São Paulo." Master thesis, FAU USP, 2006.

Sullivan, Louis Henri. *Um sistema de ornamento arquitetônico coerente com uma filosofia dos poderes do homem*. Londrina: EDUEL, 2011.

Tagliari, Ana. *Frank Lloyd Wright: princípio, espaço e forma na arquitetura residencial*. São Paulo: Annablume, 2011.

Tentori, Francesco. *P.M. Bardi*. São Paulo: Instituto Lina Bo e P.M. Bardi/Imprensa Oficial do Estado, 2000.

Toledo, Benedito Lima. *Vila Penteado: registros*. São Paulo: FAU USP, 2002.

Tota, Antonio Pedro. *O amigo americano: Nelson Rockefeller e o Brasil*. São Paulo: Companhia das Letras, 2014.

Tota, Antonio Pedro. *O imperialismo sedutor: a americanização do Brasil na época da Segunda Guerra*. São Paulo: Companhia das Letras, 2000.

Tsiomis, Yannis. *Le Corbusier: Rio de Janeiro 1929-1936*. Rio de Janeiro: Centro de Arquitetura e Urbanismo do Rio de Janeiro, 1998.

Union Pacific System. *California Calls You*. Chicago: Poole Bros., 1921.

United Nations. "A Workshop for Peace: The Creation of the United Nations Headquarters." *YouTube*, June 17, 2016 <https://bit.ly/3g7BKJo>.

United Nations. *The United Nations and Latin America: A Collection of Basic Information Material About the Work of the United Nations and the Related Agencies in Latin America*. New York: The United Nations Office of Public Information/External Relations Division, 1961.

Vivoni Farage, Enrique. *San Juan Siempre Nuevo: Arquitecture y Modernización en el Siglo XX*. San Juan: Universidad de Puerto Rico, 2000.

Vleck, Jenifer Van. *Empire of the Air: Aviation and the American Ascendancy*. Cambridge: Harvard University Press, 2013. Kindle edition.

Waisman, Marina. *O interior da história: historiografia arquitetônica para uso de latino-americanos*. São Paulo: Perspectiva, 2013.

Williamson, Edwin. *História da América Latina*. Lisbon: Edições 70, 2012.

Wilson, Richard Guy. "Reflections on Modernism and World's Fairs." In Rydell, Robert W. and Laura Burd Schiavo. *Designing Tomorrow: America's World's Fairs of the 1930s*. London: Yale University Press, 2010.

Wong, Yunn Chii. "Fuller's DDU project (1941-1944): Instrument, Art or Architecture? (Heroic design versus ad hoc pragmatism)." In *Transportable Environments: Theory, Context, Design and Technology*, edited by Robert Kronenburg. New York: Routledge, 1998.

Wright, Frank Lloyd. *Modern Architecture: Being the Kahn Lectures of 1930*. Introduction by Neil Levine. Princeton, Princeton University Press, 2008.

Xavier, Alberto, ed. *Depoimento de uma geração: arquitetura moderna brasileira*. São Paulo: Cosac Naify, 2003.

Zabalbeascoa, Anatxu and Javier Rodríguez Marcos. *Vidas Construidas: Biografías de Arquitectos*. Barcelona: Gustavo Gili, 2002.

Zein, Ruth Verde. "When Documenting is not Enough. Buildings, Dates, Reflections, and Theoretical Constructions." In *Critical Readings*. São Paulo/Austin: Romano Guerra/Nhamerica, 2019.

Zevi, Bruno. *Frank Lloyd Wright. Obras y Proyectos/Obras e projetos*. Barcelona: Gustavo Gili, 2006.

Zevi, Bruno. *Richard Neutra*. Italy: Il Balcone, 1954.

About the author

Fernanda Critelli is architect
with master and PhD degrees (FAU
Mackenzie, 2012, 2015 and 2020).
Worked for six years at Bacco
Arquitetos Associados, was volunteer
secretary at Núcleo Docomomo
São Paulo (2014-2019) and, for
seven years, worked as editor at
Romano Guerra Editora (2016-2023).
Is researcher of Richard Neutra's
works since undergraduate school,
with scientific initiation (CNPq
scholarship), master degree (Capes
and Fapesp scholarships), with a
period as a foreign researcher at
University of Texas at Austin, and PhD
(Mackpesquisa scholarship).

Romano Guerra Editora
Rua General Jardim 645 cj 31
01223-011 São Paulo SP Brasil
rg@romanoguerra.com.br
www.romanoguerra.com.br

Nhamerica Platform
807 E 44th st,
Austin, TX, 78751 USA
editors@nhamericaplatform.com
www.nhamericaplatform.com

Latin America: Thoughts
Romano Guerra Editora
Nhamerica Platform
Management Coordination
Abilio Guerra
Fernando Luiz Lara
Silvana Romano Santos

Richard Neutra and Brazil
Fernanda Critelli
Brasil 7
Editor
Abilio Guerra
Fernando Luiz Lara
Silvana Romano Santos
Graphic Design and Formatting
Dárkon V Roque
Pre-press
Nelson Kon
Translation
Odorico Leal
Translation review
Noemi Zein Telles
Support
This book is based on research supported by the following scholarships: Pibic CNPq (scientific initiation); Capes Prosup/Taxas, Fapesp for in country master degree (process n. 2013/04898-1) and for research internship overseas (process n. 2014/12996-6; master degree); and Fundo Mackpesquisa (PhD)

This book's translation to English version received support from Processo Capes n. 23038.009799/2019-96, Programa Proex n. 1135/2019, received by the Programa de Pós-Graduação em Arquitetura e Urbanismo da Universidade Presbiteriana Mackenzie

Acknowledgements

Adriana Irigoyen, Aimee Lind (Getty Research Institute), Andres Otero, Angélica Benatti Alvim, Antonio Pedro Tota, Bruno Mesquita (Biblioteca do Masp), Carla Silva-Muhammad (UT Austin), Carlos Warchavchik, Catherine R. Ettinger, Christopher Long (UT Austin), Dina Uliana, Dion Neutra (*in memorian*), Eduardo Luis Rodriguez, Swiss Embassy in Cuba, Eric Munford, Genie Guerard (Library of Special Collections, UCLA), Getty Research Institute, Isabela Ono, Ivani DiGrazia, José Geraldo Simões Júnior, José Lira, Kykah Bernardes, Lauren Weiss Bricker (Cal Poly Pomona), Marcio Cotrim, María Ofelia González (Swiss Embassy in Cuba), Meg Partridge, Nancy Hadley (AIA California), Paulo Bruna, Paulo Mauro de Aquino, Raymond Richard Neutra, Renato Anelli, Richard Cleary (UT Austin), Roger M. Kull, Ruth Verde Zein, Sarah Lorenzen (Cal Poly Pomona), Simon Elliott (Library of Special Collections, UCLA), Thomas S. Hines, University of California at Los Angeles, University of Texas at Austin, Victor Hugo Mori

Support

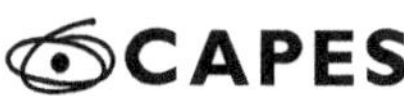

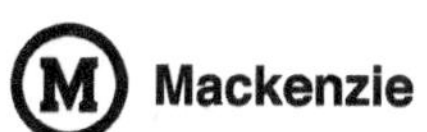

Portuguese Version
Richard Neutra e o Brasil
Fernanda Critelli, 2022
ISBN: 978-65-87205-05-2
(Romano Guerra)
ISBN: 978-1-946070-42-5
(Nhamerica)

Ebook Version
Richard Neutra e o Brasil
Fernanda Critelli, 2022
ISBN: 978-65-87205-19-9
(Romano Guerra)
ISBN: 978-1-946070-41-8
(Nhamerica)

Richard Neutra and Brazil
Fernanda Critelli, 2022
ISBN: 978-65-87205-15-1
(Romano Guerra)
ISBN: 978-1-946070-39-5
(Nhamerica)

Cover Image
Travel sketches, elevated view from Rio de Janeiro and Morro dos Dois Irmãos. Richard Neutra, 1945. Richard and Dion Neutra Papers Collection. Department of Special Collections, Charles E. Young Research Library, UCLA

This book was composed in Rotis Semi Sans and printed on papers offset 90g, couché 115g and supremo 250g

292

Critelli, Fernanda
Richard Neutra and Brazil
Fernanda Critelli
foreword
Abílio Guerra
afterword
Raymond Richard Neutra

1ª edição	São Paulo, SP: Romano Guerra;
1st edition	Austin, TX: Nhamerica Platform 2023

292 p. il.
(Latin America: Thoughts: Brasil, 7)

ISBN: 978-65-87205-18-2
(Romano Guerra)
ISBN: 978-1-946070-40-1
(Nhamerica)

1. Neutra, Richard Joseph, 1892-1970
2. Modern architecture – 20th Century – United States
3. Modern architecture – 20th Century – Brazil
4. Modern architecture – 20th Century – Latin America

I. Guerra, Abílio
II. Neutra, Raymond Richard
III. Title

CDD 724.973

Catalog sheet prepared by librarian Dina Elisabete Uliana – CRB-8/3760